SPI
Travel

LOS ANGELES

Contents

the magazine 5

Finding Your Feet 33

At the Beach 49

The Westside and Beverly Hills 75

Written by Justin Henderson
Where to... sections by Marael Johnson

Copy edited by Mary Sutherland
Verified by Bob Holmes
Indexed by Marie Lorimer

Edited, designed and produced by AA Publishing
© Automobile Association Developments Limited 2003
Maps © Automobile Association Developments Limited 2003

The contents of this publication are believed correct at the time of
printing. Nevertheless, the publishers cannot be held responsible
for any errors or omissions or for changes in the details given in this
guide or for the consequences of any reliance on the information
provided by the same.

Published in the United States by AAA Publishing,
1000 AAA Drive,
Heathrow, Florida 32746
Published in the United Kingdom by AA Publishing

ISBN 1-56251-762-7

Color separation by Leo Reprographics
Printed and bound in China by Leo Paper Products

10 9 8 7 6 5 4 3 2 1

This book makes reference to various Disney copyrighted characters,
trademarks, marks and registered marks owned by The Walt Disney
Company and Disney Enterprises, Inc.

A00933

CRUISING

Yes, it's glitzy, overdone, loud, brash and corny, but the sun never really sets on Sunset Boulevard. One of the longest streets (26 miles) in L.A., it began life as an unpaved road linking the old El Pueblo de Los Angeles (now Downtown L.A.) with the Pacific Ocean. Sunset snakes through east Downtown all the way to the Pacific, flanked by every kind of L.A. neighborhood imaginable. It works as a starting point from where you can see the Hollywood that once was, and what it has become.

Paramount Pictures is one major studio that still calls Sunset Boulevard home

In the 1920s, a 12-block segment between Western and Gower avenues became the hub of the nascent movie industry, making it an easy limousine run from studio to opulent hillside mansion.

The neon and billboard center of the world, Sunset Strip, has been famous for more than 60 years for its glitzy nightclubs, gangsters, luxury hotels and drug-over-dosed young (and dead) stars. Through the first half of the 20th century, the major movie studios – 20th Century Fox, Warner Bros., Paramount, Columbia – were located here, cheek by jowl with those lesser studios that cranked out Grade-B Westerns. Today the big-name studios are in nearby Burbank, or in

SUNSET

Burbank, or in New York, Miami or Toronto, Canada, and only Paramount remains; TV studios, corporate offices and movie museums have moved in. Tours and nostalgia rule here, but the Strip is still one of the hottest nightlife zones on the West Coast.

Take a Ride

Start at Figueroa Street a block west of El Pueblo, the historic heart of L.A. (▶ 147). Toward the east, Sunset turns into East Cesar Chavez Boulevard: L.A.'s Hispanic culture dominates this end of town. Weaving west past cantilevered Dodger Stadium, artsy Silver Lake and artsier Los Feliz, the L.A. demographic becomes evident. Here in the flatlands, the scene is primarily ethnic with Spanish street signs and other neighborhoods called "Little Armenia" and "Thai

Town." The farther west you go into Hollywood and toward the foothills, the more rarified the real estate becomes. For the most part, those well-paid workers in the city's omnipresent media industry occupy the heights.

Shortly before Vermont Avenue, Sunset straightens out for its fabled run through Hollywood. To the right, Barnsdall Park and the Frank Lloyd Wright Hollyhock House (▶ 126) fly by, then Gower Gulch on your left (now a huge shopping mall), where those 1930s and '40s black-and-white Westerns were hatched, as well as the Hollywood Freeway. Cruising west, look for the old Warner Bros. Studio at 5858 Sunset, then the Hollywood Palladium and the white-domed Cinerama movie house, now another enormous shopping/health

All neon and billboards, the Strip has been a nightlife magnet for decades

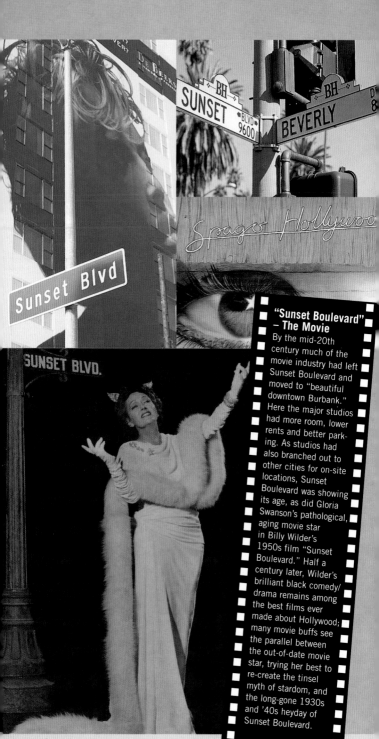

"Sunset Boulevard" – The Movie

By the mid-20th century much of the movie industry had left Sunset Boulevard and moved to "beautiful downtown Burbank." Here the major studios had more room, lower rents and better parking. As studios had also branched out to other cities for on-site locations, Sunset Boulevard was showing its age, as did Gloria Swanson's pathological, aging movie star in Billy Wilder's 1950s film "Sunset Boulevard." Half a century later, Wilder's brilliant black comedy/drama remains among the best films ever made about Hollywood; many movie buffs see the parallel between the out-of-date movie star, trying her best to re-create the tinsel myth of stardom, and the long-gone 1930s and '40s heyday of Sunset Boulevard.

club/entertainment center. The Hollywood Athletic Club at 6525 Sunset is where Charlie Chaplin and at least three Tarzans (Buster Crabbe, Johnny Weissmuller and Bruce Bennett) swam in the Olympic-size pool.

The Crossroads of the World at 6671 Sunset, a landmark 1936 building and one of L.A.'s earliest shopping malls, remains a charming piece of Streamline Moderne architecture.

Fight traffic another few miles and you'll hit Sunset Strip, a 2-mile stretch of Sunset Boulevard that runs from Crescent Heights Boulevard to Doheny Drive. The Strip has been a nightclubber's paradise since the 1920s, when one-lane Sunset linked the stars' homes in Bel Air with the studios farther east.

Gangsters ruled the clubs here in the 1930s and may still, but the high-rise luxury hotels, posh restaurants and new-style music clubs now cater to the rich-and-famous-for-a-while TV and movie stars. Check out the enormous, sky-blocking billboards along this part of Sunset to view the self-advertisements of rock stars, upcoming films and political opinions.

TV pretty much killed the old nightclubs, and so the resilient Strip reemerged as a birthplace of the rock 'n' roll era, with clubs like the Roxy and Whisky-a-Go-Go (always referred to as The Whisky) presenting the early gigs of Buffalo Springfield, Elton John, The Doors and others. The chain House of Blues, Johnny Depp's Viper Room and other hot spots compete with The Whisky.

The Strip is *the* place to go for live music in a town known for the best, the first and the most popular live music venues. Famous cool hotels along here include the Chateau Marmont and the Sunset Hyatt, with its very own on-site recording studio, the striking Mondrian and the new-but-old Hyatt West Hollywood.

The still-thriving Comedy Store (➤ 135) was the scene of early success for Robin Williams, Jim Carrey, David Letterman and Jerry Seinfeld, among others. Comics, actors and musicians of all stripes still flock here, looking for that big chance. If you hit a club on a good night and dress the part of a Someone, you might even get into one

Opposite: Images of Sunset; Billboards rule the Boulevard; Sunset slices through Beverly Hills; The stars dine at Spago; Gloria Swanson's swan song

Below: The Whisky has rocked for over 40 years

of these places to see the future of rock or TV trying out their show-biz wings.

At Doheny you enter the greener precincts of Beverly Hills, followed by Bel Air, Brentwood and Pacific Palisades: mile after lush, leafy mile of curving, gently rising and falling Sunset Boulevard lined with exclusive residential enclaves.

The understated sign of the Beverly Hills Hotel (► 41) announces its legendary presence; you can't miss it – it's still painted a peculiar shade of pink.

In Bel Air, UCLA's verdant Westwood campus (► 85–87) butts up against Sunset, opposite the Bel Air gates. The Getty Center (► 80–84) gleams on the hill to the right as you cross the 405 Freeway.

Farther west, in Pacific Palisades, Sunset glides through a sunny retail village shopping center for yet another suburb with real estate prices for multimillionaires only. Near the end of the Strip you'll pass the Self-Realization Fellowship Lake Shrine (► 67), then the air turns salty, the sun starts to set and you've traveled from the beginnings of L.A. in El Pueblo to the western edge of the continent. Will Rogers State Historic Park and Beach (► 66–67) are on the left, Topanga Canyon (► 68) is up to the right and the wide Pacific Ocean in front of you.

Left: Will Rogers State Historic Park features weekly polo matches

Below: The Self-Realization Fellowship Lake Shrine, a touch of Nirvana on Sunset Boulevard

Mulholland Drive

Dancing along above Sunset on the rim of the Hollywood Hills, Mulholland Drive, named for the designer/architect of the Los Angeles Aqueduct, which in turn created the highly populated San Fernando Valley, offers some of the best views in L.A., as well as some of the most exclusive real estate (Marlon Brando, Jack Nicholson and Warren Beatty all have Mulholland addresses). Farther northwest it includes a 7-mile stretch of barely passable dirt track and snakes a scenic, curvaceous route all the way to the Pacific at the far end of Malibu, providing hours of intense driving and spectacular scenery. Pick it up off the 405 Freeway or from one of the canyon roads winding up from Sunset. And back in town, don't miss David Hockney's monumental view of Mulholland at LACMA, the Los Angeles County Museum of Art (► 108–112).

Quake! Rattle and Roll

In case you're wondering what the odds are that you'll experience an earthquake while visiting Los Angeles, rest assured: You will. However, chances are you won't know it. Of the 200,000 earthquakes that have rattled L.A. in the past decade, only a few caused damage worth mentioning, and several others shook the ground enough to be noticeable.

Above: Cars were crushed and left: Apartment buildings suffered extensive damage in the Northridge quake of 1994

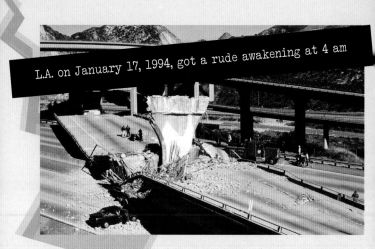

L.A. on January 17, 1994, got a rude awakening at 4 am

This is not to say it isn't possible that you'll be here for a Big One. Those (un)lucky enough to be in L.A. on Jan. 17, 1994, got a rude awakening at 4 am when King Kong himself picked up and shook every house in Northridge and Santa Monica. This temblor (the name scientists apply to earthquakes), rocketing out of an especially dangerous type of crack in the earth known as a blind thrust fault, hit an imposing 6.8 on the Richter scale (▶ opposite), claiming 61 lives, leaving 20,000 people homeless and causing more than $40 billion in damage. At the same time a secondary epicenter slammed Santa Monica, collapsing every brick chimney in the area.

You might ask, how could a city survive 200,000 quakes in 10 years? That averages nearly 55 quakes a day, or over two every hour. You begin to wonder why anyone could possibly want to live here.

Most quakes, fortunately, are tiny tremors, detectable only by a seismograph. The number 200,000 serves only to reinforce an inescapable geological truth, revealed on a seismic map of Los Angeles County: fault lines are indeed more plentiful than freeways. Southern California straddles the Pacific and North American tectonic plates, two major pieces of the Earth's crust that are engaged in a grinding slow dance, as the Pacific plate moves northwest about 1.6 inches per year. For much of the length of this boundary, most visible in the north–south slash of the San Andreas Fault, the plates run parallel; in Southern California though, the San Andreas takes a turn to the west. This causes the plates to push more fiercely into each other, producing countless faults and near-constant earthquakes. An estimated 200 of these faults could produce a quake of magnitude 6 or higher on the Richter scale.

The San Andreas, perhaps the most famous fault line in the world, is the queen mother of the fault network woven into Southern California's sun-baked skin. An

Freeway damage from the 1994 earthquake

Stretches of the San Andreas Fault are visible on the surface

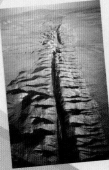

800-mile band of broken and crushed rock, the San Andreas comes onshore near Eureka in Northern California and extends south all the way into Mexico, passing just east of Los Angeles in the Cajon Pass area near San Bernardino. The fault reaches 10 miles deep into the earth, ranging in width from a few hundred feet to a mile.

For all its notoriety, the San Andreas Fault itself has not produced a major quake since 1857. This sounds like a good thing, but not necessarily; for every year the San Andreas goes without a quake, it stores a little more energy for the next one. And it may come soon, since seismologists have calculated that major quakes along the San Andreas occur on average every 150 years. The next one on the San Andreas could very well be "The Big One."

Yet life goes on in "Quake City." Most residents remain oblivious, thinking little about the probability of an earthquake except during or just after one, when there's the usual run on pricey earthquake insurance and emergency supplies. At this time small numbers of people decide to move out, headed for what they hope to be more stable ground. Los Angeles is so disaster-prone –

A quake rocked Downtown L.A. in March 1933

between quakes, the city faces intermittent droughts, regular landslides, annual raging wildfires and daily traffic jams – that people have grown used to it. A certain unreality pervades the atmosphere, and perhaps it's best that way. Mitigating in advance the effects of a major quake would be impossibly expensive, and living too close to the thought of its imminent arrival takes a huge psychological toll.

So Southern California's millions of fatalistic citizens carry on as if "The Big One" will never come – at least not in *their* lifetime.

Charles Richter

An American seismologist, Charles Richter (1900–85), developed a logarithmic equation that measures the energy released by those earth-shattering waves when an earthquake happens. Richter scale numbers begin with zero (noticeable only on a graph) to nine (showing devastating damage).

First

Angelenos:

The Chumash and the Gabrielinos

Anyone native or resident of Los Angeles is an Angeleno. While Mexican-Americans often brag that Los Angeles' historic roots lie in Mexico (▶ 147–148), these early Spanish-speaking Angelenos were hardly here first. Native Americans inhabited California for thousands of years before the Spanish soldiers, settlers and missionaries showed up. In Southern California, along the Santa Barbara Channel from San Luis Obispo to Malibu and out in the Channel Islands, the ocean-going Chumash people thrived since well before BC turned to AD. The Tongva people, later known as the Gabrielinos, occupied villages on Santa Catalina Island (▶ 27–28) and in the regions around what is now L.A.

Then came the colonizers. After a few brief encounters in the 16th and 17th centuries (Juan Cabrillo showed up off the Malibu coast in 1542) the Southern California natives were left alone until the late 18th century, when bands of settlers were sent in from Mexico to shore up Spain's claim to Southern California. Entire cultures were nearly wiped out by the usual imperialist suspects: European diseases, abuse of women, forced religious conversion, enslavement, wholesale theft of land and destruction of a way of life. By the 20th century, only a few Chumash remained. In recent years the last Chumash survivors managed to reestablish themselves as a recognized cultural group, with a revital- ization of traditional languages and crafts and a casino, located near modern-day Santa Barbara.

Research ranging from site excavations through oral histories to written accounts by Spanish explorers has created a fairly accurate account of life in pre-colonial Southern California. Not surprisingly, this life was relatively sweet. You might say that many of the millions of Southern Californians alive today appreciate the same regional verities that the estimated 13,000 Chumash reveled in 300 or 400 years ago: nature is bountiful and benevolent, but for the odd fire, drought or earthquake.

Inhabiting coastal villages and the islands, the Chumash relied on ocean-going plank canoes with double-bladed paddles for travel. They developed high-quality stonework, including flint blades, large flat-rimmed mortars and steatite (soapstone) animal figures. They also wove useful and elegant baskets. The Gabrielinos, who lived farther south, were said to have initiated the Chinigchinich cult, a mission- era phenomenon that spread over Southern California.

The cult's moral and ethical philoso- phies closely paralleled

Opposite: Cave paintings from early Californians

Above: Chumash survivors circa 1890

Left: A traditional Chumash presentation basket

Chumash Canoes

The most innovative Chumash inven- tion was the plank canoe, which allowed them to colonize the Channel Islands and to travel quickly up and down the coast. Fashioned by hand with tools made from stone, animal bones or shells, the canoes were the most valuable property in any village, owned only by the wealthy. Ranging in size from roughly 12 feet to as long as 30 feet and made of redwood or pine, the canoes were painted with a mix of tar, pitch and ocher coloring, and decorated with abalone shells. When finished, each was launched with appropriate ceremony.

Christianity, leading many to suspect that it actually emerged after the first missions had been established. However, the Christians did not take psychoactive herbs such as the toloache plant, or jimsonweed, used by the Gabrielinos to attain visionary states.

A Chumash fish effigy pipe with inlaid shells

The Chumash traded with the Gabrielinos of Catalina for steatite, used because it can be carved easily. The Chumash made effigies, pipes, fancy beads and cooking pots from this valuable commodity. Catalina Island was so rich in this stone that the Chumash called the island *huya*, their word for steatite.

The Chumash calendar almost exactly parallels the Gregorian calendar of the Old World, except that their New Year begins on the winter solstice, around Dec. 22. The Chumash year is divided into 12 months of 30 days each. As with Western astrology, Chumash individuals were assumed to be graced (or cursed) with personality traits inherent in the month of their birth.

What's In a Name?

A number of Chumash villages survive in the names of modern California towns and places, including Point Mugu (Muwu), Simi Valley (Shimiyi), Lompoc (Lompo), Ojai (Ahwa'y), Pismo Beach (Pismu) and, most famously, Malibu (Humaliwo).

The Chumash have revived their cultural traditions in recent years

Great Locations

Considering all the TV series, videos, commercials and movies filmed in and around L.A.'s perpetually sunny streets and beaches, you might view the whole city as one big movie location. In spite of some movement to Vancouver and Toronto in Canada and New York, Miami and other U.S. locations, most TV and film shows are still shot in and around L.A.

On any given day L.A. swarms with cinematic and video action, ranging from game shows, talk shows and sitcoms (primarily shot indoors at studio soundstages) to location shoots for the latest new movie or commercial.

Tracking these locations down is a relatively simple matter, thanks to an organization called the Entertainment Industry Development Corporation, or EIDC. You can call the EIDC (tel: 323/957-1000) to get the scoop, or go online at www.eidc.com. You could also plug into

Star for a Day

For those with wily intellects and nerves of steel, there is the chance to actually perform on a game show such as "Jeopardy" or "Wheel of Fortune." To try for an audition, call the following: "Jeopardy" (tel: 310/244-5367); "Wheel of Fortune" (tel: 213/520-5555); "Win Ben Stein's Money" (tel: 213/520-4BEN); "Rock 'n' Roll Jeopardy" (tel: cable 800/482-9840, or sign up online at www.rock-jeopardy.com); "The Price is Right" (The Price is Right, CBS Television City, 7800 Beverly Boulevard, Los Angeles, CA 90036).

L.A.'s movie culture by exploring locations from movies of the recent or distant past: There are hundreds of very familiar ones. Top spots that are covered in this guide include the Griffith Park Observatory (➤ 118; "Rebel Without a Cause," 1955) and Santa Monica Pier (➤ 57–59; "The Sting," 1973). Other famous movie sites are: the mansion and grounds at 1011 Beverly Dr. in Beverly Hills, which stood in for a New Jersey manse in "The Godfather" (1972); 1017 N. Crescent Dr. in Beverly Hills, where John Travolta tracked down Danny DeVito (using a Star Map) in "Get Shorty" (1995); the Regent Beverly Wilshire Hotel that served as a primary location in "Pretty Woman" (1990). When Woody Harrelson and Rosie Perez win big at "Jeopardy" in "White Men Can't Jump" (1992), they hole up in a suite at the Shangri-La Hotel on Ocean Avenue in Santa Monica. Other scenes from that movie were shot in Palisades Park (➤ 182) across the street, and at the basketball courts on Venice Beach (➤ 54–56). Fans of the surfside voluptuaries of "Baywatch" will fondly recall scenes from the series as they tour the

Top Tips
Tickets to the recordings of a sitcom, talk show or game show are free, usually limited to two per person and distributed on a first-come, first-served basis. Kids under ten years are generally not allowed in. If you decide to do this at the last minute, you might be able to obtain tickets on the street, in nearby shops around Mann's Chinese Theatre or outside the entrance to Universal Studios.

beaches of Santa Monica and Malibu.

Another means of visiting a "location" is to get into an audience taping for a sitcom, talk or game show. Demand is high, so requests should be made at least six months in advance. **Audiences Unlimited** (tel: 818/506-0043/0067) distributes tickets for most of the top sitcoms. Well organized and sanctioned by the networks and production companies, Audiences Unlimited may be the best way into an actual show.

To obtain tickets for game and talk shows, try **Television Tickets** (tel: 323/467-4697).

Aside from the network **ABC** (www.abc.com), which uses Audiences Unlimited exclusively, other networks may also have their own ticket offers.

Also contact **CBS** (7800 Beverly Boul., tel: 323/852-2458, www.cbs.com) or **NBC** (3000 W. Alameda St., Burbank, www.nbc.com).

"Rebel Without a Cause" James Dean at the Griffith Park Observatory

Far left: Newman and Redford plot "The Sting" on the Carousel on Santa Monica Pier

Left and above: TV buffs can watch shows taped at CBS and NBC

L.A. BY

L.A.'s architectural dynamic defies easy characterization. Essentially anything goes, from Aztec Modernism to high-tech "Googie-ism," a word coined to mean the slick, brightly colored look of a coffee shop or deli. The history of the city's construction begins with Hispanic influence – the adobe walls of sunny Spain and Mexico – but the shift from Hispanic to Anglo rule in the mid-19th century altered the design culture, with East Coast-style wood and masonry structures increasingly evident after about 1850.

In the 150 years since, waves of immigration, benevolent weather and the ubiquitous influence of the car culture and the movies have cast a collective spell over the urban environment. Dozens of great designers and architects have raised their individualistic roofs all over town; Mission Revival, Mediterranean Revival, Craftsman, neoclassic, beaux arts, art deco, Streamline Moderne, Egyptian Revival, pre-Columbian Revival, Los Angeles Modernism and other stylistic trends have all left their mark. L.A.'s architects and designers, like filmmakers, have always felt free to pursue their visions, however iconoclastic or non-contextual they might be.

Non-contextual is key: L.A. has never possessed a cohesive urban "design" – Downtown's relatively new skyline aside. The overriding visual image of L.A. is that of an endless, shapeless sprawl of suburbs and subdivisions, a sea of low-rise buildings interrupted by an occasional skyscraper cluster or bank of hills scarred with strip malls, billboards and other manifestations of consumer culture. All of it is ruled by vast humming hordes of ant-like automobiles and the infinite grid of roads necessary to accommodate them. This sea of structures and roads is contained by impassable mountains on one side and the ocean on the other. It all looks as if it were built without any clear plan.

Yet there are architectural riches here. The ocean, mountains and the elemental lushness of the land (it's really a desert but is fed by water piped in from hundreds of miles away) set a beautiful scene for L.A., its suburbs and encircling towns and their cache of inspired structures.

Architect Richard Meier's Museum of Television & Radio in Beverly Hills

Best Way to See L.A. Architecture

L.A.'s architectural riches spread far and wide, but they're easily accessible for those with patience and a car. There's something to see in almost any neighborhood, so take it slow, use a guidebook and a map, and you'll find dozens of memorable buildings. To more fully explore the design scene, get Michael Webb's *Architecture and Design LA,* or *Los Angeles: An Architectural Guide* by David Gebhard and Robert Winter and take the tour.

DESIGN

Los Angeles Airport

The control tower at Los Angeles International Airport (LAX) was created by local architect Kate Diamond, whose 1995 design evokes a stylized palm tree. It makes a fine counterpoint to the nearby Theme Building, the spidery structure that has long been the symbol of LAX and now contains the space-fantasy restaurant called Encounter.

Venice Beach and Canals

Heading north, in Venice and along the Marina Peninsula, you'll find a number of standout houses, including a few restaurants and offices. The **Norton House**, from Frank Gehry in 1984, with a lifeguard tower office that made Gehry famous, can be found at 2509 Ocean Front Walk; not far away Antoine Predock built a luminous split-level house at 2315 Ocean Front Walk. In the Venice Canals, the **Irani-Beaucage House** at 419 Linnie Canal Court is a sharp-looking two-story living/working space. Fred Fisher's design for **L.A. Louver Gallery**, at 55 N. Venice, set the standard for hard-edged yet arty galleries. The design by Morphosis for the **72 Market Street** restaurant sets mixed elements against each other in L.A. eclectic fashion. **Chaya Venice**, from Grinstein Daniels, offers a stylish Japanese/Modern interior

This spidery LAX landmark houses the fantasy restaurant, Encounter

Art or architecture? A Frank Gehry building on Main Street

for Pan-Asian dining at 110 Navy at Main Street. Don't miss the big binoculars in front of the **Chiat/Day/Mojo Headquarters**, by Frank Gehry at 340 Main Street, or Gehry's **Edgemar complex**, to the north at 2345 Main.

Main Street, Santa Monica

Also on Main, but now in Santa Monica, Barbara Lazaroff's interior design for **Chinois on Main** (2709) is an exercise in excess but lots of fun. The **Horatio West Court** at 140 Hollister Avenue delivers a 1919 classic from Irving Gill: Mission Modernism at its best. Frank Gehry's own Santa Monica house, at 22nd and Washington Avenue, is worth a drive by to see where he began. Gehry called it "a dumb little house with charm," which he wrapped in chain-link fencing, corrugated metal and plywood. At **Bergamot Station**, Fred Fisher again transformed a light industrial complex into one of the liveliest art gallery scenes in L.A.

DON'T MISS THE UNION 76 GAS STATION, NEAR THE CIVIC CENTER, A CLASSIC FROM THE BUDGET-GAS ERA OF THE 1950s.

Culver City

In Culver City, architect Eric Owen Moss has been on an inspired run, creating new and retrofitting old buildings for a roster of enlightened clients. See his impressive range of work at the following addresses: 8520 and 8522 National Boulevard, 3520, 3524, 3530, 3540, 3535 and 3542 Hayden Avenue and 3457 La Cienega. Moss is one of L.A.'s finest architects, and tourist-free Culver City has emerged as his primary showcase.

Pacific Palisades

In Pacific Palisades, Charles and Ray Eames and several inspired Modernists and contemporary iconoclasts have created dozens of striking homes such as **Lee Kappe houses** at 715 and 680 Brooktree, 14629 Hilltree and 596 Dryad. **The House** at 444 Sycamore Road by Pierre Koenig, and the one and only **Eames House**, at 203 Chautaqua Boulevard, are considered the greatest of the Case Study Houses from the late 1940s. These houses are all in or on the edge of Santa Monica Canyon.

Brentwood and Westwood

Look at UCLA's classic old campus buildings (especially Royce Hall and Powell Library) by George W. Kelham, from the 1920s. Two of the later UCLA classics include the University Elementary School by Richard Neutra and the Student Placement & Career Planning Center by Frank Gehry. The two major architectural projects of the last 10 years in this area are the elegantly complex **Skirball Cultural Center** (► 102) by Moshe Safdie and, down the hill,
the monumental **Getty Center**, Richard Meier's masterwork. On a smaller scale, Frank Gehry designed the **Schnabel House** at 526 Carmelina, and Ricardo Legorreta created the colorful **Greenberg House** at 223 Carmelina. Frank Lloyd Wright crafted the **Sturges House** at 449 Skyeway.

Royce Hall, from the 1920s, still reigns at UCLA

Beverly Hills

Land of monied mansions, Beverly Hills has its share of fine buildings, beginning with its own **Civic Center** at Santa Monica Boulevard and Rexford, a 1930s creation with a 1980s remodel/expansion by Charles Moore. Not far away is Richard Meier's **Museum of Television and Radio** at 465 N. Beverly. The late Frank Israel executed a fine office building for Virgin Records at 338 N. Foothill Road. Don't miss the **Union 76 gas station**, near the Civic Center, a classic from the budget-gas era of the 1950s.

Anderton Court at 328 Rodeo is a Frank Lloyd Wright number, one of a dozen high-design statements along "retail row." Nearby, the restaurant **Kate Mantilini**, by Morphosis, is one of L.A.'s great contemporary statements at 9101 Wilshire.

Architecture Tours

Architours (tel: 323/294-5821, www.architours.com) offer focused tours at the discretion of individual clients or all-day group tours that cover a specific topic (for example art-deco buildings, houses by Frank Lloyd Wright and Rudolf Schindler). The **Los Angeles Conservancy** (523 W. Sixth, Suite 1216, Los Angeles, tel: 213/623-2489, la-conservancy.org) has about a dozen different tours of historic Downtown L.A. focusing on different aspects of the area, including architecture. The **Googie Tour** (tel: 323/980-3480) covers space-age diners and other buildings with architectural motifs drawn from eclectic cultural references. **Pasadena Heritage** (tel: 626/441-6333) offers tours of historic Pasadena architecture. Call for tour schedules and prices. The **Pasadena Convention and Visitors Bureau** (171 S. Las Robles, Pasadena, tel: 626/795-3111) has brochures with 10 self-guided tours of historic Pasadena, several with an emphasis on architecture.

Hollywood

There are hundreds of interesting buildings in the Hollywood area. Here are a few of the greats.

Mann's Chinese Theatre (6925 Hollywood Boulevard), the **El Capitan Theater** (6838 Hollywood), the **Pantages** (6233 Hollywood) and the **Egyptian Theater** (6713 Hollywood, now American Cinematheque) are four great old movie palaces worth seeing. The **Hollywood Bowl** (2301 N. Highland) remains one of the country's most sublime outdoor music venues.

Houses designed by Frank Lloyd Wright here include **Ennis-Brown** (2655 Glendon), **Hollyhock House** (4800 Hollywood Boulevard), Wright's first and some say his best, and the **Storer House** (8161 Hollywood Boulevard).

Below: An interior view of the Los Angeles Times Building Downtown

Bottom: The Bradbury Building, L.A.'s most enchanting interior

Downtown

Here the old greats include the **Los Angeles Times Building**, the **Central Library**, the **Regal Biltmore Hotel** and the **Bradbury Building**, the latter for the interior atrium alone. Among the newer standouts are the **Museum of Contemporary Art (MOCA)**, the **Geffen Contemporary**, the **Walt Disney Concert Hall** by Frank Gehry, and the new **Cathedral of our Lady of Angels** by Jose Rafael Moneo.

Pasadena

In Pasadena the **Gamble House** reigns supreme as America's greatest Arts and Crafts house. Check out the mansions in San Marino; old and downtown Pasadena offer a wealth of impeccably maintained period buildings from the 19th century and several Greene & Greene houses as well.

The Channel Islands... and Catalina

If you've ever dreamed of going to the Galapagos Islands, where an assortment of unique animals shaped Darwin's theory of evolution, consider as an alternative a quick trip to the Channel Islands. Accessible by day-trip from Santa Barbara and Ventura (the Chumash used to paddle out there), the uninhabited Channel Islands have been described as California's Galapagos. Here, in their inbred isolation, over 75 different plant species and 60 animal species have evolved into endemics – life forms unique to one or more of the islands. Often these endemics are simply smaller or larger versions of mainland critters like the Island fox, the size of a house cat, or the Santa Cruz Island scrub jay, a quarter again as large as coastal jays and a brighter shade of blue.

SAN MIGUEL

Channel Islands

Aside from evolutionary intrigues, the Channel Islands offer a wonderful opportunity to explore pristine environments that illustrate what much of California and its coastal waters looked like prior to colonization. The **Channel Islands National Park** (created by President Carter in 1980) encompasses 200 square miles of ocean and five islands totaling about 250,000 acres. From north to south, they are (forming the main cluster) San Miguel, Santa Rosa, Santa Cruz and Anacapa and Santa Barbara Island farther south.

Three other islands are also part of the Channel Islands but are not protected with national park status. San Nicolas and San Clemente Islands belong to the U.S. Navy, which has used San Clemente for practice bombing runs for decades. San Nicolas, home to an array of ancient petroglyphs of dolphins, sharks and whales, was used to track Russian subs through the Cold War. The same equipment now tracks whales. The southernmost Channel Island is Santa Catalina (► opposite).

Protected 6 miles out from each island, park waters offer sanctuary to numerous ocean-going creatures, including gray whales passing through on their annual migrations and a large population of endangered blue whales. Other marine mammals evident in large numbers are dolphins, porpoises, sea lion and seal species and sea otters.

San Miguel, farthest west, is a 9,325-acre refuge for around 30,000 sea lions and seals every summer.

Santa Rosa offers 52,794 acres of windswept terrain, a number of endemic species and one of two surviving natural stands of Torrey pines (the other is near La Jolla). Santa Rosa also shelters some 2,000 archaeological sites relating to Chumash settlements (► 14–16) and later settlements of Chinese abalone gatherers.

Santa Cruz, the largest island in the chain at 60,645 acres, is also the greenest. Two mountain ranges traverse the island, with a beautiful central valley between, where a man named Justinian Caire ran a successful winery early in the 20th century. Prohibition closed the winery, but the ranch and buildings have been preserved.

Fascinating Fossils

During the last Ice Age, hundreds of woolly mammoths swam there from the mainland. Over many generations, these island mammoths shrank down in size, from about 12 to 14 feet at the shoulder to just 6 or 7 feet, becoming *Mammuthus exilis*, a unique pygmy mammoth species. Radiocarbon testing of their fossilized remains suggests these mammoths died out about 11,000 years ago, roughly 400 years before humans arrived.

Just 11 miles from Oxnard's Channel Islands Harbor, 699-acre **Anacapa**'s proximity to the mainland has made it a day-tripper's destination.

Finally, **Santa Barbara**, the island, not the city, has 639 acres of raw, deserted, windswept, clifftop turf, with no trees, no beaches and no fresh water.

Santa Catalina Island

Twenty-two miles from the mainland, Santa Catalina Island is another world, as remote from the remoteness of the other Channel Islands as it is from San Pedro and Long Beach, the L.A. towns whose harbors offer the fastest rides out there (although you can also go from the Balboa Pavilion, 400 Main Street, Newport Beach).

For one thing, it has a real town on it – **Avalon**, a little jewel of a resort town nestled into a balmy bay, with 3,200 residents. Day-trippers love Avalon's waterfront restaurants and bars, its colorful hillside homes and its fabulous tilework. Fantastic displays of 1930s California tilework blanket the town, especially around the waterfront plaza, the walkways

Top: Ruggedly beautiful Anacapa lies just 11 miles off the coast

Above: California sea lions love the Channel Islands' rocky shores

The Catalina town of Avalon is a favorite L.A. boaters' destination

that climb the hilly town and at the Moorish Casino on Avalon Bay, an art-deco masterpiece. The other popular spot on Santa Catalina is **Two Harbors**, just about in the middle of the island. Camping, snorkeling and diving are the main diversions; get off the boat in Isthmus Cove on the side facing the channel/mainland, and stroll the half-mile trail over to Catalina Harbor on the ocean side. It's an easy walk, but watch out for buffalo (descendants of the 14 buffalo brought here to film "The Vanishing American" in 1924 by Zane Grey, American author of books about the Old West, the most famous of which was *Riders of the Purple Sage*).

You can get on a tour bus to explore parts of the island, but by far the best way is by hiking or mountain-biking. You can see the island's unusual ecosystems, along with breathtaking 360-degree views of the ocean. A network of trails make it possible to trek or bike the island for anywhere from an hour to several days. Call the **Santa Catalina Island Conservancy** (tel: 310/510-2595) for information and permits. Guided hikes can also be booked via **Catalina Fitness Company** (tel: 310/510-9255), and bus tours can be booked through **Discovery Tours** (tel: 310/510-8687). Get there on the *Catalina Express* from San Pedro, Long Beach and Dana Point (tel: 310/519-1212, 800/315-3967).

Access and Activities

Each island offers different levels of access and sites for landing, swimming, camping, hiking and other activities. For specifics go to www.nps.gov/chis or visit the **Channel Islands National Park Visitors Center** (1901 Spinnaker Drive, Ventura, tel: 805/658-5730). From Ventura, **Island Packer Cruises** (1867 Spinnaker Drive, Ventura, tel: 805/642-1393, www.islandpackers.com) offers tours with snorkeling, kayaking and other options. In Santa Barbara, try **Truth Aquatics** (301 W. Cabrillo Boulevard, Santa Barbara, tel: 805/962-1127, www.truthaquatics.com). Flyovers and drop-offs can be arranged through **Channel Islands Aviation** (305 Durley Avenue, Camarillo, tel: 805/987-1301).

Goin' to Surf City

Surfing! The Hawaiians or the Polynesians invented it around a thousand or more years ago. It's the national sport of Australia, now practiced in Europe, Asia and Africa as well as in just about every state with a coastline from Maine to Washington.

California's surf culture conquered the world with 1960s beach blanket flicks like "Gidget"

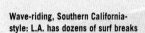
Wave-riding, Southern California-style: L.A. has dozens of surf breaks

In big cities all over the U.S., far and near from the coast, trendy shops sell surfing clothes and surfing gear to style-conscious wannabe surfers. Yet for all its international appeal, surfing is eternally linked with life in Southern California. For this we can thank the Beach Boys and a couple of movies about a girl named Gidget, a Beach Party and an Endless Summer. These pop-cultural products spawned in the late 1950s and 1960s produced a groove that has vibrated around the world ever since.

L.A.'s waves are perhaps second-class by international standards, but Southern California remains one of the primary centers for surf culture. L.A., or at least a few of its coastal suburbs, continues to claim the crown of Surf City.

Malibu Point still offers those long, slow, perfect right-point break waves all summer long; **Huntington Beach** not only hosts California's biggest surfing event, the Pro-Am, every summer, it also offers a consistent beach break year-round and is the home of the **International Surfing Museum and Hall of Fame** (411 Olive Avenue, Huntington Beach, tel:

714/960-3483, Wed–Sat noon–5, inexpensive).

Aside from these two hot spots, you'll find surfers at almost every beach up and down the Southern California coast. Old guys on longboards, 10-year-olds on dinky shortboards, teenage girls carving up the waves: it's been an integral part of the L.A. scene for 50 years and the foundation for one of pop culture's most enduring myths. Since 1960, being a surfer, a babe or a dude has been and still is, way cool.

BEST OF L.A.

⮑ Best Beach Day

A hot summer day at **Matador Beach**, northwestern Malibu. Bring food, drink, snorkeling gear and/or a kayak; hit **Surfrider Beach, Malibu** during a south swell and watch the surfers ride one of California's great waves. For lovers of urban craziness there's the **Venice Boardwalk** (► 54–56) on a sunny weekend afternoon for a full-tilt experience of California's Bohemia-by-the-sea.

L.A. at its zany best; a hot and busy day on the Venice Boardwalk

⮑ Best Sports Event

Any **basketball** game that features the Los Angeles Lakers, live at the **Staples Center** (► 164), including multimillion-dollar basketball stars on the court and mega-million-dollar movie stars courtside: this is Hollywood meets the NBA.

Above: For upscale shoppers, Rodeo Drive is heaven on earth

Right: Two's company on Venice Beach

Bottom: Sunset-watching from the Getty Center can be a sublime experience

⮌ Best Meals

Middle of the night breakfast: Insomnia Café (► 131), where you can hang out with movie moguls.

Breakfast: Back to the Beach (► 185), just off the cycle path north of the Santa Monica Pier. Substantial food, gull and wave sounds rolling across wide white sand, the Palisades overhead lined with palms: this is coastal bliss.

Brunch: by the Swan Pool at the Bel Air Hotel (► 95) in Stone Canyon, L.A.'s most beautiful hotel.

Lunch: at the Polo Lounge (► 99), watch the Hollywood gamesters in action.

Vegetarian meal: the low-key Inn of the Seventh Ray in Topanga Canyon (► 68).

Afternoon tea: The Rose Garden Room at the Huntington (► 155 and 162).

Evening meal: Patina (► 131) Crustacean (► 97). L.A. has at least a dozen great restaurants.

⮌ Best Views

From the **Getty Center** (► 80–84) or **Griffith Park Observatory** (► 118) at sunset, or from anywhere along **Mulholland Drive** in the Hollywood Hills (► 10).

⮌ Best Recreational Activity

Take the **South Bay Cycle Ride** (► 184–186) from end to end and back on an early morning. You'll love every waterfront mile.

⮌ Best Garden

The acres of exotic succulents in the **Desert Garden at the Huntington Botanical Gardens** (► 155).

⮌ Best Night on the Town

A concert at the new Frank Gehry-designed **Walt Disney Concert Hall** (► 157), after dinner at Bernards in the Millennium Biltmore Hotel (► 43). In summer, trade that for a concert at the **Hollywood Bowl** (► 128 and 136), with a catered box dinner and a bottle of wine.

⮌ Best Shopping

For the rich and trendy, **Rodeo Drive** (► 88–91). For the less rich but more trendy, **Melrose Avenue** (► 133–134).

⮌ Best Weird Place

The **Museum of Jurassic Technology** (9341 Venice Boulevard, Culver City, Thu 2–8, Fri–Sun noon–6, inexpensive) a compendium of vividly displayed weirdness.

⮌ Best Hotel

The **Bel Air** (► 95), for style, atmosphere, service and its location high in the hills.

⮌ Best Drives

Mulholland Drive (► 10) at night, or the **Pacific Coast Highway** by day from Santa Monica (not at rush hour).

Finding Your Feet

First Two Hours

Arriving by Air: Los Angeles

- Most visitors to L.A. arrive at the vast, perpetually busy **Los Angeles International Airport** or **LAX** (tel: 310/646-5252), located in Westchester about 15 miles from Downtown L.A. near the beach south of Marina del Rey and west of Inglewood. LAX is huge but easy to manage, with shuttle buses (tel: 310/646-2911) connecting the airport's eight terminals.
- If you need help, inquire at **Traveler's Aid** booths or try the **computer kiosks** located outside the baggage-claim areas. The kiosks offer information on shuttles, taxis, buses, limousines and rental cars.
- Airport curbside **pick-up locations** are color-coded for vans, cabs, buses and shuttles. There are lots of vans headed for Disneyland, Long Beach, Santa Barbara and other places, so if you want to head out of town as soon as you arrive, you'll have no trouble finding transportation.
- Inside the terminals near the baggage-claim areas you'll also find banks of **dedicated phones** and lists of phone numbers that will connect you with dozens of hotels as well as multiple means of transportation.

Arriving by Air: Outside Los Angeles

- If you are flying in from nearby states or cities, you may arrive at one of the region's many smaller airports, which include **Burbank/Glendale/Pasadena Airport** (tel: 818/840-8840) in Burbank; **John Wayne Airport** (tel: 714/252-5200) in Anaheim; **Long Beach Municipal Airport** (tel: 562/570-2600); or **Ontario International Airport** (tel: 909/373-2700) in Ontario, convenient only if you are headed first to the desert.

Arriving by Train

- **Amtrak** trains arrive from most major U.S. cities at **Union Station** (tel: 213/624-0171 or 213/683-6729) in Downtown Los Angeles. For information call Amtrak (tel: 800/872-7245; www.amtrak.com).

Arriving by Car

- If you're driving in, you'll probably come in on **Interstate 5**, **U.S. 101**, **or U.S. 1** from the north or south, or **Interstate 10 or 15** from the east.
- Use a **map** to plan your entry, and try to avoid arriving at rush hour.

Renting a Car

- In spite of the car services, buses, taxis and L.A.'s new Metro system, you are best off in Los Angeles with a **rented car**. The city sprawls, and without one you're at the mercy of tour operators or limited public transportation options if you really want to see the sights. With some luck, skill and good timing, you can avoid the worst of the traffic jams that plague the city from dawn till dusk and often into the night.
- You can arrange for a rental car from your **hotel**. However, there is one advantage to **renting at the airport**: The rental companies have user-friendly computers set up in their airport offices. These allow patrons to print out maps and detailed directions on how to get from the rental agency (at the airport) to their various destinations.
- Unless there's something huge going on in the city, it's not necessary to reserve a car **in advance** except at the height of summer and around New Year, when the Tournament of the Roses Parade brings in big crowds.
- There are thousands of rental cars available through dozens of agencies (▶ 37); all you need to do is **call a couple of agencies** to track down the

type of car you want, then take the agency's own free bus to the company office (the car rental agencies are all located within five minutes' drive of the airport) to pick up your car.

Driving in L.A.

- L.A.'s experienced drivers are generally **courteous**.
- L.A. offers reasonably priced **parking** in lots or on metered streets.
- If you'd rather not jump into driving a car right out of the airport, **take a ride** to your hotel. Most hotels have their own shuttles, so it may not be necessary to pay for a cab.

Orientation

- Aside from Pasadena to the north of Downtown and several excursions out of town, all the destinations in this guide can be found **north of the airport**, west of Downtown.
- **From east to west** the areas lie as follows: Downtown (and Pasadena), Mid-Wilshire/Hollywood, Westside and Beverly Hills, the Beach.
- There are **distinct districts and neighborhoods** within each of the areas, and hundreds of other suburbs, separate cities and towns, districts, *barrios* and neighborhoods spreading in every direction from Downtown. They are all part of the Greater Los Angeles area.

Tourist Offices

Most L.A. districts have their own tourist offices. The following cover the primary areas:

- **Downtown**: Los Angeles Convention and Visitors Bureau, 633 W. Fifth Street, Suite 600, Los Angeles, tel: (213) 624-7300, www.lacvb.com; Visitors Information Center, 685 S. Figueroa Street between Wilshire and Seventh, Mon–Fri 8–5, Sat 8:30–5.
- **Beverly Hills**: Beverly Hills Visitors Bureau, 239 S. Beverly Drive, Beverly Hills, tel: (800) 345-2210 or (310) 248-1015, www.bhvb.org, Mon–Fri 9–5.
- **Hollywood**: Visitor Information Center Hollywood, Janes House, 6541 Hollywood Boulevard, Hollywood, tel: (213) 689-8822, Mon–Fri 9–5:30.
- **Pasadena**: Pasadena Convention and Visitors Bureau, 171 S. Los Robles Avenue, Pasadena, tel: (626) 795-9311, www.pasadenavisitor.org, Mon–Fri 8–5, Sat 10–4.
- **West Hollywood**: West Hollywood Convention and Visitors Bureau, 8687 Melrose Avenue, M-26, West Hollywood, tel: (800) 368-6020 or (310) 289-2525, www.visitwesthollywood.com, Mon–Fri 8–6.
- **Santa Monica**: Santa Monica Convention and Visitors Bureau, 1400 Ocean Avenue, Santa Monica, tel: (310) 393-7593, www.santamonica.com. The Santa Monica Visitors Bureau in Palisades Park is also at 1400 Ocean Avenue (between Santa Monica Boulevard and Broadway), daily 10–5.
- **Marina del Rey**: Marina del Rey Chamber of Commerce/Visitor and Convention Bureau, 4371 Glencoe Avenue, B-14, Marina del Rey, tel: (310) 645-5151, www.wlaxmdrchamber.com, Mon–Fri 9–5.

Admission Charges

The cost of admission for museums and places of interest mentioned in the text is indicated by the following price categories.
Inexpensive under $5 **Moderate** $5–$10 **Expensive** over $10

Getting Around

There are surface street routes connecting all of L.A. These "alternate" routes may be less crowded and thus faster than the freeways at rush hour or other busy times. For example, the San Diego Freeway (405) is a traffic-plagued mess for hours every day. Crafty L.A. drivers know that in certain parts of town (for instance getting to and from the Getty Center or the Skirball Center from Wilshire or Sunset Boulevard) you can take Sepulveda, which runs parallel to 405, and save precious minutes.

Driving

The following offer basic freeway or street routes from LAX to the primary in-city areas.

- To reach **Marina del Rey, Venice, Santa Monica** and **Malibu**, follow the signs to Sepulveda Boulevard north; get off Sepulveda onto Lincoln Boulevard (here serving as Highway 1) and go north. Marina del Rey, Venice and Santa Monica are around 10–30 minutes away. Malibu lies another 20–30 minutes plus up the Pacific Coast Highway, Highway 1. (To reach the South Bay go south on Sepulveda.)

- To reach **Westside and Beverly Hills**, exit at the airport and follow the signs to the Century Freeway (105) or take Century Boulevard east to the San Diego Freeway (405). Head north on 405 until you cross 10 (the Santa Monica Freeway), then exit on Santa Monica, Wilshire or Sunset Boulevard, depending on your destination. This could take anywhere from 30 minutes to an hour.

- **Downtown Los Angeles** is roughly 20 minutes to an hour away from LAX. Take the Century Freeway (105) east to the Harbor Freeway (110) north; or take 105 to the San Diego Freeway (405) north to the Santa Monica Freeway (10) east to the Harbor (110) north. One big thing to watch out for: Heading east on the Santa Monica Freeway (10) as you approach the interchange with the Harbor Freeway (110) near Downtown L.A., there is no sign that mentions either Downtown or Los Angeles. Take 110 north toward Pasadena to reach the Downtown L.A. exits.

- To reach **Pasadena** follow directions to Downtown and continue north on 110 (the name changes to the Pasadena Freeway once you're north of L.A.) to the end. From Downtown L.A. to Pasadena can take anywhere from 15–30 minutes plus.

- To reach **Hollywood or Mid-Wilshire**, take 105 east to 405 north to 10 east to 110 north (toward Pasadena), then take the Hollywood Freeway (101) toward Hollywood. Alternately, take 405 north to 10 east and get off at La Brea, La Cienega or Fairfax, and head north toward West Hollywood and the Hollywood Hills. Figure on 30–60 minutes.

Car Rentals

- Most rental companies honor **foreign driver's licenses**, but you might want to make sure when making your reservation.

- It is also helpful to have your **passport** or **international driver's license** available.

- Drivers **under the age of 25** will be charged a higher rate (for insurance purposes), and you will definitely need a major credit card.

- **Rates vary widely** depending on size and style of car and the time of year as well as the number of days you're renting. You'll get a better deal on weekly rates. Although L.A. doesn't really have a season, prices follow demand, so they're higher in summer.

- **Competition** is fierce, so look for deals. All the major companies have websites where you can shop in advance to track down specific models, prices and discounts. Look for links to Special Offers: you can get amazing deals!
- Check to see if your **insurance company** at home covers you for car rentals. Otherwise you may have to pay for per-day surcharges that all rental companies try to impose for liability insurance.
- The best places for specialty car rentals are: **Budget**, The Beverly Hills Collection, 9815 Wilshire Boulevard, tel: (800) 227-7117, www.budgetbeverlyhills.com, and **Beverly Hills Rent a Car**, 9220 South Sepulveda Boulevard, L.A., tel: (800) 479-5996, www.bhrentacar.com

---

Here are some useful car rental numbers:

Alamo tel: (800) 327-9633	**Hertz** tel: (800) 654-3131
Avis tel: (800) 331-1212	**National** tel: (800) 227-7368
Budget tel: (800) 527-0700	**Payless** tel: (800) 729-5377
Dollar tel: (800) 800-4000	**Rent-A-Wreck** tel: (800) 535-1391
Enterprise tel: (800) 325-8007	**Thrifty** tel: (800) 367-2277

Public Transportation

Metro

- **Metro information**, tel: (800) 266-6883; **Metro Art information**, tel: (213) 922-2727.
- L.A.'s **subway** and **light-rail system** (the Metro) finally kicked into gear in the 1990s, but its three lines, covering about 60 miles, can be useless when trying to get from one part of town to another. However, the Metro does feature interesting **original art** in every one of its 50-odd stations.
- Trains run every 5–10 minutes during rush hours, every 15–20 minutes otherwise, and the **cost is minimal**.
- **The Red Line** runs from Union Station near Downtown through Hollywood to North Hollywood and beyond into the San Fernando Valley. This line is useful for getting to Hollywood and Universal Studios (▶ 120–123) from Downtown.
- The above-ground **Blue Line** links Downtown with distant Long Beach and serves as the most heavily used commuter line. You can take this one to avoid a dreary drive to see the Watts Towers (▶ 157) (get off at the 103rd Street stop) or to reach the *Queen Mary* and other sights in Long Beach (▶ 173–175).
- The nowhere-to-nowhere (for tourists anyway) **Green Line** connects Norwalk, southeast of L.A., with Redondo Beach, southwest of L.A.

Bus

- The system covers the **entire metropolitan area.**
- Local city lines such as **Santa Monica's Big Blue Bus** handle the territory not covered by the Metro. For information tel: (800) COMMUTE or (213) 626-4455, Mon–Fri 7–3:30.
- One-way fares cost $1.35, with transfers an extra 25 cents. **Express** buses cost from $1.85 to $3.85. **DASH** (Downtown Area Short Hop) buses charge 25 cents; one travels around Hollywood, while five others go through Downtown every ten minutes or so. DASH routes also take in parts of Mid-Wilshire, Venice, South Central L.A. and Pacific Palisades.

Cabs

- You'll find it **hard to hail a cab in L.A.**, except at the airport, train station and major hotels. Phone ahead and have one dispatched by radio.
- Cab companies can be found in the **listings in the Yellow Pages**.
- Some useful cab companies: **Checker Cab** tel: (213) 482-3456; **Independent Cab** tel: (213) 385-8294; **L.A. Taxi** tel: (310) 859-0111.

Walking, Cycling and Hiking

- Some **good areas for strolling** include Downtown L.A., Old Pasadena, Hollywood Boulevard, Melrose Avenue in West Hollywood, Sunset Strip, Rodeo Drive and the Golden Triangle in Beverly Hills, Westwood Village and the UCLA campus, Main Street in Santa Monica, the Third Street Promenade in Santa Monica, Palisades Park in Santa Monica and the piers and boardwalks on the beach in both Santa Monica and Venice.
- The best cycle route by far is the beachfront path that covers a significant stretch of the **Santa Monica Bay** shore (► 184–186).
- The **Santa Monica Mountains** and **Griffith Park's Hollywood Hills** each have an extensive network of hiking and mountain-biking trails. For information call the **Sierra Club** (tel: 323/387-4287), the **Santa Monica Mountains National Recreation Area** (tel: 805/370-2301) or **California State Parks** (tel: 818/880-0350).

Tours

- Guided bus tours, studio tours and various specialty tours abound. The granddaddy of them all is the **Movie Stars' Homes Tour** (► 117).
- **You can book** these mainstream Hollywood tours at any hotel, at various shops or from hawkers around Mann's Chinese Theatre in Hollywood.
- Established mainstream tour companies include **Casablanca Tours** (tel: 323/461-0156), **GrayLine Tours** (tel: 213/689-8822) and **Hollywood Fantasy Tours** (tel: 323/469-8184).
- Many areas feature **local walking or driving tours** highlighting architecture, historic buildings and other points of interest. Check with your hotel concierge or the appropriate tourist office or consult the free, available-everywhere *L.A. Visitors Guide* for details and other choices.
- **Nightclub Tours**: L.A. NightHawks, Box 7642, Santa Monica, tel: (310) 392-1500. Complete with guide, limo and club passes.
- **Haunted Hearse Tours**: tel: (323) 782-9652. Ride in a hearse for a few hours and view select famous locations of Hollywood deaths, scandals, sexual perversions and drug disasters. Daily at 7 pm; expensive.
- **NBC Studio Tour**: 3000 W. Alameda, Burbank, tel: (818) 840-3537, Mon–Fri 9–3; moderate.
- **Warner Bros. VIP Studio Tour**: 4000 Warner Boulevard, Burbank, tel: (818) 972-TOUR, Mon–Fri 9–4; expensive.
- **Universal Studios**: The Studio Tour is one of the many rides at this theme park/studio (► 121).

CityPass

L.A. is part of the CityPass network, a money-saving, multiattraction pass that gets half-price admission at eight major L.A. attractions. Good for nine days from the first use, and priced at $49.95 ($38 for kids under 12), passes can be bought at any of the attractions or online at www.citypass.net. The list includes Universal Studios Hollywood, the Museum of Television & Radio, the Petersen Automotive Museum, the Museum of Tolerance, Hollywood Entertainment Museum, American Cinematheque at the Egyptian Theatre, the Reagan Presidential Library & Museum and the Autry Museum of Western Heritage. Tel: (707) 256-0490 for information.

Accommodations

Big city, lots of choices! When it comes to accommodations, visitors to
Los Angeles can choose from the hip to the haute, with plenty of low-key
(but not low-class) establishments tossed into the mix.

The city encompasses the pulsing Downtown, surf-and-sun beaches, the
chic Westside and Beverly Hills, traditional old Pasadena and the undeni-
able lure of Hollywood. Within each of these areas lies a trove of quality
brand-name hotels and motels, offering a broad range of prices.

A celebrity haunt on the Westside or Beverly Hills will be accompanied
by sky-high rates, while a less flashy motel or hotel in another neighborhood
may be less expensive than expected. L.A. caters to all budgets. If you're
here for a convention or business, one of Downtown's full-service high-rises
may serve well, but for ocean breezes with your latte try Santa Monica.
All of the major hotel and motel chains are here. Additional options include
bed-and-breakfasts and efficiency apartments.

Visitors should take into consideration the city's vast size – and its
inadequate (and, in places, nonexistent) public transportation system.
A Metro subway system now links Downtown to Hollywood, and buses
operate in many parts of the city; nonetheless, almost everyone will want
a car to make the most of a visit. Most types of accommodations provide
parking facilities, but some tack on surcharges, and others offer only
valet parking. Accessible rooms are readily available for travelers with
disabilities, and nonsmokers can request a smoke-free room.

When to Go

Weather is rarely a factor in L.A.'s moderate climate. Summer months
and holidays usually glean the most visitors, especially to the beaches and
theme parks. Flexible travelers will often be able to pick up some great
deals during off-peak times. At any time, it's best to make advance reservations – especially if you have your heart set on one of the ritzier spots.

Information

- AAA, Automobile Club of Southern California, 2601 S. Figueroa Street,
  90007, tel: (213) 741-3111
- Los Angeles Convention and Visitors Bureau, 633 W. Fifth Street, Suite
  600, 90071, tel: (213) 624-7300, fax (213) 624-9746

Diamond Ratings

- AAA tourism editors evaluate and rate lodging establishments based on
  the overall quality and services. AAA's diamond rating criteria reflect the
  design and service standards set by the lodging industry, combined with
  the expectations of our members.
- Our one (♦) or two (♦♦) diamond rating represents a clean and
  well-maintained property offering comfortable rooms, with the two-
  diamond property showing enhancements in decor and furnishings. A
  three (♦♦♦) diamond property shows marked upgrades in physical
  attributes, services and comfort and may offer additional amenties. A
  four (♦♦♦♦) diamond rating signifies a property offering a high level
  of service and hospitality and a wide variety of amenities and upscale
  facilities. A five (♦♦♦♦♦) diamond rating represents a world-class
  facility, offering the highest level of luxurious accommodations and personalized guest services.

Prices

The price ranges below are for the least expensive double room, excluding 14 percent hotel tax.
$ = under $125   **$$** = $125–$225   **$$$** = over $225

At the Beach

▼▼ Best Western Ocean View Hotel $

This good, solid choice, across from the beach and the Santa Monica Pier, will give you the ocean but won't mess with your budget. All of the 65 rooms are clean and modern and many come with ocean views, private balconies and refrigerators. Leave your car in the covered garage, and walk to Santa Monica's shopping and entertainment district.

➕ 202 D2   ✉ 1447 Ocean Avenue
☎ (310) 458-4888 or (800) 452-4888;
fax: (310) 458-0848;
www.bestwestern.com

▼▼▼ Channel Road Inn Bed-and-Breakfast $$

Tucked into Santa Monica Canyon, just one block from the beach, this architectural prize consists of the original 1910 shingle-clad Colonial Revival house plus a third-story addition. The house is filled with period antiques, and all 14 rooms are individually decorated and have private baths; some rooms boast fireplaces, ocean views and decks. Breakfast is served on the patio or in the cheery breakfast room, and wine and cheese is set out each afternoon. A hot tub is on hand for soaking and centering. Bikes are provided, and some fine restaurants are within walking distance.

➕ 202 D2   ✉ 219 W. Channel Road
☎ (310) 459-1920; fax: (310) 454-9920; www.channelroadinn.com

▼▼ ▼▼ Fairmont Miramar Hotel Santa Monica $$$

Known locally as the "Miramar," this fine property evolved from Santa Monica founder Sen. John P. Jones's private mansion. Past guests have included notables such as J.F.K. (when he was a senator) and Jackie, Greta Garbo and Clark Gable. Today's Miramar draws international visitors and families primarily. Accommodations are in the original character-soaked brick building, charming bungalows or contemporary Ocean Tower. The lushly landscaped property is just across from the Palisades bluff and beach access, and a short walk from Santa Monica Promenade.

➕ 202 D2   ✉ 101 Wilshire Boulevard
☎ (310) 576-7777 or (800) 441-1414;
fax: (310) 458-7912; www.fairmont.com

▼▼▼ Hotel Casa Del Mar $$$

Sitting directly on the sand, this local landmark sprang to life in 1929 as the glamorous Club Casa Del Mar. After a $60 million renovation, the eight-story Italian Renaissance building reopened in time for the millennium. Many of the rooms and suites face the water, while others are just a tiptoe away. All units are beautifully appointed with such niceties as fresh flowers, excellent sound systems and fabulous white marble bathrooms. Fine dining is offered in the Oceanfront Restaurant and the bar features lighter fare (and the same view).

➕ 202 D2   ✉ 1910 Ocean Front Walk   ☎ (310) 581-5533 or (800) 898-6999; fax: (310) 581-5503; www.hotelcasadelmar.com

▼▼▼ The Inn at Venice Beach $

This modern motel sits just a couple of blocks from the beach and the delightfully eccentric Venice Boardwalk. Though not luxurious, the flavor is that of a European inn, making it a sterling choice for moderately priced accommodations near the ocean. Airy rooms feature high-beam ceilings, and complimentary continental breakfast is served.

🏠 202 D2 ✉ 327 Washington Boulevard ☎ (310) 821-2557 or (800) 828-0688; fax: (310) 827-0289; www.innatvenicebeach.com

Westside and Beverly Hills
▽▽▽ Avalon Hotel $$

Slightly out of the Beverly Hills loop, this former apartment building-turned-hotel offers 88 retro-50s-style guest rooms and suites that provide a homey feel. Most units face the courtyard pool, and all have such cozy amenities as cable TV, CD players, voice mail and safes.

🏠 198 B1 ✉ 9400 W. Olympic Boulevard ☎ (310) 277-5221 or (800) 535-4715; fax: (310) 277-4928; www.avalon-hotel.com

▽▽▽▽ Beverly Hills Hotel $$$

Known as the "Pink Lady," this has been the quintessential Los Angeles glamour spot since 1912. Just about anyone who is, was or wants to be anyone in Tinseltown has either stayed, dined or cocktailed in this classic property. Impeccably renovated, the hotel still sports its signature banana-leaf wallpaper in the corridors, and acres of lush tropical landscaping. Most of the celebs bed down in one of the high-priced bungalows, but all rooms are beautifully appointed, with pampering staff at your beck and call. Dealmakers and stargazers still congregate in the famous Polo Lounge.

🏠 198 C3 ✉ 9641 Sunset Boulevard, 90210 ☎ (310) 276-2251 or (800) 283-8885; fax: (310) 887-2887; www.thebeverlyhillshotel.com

▽▽▽▽ Beverly Hilton $$

The Beverly Hilton, a venerable Beverly Hills hotel that had become embarrassingly lackluster, found a savior in celebrity-owner Merv Griffin. A complete renovation re-glitzed this popular behemoth,

with spacious rooms, elegant ballroom and Trader Vic's Polynesian restaurant (one of L.A.'s long-time favorite haunts) for tiki ambience and knockout rum concoctions.

🏠 198 C2 ✉ 9876 Wilshire Boulevard ☎ (310) 274-7777 or (800) 922-5432; fax: (310) 285-1313; www.merv.com

▽▽▽ Hotel Del Capri $

This privately owned little gem, dwarfed by neighboring high-rise condos, is close to Westwood Village, UCLA, and it's only a short drive from Beverly Hills. Lucky guests (who often include visiting performing artists) cocoon themselves in one of the spacious units, many with kitchenettes. Free parking, complimentary continental breakfast, a courtyard and swimming pool are big bonuses.

🏠 198 C2 ✉ 10587 Wilshire Boulevard ☎ (310) 474-3511 or (800) 444-6835; fax: (310) 470-9999; www.hoteldelcapri.com

▽▽▽ Le Meridien at Beverly Hills $$

Until mid-1999 this property was the Hotel Nikko. Then came Le Meridien, resulting in a superb blend of French flair, Zen-like bliss and high-tech gadgetry. The Panacea Restaurant and lobby meditation garden are cool, but it's the guest rooms that hit the button with business travelers and techno-dreamers. Aside from Japanese decor with sliding shoji screens and soaking tubs, a bedside command post allows guests to access the comprehensive entertainment system and an array of information systems.

🏠 199 E2 ✉ 465 S. La Cienega Boulevard ☎ (310) 247-0400 or (800) 645-5624, fax (310) 247-0315; www.lemeridienbeverlyhills.com

▽▽▽▽ Peninsula Beverly Hills $$$

Chic and elegant, this relative of Hong Kong's famed Peninsula Hotel is a hit with anyone who demands the perfect discreet hotel experience. Noted for its personalized service, this boutique property garners high marks for its lovely rooms filled with finery, elite spa treatments, and the excellent Belvedere restaurant. No need to walk over to nearby Rodeo Drive – one of the hotel's Rolls Royce's will slink you to and fro. Entertainment industry agents and their clients crowd the Club Bar, known as *the* premier deal-making spot.

➕ 198 C2 ✉ 9882 Little Santa Monica Boulevard ☎ (310) 551-2888 or (800) 462-7899; fax: (310) 788-2319; www.peninsula.com

Hollywood, Midtown and Universal Studios

▼▼▼ Argyle Hotel $$

Formerly the Sunset Towers, this art-deco landmark – smack on Sunset Strip – once housed Marilyn Monroe, Clark Gable and other celebrities. Standing 16 stories tall with 64 luxe rooms, the Argyle boasts a cool rooftop pool and spa with great city views as well as a sundeck where the oiled and famous can work on their tans. The in-house restaurant, Fenix, consistently gets favorable reviews.

➕ 199 E4 ✉ 8358 Sunset Boulevard ☎ (323) 654-7100 or (800) 225-2637; fax: (323) 654-9287; www.argylehotel.com

▼▼▼ Best Western Sunset Plaza Hotel $

It doesn't draw the hippest crowd in town, but its heart-of-the-Sunset-Strip location and reasonable rates are hard to beat. All 100 rooms feature modern appointments, refrigerators and voice mail, while some are fitted with kitchenettes. Complimentary continental breakfast, a swimming pool and tours that depart from the hotel lobby make this a particularly attractive choice.

➕ 199 E4 ✉ 8400 Sunset Boulevard ☎ (323) 654-0750 or (800) 421-3652; fax: (323) 650-6146; www.bestwestern.com

▼▼▼ Hollywood Roosevelt Hotel $

Site of the first Academy Awards presentation since opening in 1927, the legendary Hollywood Roosevelt is synonymous with stardom. Across from Mann's Chinese Theatre, the hotel reeks with Tinseltown's glory years when the likes of Ernest Hemingway, F. Scott Fitzgerald, Errol Flynn and W.C. Fields were permanent fixtures – especially in the Cinegrill Bar. The guest rooms vary in size, but all have comfortable decor, and some even come with resident ghosts.

➕ 199 F4 ✉ 7000 Hollywood Boulevard ☎ (323) 466-7000 or (800) 950-7667; fax: (323) 462-8056; www.hollywoodroosevelt.com

▼▼▼ Le Reve Hotel $$

Le Reve snugs into the foothills just off the Sunset Strip – off the beaten path, but not far from the madding crowd. This secluded boutique hotel has only 80 luxurious units, most with fireplaces, kitchenettes and balconies, and all have refrigerators, cable TV and VCRs. The rooftop pool and garden provide even more respite.

➕ 199 D3 ✉ 8822 Cynthia Street ☎ (310) 854-1114 or (800) 835-7997; fax: (310) 657-2623; www.lerevehotel.com

▼▼▼ Renaissance Hollywood $$

This 20-story hotel is so new and big, that it's possible you'll be the first to sleep on the mattress. The ambience and decor of this cornerstone to the glitzy Hollywood-Highland retail and entertainment complex reflects the city's 1950s residential-style architecture. Public areas are gleaming, amenities are top-notch and you're just steps away from shops, movie theaters and Hollywood Boulevard, and a short drive from Universal Studios.

➕ 199 F4 ✉ 1755 N. Highland Avenue ☎ (323) 856-1200 or (800) (468-3571); fax: (323) 856-1205; www.renaissancehollywood.com

▼▼▼ Wyndham Bel Age Hotel $$

All the units in this luxurious hotel are suites with living rooms, work areas, kitchens and private balconies (some with terrific city views). Art lovers appreciate the paintings and antiques placed throughout, business travelers enjoy the extra space and connoisseurs of Russian cuisine and flavored vodkas make a beeline for the elegant and pricey Diaghlev restaurant.

➕ 199 D3 ✉ 1020 N. San Vicente Boulevard ☎ (310) 854-1111 or (800) WYNDHAM (996-3426); fax: (310) 854-0926; www.wyndham.com

Downtown and Pasadena
▼▼▼ Millennium Biltmore Los Angeles $$

The Biltmore, opened in 1923, is one of L.A.'s most cherished hotels. Designated a Historical Cultural Landmark, the restored Italian Renaissance-style structure was used for early Academy Awards presentations, headquarters for JFK's 1960 presidential campaign, and other high-profile events. Public areas are exquisite and ornate, but many of the units are smallish. Thoughtful service, a health club and an upscale bistro-and-sports bar add to the allure.

➕ 197 D4 ✉ 506 S. Grand Avenue ☎ (213) 624-1011 or (800) 245-8673; fax: (213) 612-1628; www.millennium-hotels.com

▼▼▼ New Otani Hotel $

Located in Little Tokyo, this contemporary high-rise is close to the Convention Center, the Performing Arts Center and Union Station. Rooms edge toward minimalism, but all the comforts are in place. You'll also be treated to such delights as the tranquil half-acre Japanese garden and spa with shiatsu massage.

➕ 197 E4 ✉ 120 S. Los Angeles Street ☎ (213) 629-1200 or (800) 273-2294; fax: (213) 622-0980, www.newotani.com

▼▼▼▼ Ritz-Carlton, Huntington Hotel and Spa $$$

Situated in a prestigious residential neighborhood, close to Pasadena's shops and sights, this 1906 landmark property is a bastion of elegance and tradition. All 392 units are impeccably decorated, and the public rooms are reminiscent of a fabulous country estate. Acres of landscaped gardens, a swimming pool, tennis courts, fitness center and delectable cuisine add up to another winner in the ritzy Ritz-Carlton family.

➕ 201 E4 ✉ 1401 S. Oak Knoll Avenue, Pasadena ☎ (626) 568-3900 or (800) 784-3748; fax: (626) 568-3700; www.ritzcarlton.com

▼▼▼ Westin Bonaventure Hotel and Suites $$$

The 35-story-tall, futuristic-looking Bonaventure is usually filled with conventioneers and business travelers – many trying to find their way. The dramatic lobby and "cylinder-like" glass towers can be confusing to maneuver around (and easy to get lost in), so helpful staff are usually on hand to set you straight. The hotel is always bustling, and many people stop in just for a ride on the exterior glass elevator, a drink in the 34th-floor revolving bar, or a meal in the sky-high restaurant with panoramic views of the city.

➕ 197 D4 ✉ 404 S. Figueroa Street ☎ (213) 624-1000 or (800) 937-8461; fax: (213) 612-4800; www.westin.com

▼▼▼ Wyndham Checkers Hotel $

This stylish, intimate establishment is well positioned for business travelers and others who prefer a bit more respite than the larger hotels offer. Lovely rooms provide all amenities, and pluses include room service, a business center, rooftop lap pool, spa and a fine contemporary restaurant.

➕ 197 D4 ✉ 535 S. Grand Avenue ☎ (213) 624-0000 or (800) (996-3426); fax: (213) 626-9906; www.wyndham.com

Food and Drink

Angelenos are devoted "foodies" – in fact this is where the label originated. Celebrity chefs Wolfgang Puck, Michel Richard, Joachim Splichal and others (many others) rose to superstar status at their L.A. restaurants. While a plethora of places are relegated to the "see and be seen" crowd, they are still outnumbered by a staggering assortment of casual cafés and inexpensive take-out stands.

- Thanks to L.A.'s diverse population, **ethnic eateries** can be found in just about every neighborhood.
- The mild climate and low rainfall mean that **alfresco dining** is available in every season, and many establishments have installed outdoor heaters on their patios to ward off any chill.
- **Fresh produce** is abundant and incorporated into almost all menus.
- **Vegetarians** need not worry about finding suitable fare; both casual eateries and fine restaurants offer meatfree dishes, and vegetarian cafés and health food stores are prevalent in most areas of the city.
- You can choose from **trendy clubs, clubby lounges, hip bars, neighborhood pubs and local dives**. California wine, imported beer, martinis and margaritas are perennial favorites. However, in this land known as the "cocktail nation," you'll be able to order just about any concoction.
- Make **reservations** in advance for the most popular spots, especially those that cater to celebrities.

Eating and Drinking on a Budget

- Many of the finest restaurants allow walk-ins to sit at the bar and order off a far **less expensive**, yet still high-quality **bar menu**.

Guide to Neighborhoods

Most neighborhoods have a conglomeration of eateries, ranging from inexpensive and quick to savor-every-crumb. Here's a snapshot.

- **At The Beach** The Santa Monica Promenade is chock full of restaurants, bars and sidewalk cafés. The Venice Boardwalk can't be beat for budget eats. Many plush seaside hotels combine fine dining with ocean views. Along the Pacific Coast Highway, you'll find some pricey seafood restaurants, though the occasional supermarket (on the east side of the highway) offers picnic fixings for a pittance.
- **Westside and Beverly Hills** Dress up and dig deep in your wallet for the famous restaurants near Rodeo Drive and those associated with glamorous hotels. Dine with the less-affluent student population in Westwood Village and on the UCLA campus.
- **Hollywood** The Hollywood-Highland complex is filled with dining outlets, and Hollywood Boulevard offers more. Sunset Strip's luxury hotels and the notable restaurants on and around Melrose Avenue can't be beat for trendy food and star clienteles.
- **Downtown and Pasadena** Nearly all of the large hotels and boutique operations feature multiple dining facilities – from refined, white-glove service to brasseries and poolside terraces. Old Pasadena is crammed with popular bistros and sidewalk cafés.

- **Lunch** at the fancier spots is often as delightful as dinner (particularly when there's an ocean or city view) and can reduce the check by heaps.
- **Early-bird dinners** can be especially good value and are offered by many restaurants including some of the high-end establishments.
- **Fast food and take-out** in L.A. doesn't necessarily mean a trip into one of the ubiquitous outlets. You'll find many one-of-a-kind ethnic food stands.
- Put together a **picnic** to eat at the park or beach. Groceries are relatively inexpensive, and fruits and vegetables are year-round fresh.

Practical Tips

- **Dress codes** are rarely enforced in this casual town; however, some of the more elegant restaurants require that men wear coats and ties, otherwise "smart casual" reigns.
- **Lunch** is usually served from around noon to 2 pm, **dinner** from 5 pm until 10 or 11 pm. Various **coffee shops, delis and take-outs** work 24 hours a day, as do a large number of **supermarkets**.
- The legal **drinking age** is 21. Most bars stop serving alcohol at 2 am, with some after-hours clubs continuing to pour until dawn.
- **Sales tax** will be added to the check. Expect to leave a 15 percent to 20 percent tip, depending on service. Restaurants sometimes tally the check with a tip included for groups of six or more.

Recommended Places to Eat and Drink

Each of the major chapters features a list of recommended places to eat and drink. This is by no means exhaustive, but rather a select group of some of the more interesting, memorable and famous locales.

Diamond Ratings

As with the hotel ratings (► 39), AAA tourism editors evaluate restaurants on the overall quality of food, service, decor and ambience – with extra emphasis given to food and service. Ratings range from one diamond (▼), indicating a simple, family-oriented establishment to five diamonds (▼▼▼▼▼), indicating an establishment offering such culinary skills as an ultimate dining experience.

Bests...
...**breakfast:** Campanile (► 130)
...**celebrity hangout:** Spago Beverly Hills (► 98)
...**chili dog:** Pink's (► 132)
...**dim sum:** The Empress Pavilion (► 160)
...**French:** L'Orangerie (► 131)
...**hotel dining:** Peninsula Hotel (► 41)

...**Italian:** Valentino (► 71)
...**nostalgia bar:** Cinegrill (► 42), Polo Lounge (► 41)
...**ocean view dining:** Geoffrey's (► 70)
...**old-timer:** Musso and Frank Grill (► 131)
...**prime rib:** Lawrys (► 98)
...**seafood:** Crustacean (► 97)
...**sushi:** Matsuhisa (► 98)

Prices
The $ amounts indicate the average price for a three-course meal, excluding tax, drinks and service, for one person.
$ under $15   **$$** $15–$25   **$$$** over $25

Shopping

Enormous malls, elite shopping "streets," ethnic districts and street vendors all provide a bounty of goods running the gamut of the price scale.

Malls and Department Stores

- **Talk of the Town** is the new five-story Hollywood and Highland complex adjacent to Mann's Chinese Theatre (► 115–117).
- **Other popular malls** are located throughout the city and include Beverly Center, Century City Shopping Center & Marketplace, and Westside Pavilion (Westside and Beverly Hills); Santa Monica Place; and ARCO Plaza, Broadway Plaza, and Seventh Market Place (Downtown).
- **The Grove at Farmers Market** is under construction and, when complete, will offer yet another mall experience near the Mid-Wilshire area.
- Almost all the malls are anchored by at least one department store. **Macy's** and **Robinsons-May** are the biggest entries in the mid-price category. **Nordstrom, Neiman Marcus, Barney's Beverly Hills** and **Saks Fifth Avenue** are the high-end entries.

Specialty Districts

- The crème de la crème is famous **Rodeo Drive** in Beverly Hills, where both sides of the street are lined with some of the world's most exclusive (and expensive) jewelers, boutiques, designer showrooms and salons.
- **Melrose Avenue** shifted gears from the old "super hip" days, with vintage wear and trinkets dominating the strip between La Brea and Citrus avenues and high-end home decor showcased along the western edge near the Pacific Design Center.
- Though still a tourist haven, in recent years Santa Monica's **Third Street Promenade** has usurped Melrose. Once a forlorn strip of old-fashioned stores, this three-block pedestrians-only thoroughfare (anchored by Santa Monica Place mall) is packed with hip shops, hot restaurants and cool nightlife; it's the favorite jaunt for locals and visitors in the know.
- You'll find even more swank shops and art galleries along **Montana Avenue** and **Main Street** (both in Santa Monica), or join the UCLA crowd in **Westwood Village**, where Westwood Boulevard and adjacent streets still offer a "village-type" shopping experience.
- In **Pasadena**, Colorado Boulevard and South Lake Avenue are centers of shopping action.
- **Universal CityWalk** at Universal Studios Hollywood (► 120–123) features an eclectic mix of retail outlets among the nightclubs and eateries.

Ethnic Shopping

- **Olvera Street**, a pedestrians-only historic park across from Union Station, is steeped in Mexican clothing, trinkets, pottery and other goods.
- **Chinatown and Little Tokyo**, both nearby, are the perfect areas to pick up exotic treasures from the Far East.
- Near Museum Row, **Fairfax Avenue** – headquarters for the Jewish community – is the place to purchase Judaica, curios and deli, deli, deli.

Other Shopping Options

- Don't overlook **museum shops**, rich in books, prints and other items.
- Downtown's **Garment District** offers blocks and blocks of discounted merchandise, with the Cooper Building (860 S. Los Angeles Street) as the focal point.

- On the second Sunday of each month **Pasadena's Rose Bowl** becomes a gigantic **flea market** where you can barter for just about anything.

Practicalities

- Malls and most shops are **open** daily from approximately 10–9.
- Those in the tourist areas often **keep later hours**.
- Some of the more exclusive Rodeo Drive establishments are **open by appointment only**.
- An **8.25 percent sales tax** will be added to any purchase price.

Bests...
...**accessories:** Fred Segal (► 72)
...**bookstores:** Book Soup (► 134), Midnight Special (► 72)
...**department store:** Barney's Beverly Hills, Neiman Marcus (► 101)
...**designer wear:** Prada (► 100)
...**flea market:** Rose Bowl (► 159)
...**jewelers:** Tiffany & Co., Cartier, Harry Winston, Bulgari (► 100)
...**lingerie:** Frederick's of Hollywood (► 133)
...**museum shop:** The Getty Center (► 80–84), LACMA (► 108–112)
...**non-mall shopping:** Rodeo Drive (► 100), Montana Avenue (► 73)
...**vintage wear:** Aardvark's Odd Ark (► 133)

Entertainment

As the undisputed entertainment capital of the world, Los Angeles stands at the forefront of the movie, television and music industries.

Movies and Television

- Many of the **Golden Era movie theaters** still reside on Hollywood Boulevard, with others in Westwood Village and the Downtown area.
- **Independent movie houses**, although a rare breed, can be found in the Los Feliz, Westside and Santa Monica areas.
- **Multiplexes** are ubiquitous at malls and shopping centers. Check out **UCLA** (tel: 310/825-8989, www.events.ucla.edu), **USC** (tel: 213/740-2311, www.usc.edu) and the **American Film Institute** (tel: 323/856-7600, www.afi.com) for independent releases and film festivals.
- In L.A. seeing a movie takes on a different meaning: not only can you watch one on screen but you can also view the **behind-the-scenes** creative process at **Universal Studios Hollywood** (tel: 800/864-8377) and **Warner Bros.** in Burbank (tel: 818/954-1669).
- **Television** runs nonstop, offering choices from movie classics and foreign films to sports and sitcoms. **Cable** is available at most hotels, and premium pay-for-view stations are often thrown in as a bonus. To be part of the television audience, **tickets** to most shows (free and on a first-come basis) should be requested in advance (► 19).

Theater, Dance and Music

- Downtown's **Performing Arts Center** (tel: 213/972-7211) hosts major musicals, comedies, dramas and new works, and is the seasonal home to the Los Angeles Opera, Los Angeles Philharmonic Orchestra and the Los Angeles Master Chorale.

- The **Pantages Theater** (➤ 135) and **James A. Doolittle Theater** (➤ 135) in Hollywood also host spectacles.
- Other notable venues include the new **Kodak Theatre** (➤ 136) at the Hollywood and Highland complex, the landmark **Pasadena Playhouse** (➤ 164), the **UCLA Center for the Arts** (➤ 102) and the **Geffen Playhouse** near UCLA (➤ 102).
- Major concerts are held at the **Staples Center** (➤ 164) and **Shrine Auditorium** (➤ 164) and in the enclosed **Universal Amphitheater** (➤ 123). Come May or June, locals pack picnics for the extraordinarily popular **Hollywood Bowl** (➤ 128) concerts with a roster of prestigious jazz and classical music series, top-name individual performances and the Philharmonic's summer season.
- The **Greek Theatre** (➤ 135) in Griffith Park also presents well-known performers in an **outdoor** setting.
- **Clubs, lounges and bars** around town (particularly in West Hollywood and along Sunset Strip) are filled with blues, jazz, rock and dance music every night of the week.

Outdoor Activities

- With the ocean at the front door and a mild climate, **water** enthusiasts can surf, swim, windsurf and kayak from Venice to Malibu. (Some **beaches** are designated for swimmers or surfers only, and lifeguards are not always on hand, so be wary of riptides.)
- **Cyclists and joggers** will find specially designated paths throughout the entire city (Palisades Park, Brentwood's San Vicente Avenue and the Venice Boardwalk are local favorites) and in **Griffith Park** (➤ 118).
- **Golf and tennis** can be played at public courses and parks. Many high-end hotels have tennis facilities and can arrange country club access.
- **Hikers** will find excellent trails at **Will Rogers State Historic Park** (➤ 66–67) in Pacific Palisades or farther afield in the **Angeles National Forest** (north of Pasadena, in the San Gabriel Mountains, tel: 626/574-1613, www.r5.fs.fed.us/angeles).
- In winter, **skiing** and other **snow sports** can be enjoyed in the San Gabriel or San Bernardino mountains.

Spectator Sports

- Downtown's **Staples Center** (➤ 164) is home to the **Los Angeles Lakers** and **Los Angeles Clippers** basketball teams as well as the women's **Los Angeles Sparks**. The NHL's **Los Angeles Kings** play hockey at Staples.
- The National League's **Los Angeles Dodgers** play professional baseball at **Dodger Stadium** (near Downtown) and the American League's **Anaheim Angels** hold forth at **Edison International Field** (near Disneyland, tel: 714/634-2000, www.angelsbaseball.com).
- L.A. still lacks a professional **football** team, but you can watch the **UCLA Bruins** at Edwin Pauley Pavilion on the UCLA campus (tel: 310/825-2101, www.uclabruins.com) and the **USC Trojans** at the Los Angeles Memorial Sports Arena (tel: 213/748-6131, www.ci.la.ca.us).
- Play the **ponies** at Hollywood Park (in Inglewood, near LAX; tel: 310/419-1500, www.hollywoodpark.com) or famous Santa Anita Park (in Arcadia, tel: 626/574-7223, www.santaanita.com), both with seasonal schedules of thoroughbred racing.

Practical Information

The "Calendar" section in Sunday's *Los Angeles Times* provides complete listings for all events (www.latimes.com). Call the Los Angeles Convention and Visitors Bureau's multilingual events hotline (tel: 213/689-8822; www.lacvb.com) for detailed information, or ➤ 193–194.

At the Beach

Getting Your Bearings

The beaches of Los Angeles stretch from the northwest end of Malibu down to the south end of Santa Monica Bay and beyond, but connoisseurs generally agree that those strands north of LAX, from Marina del Rey to Malibu, provide visitors with the most compelling selection of seaside activities. The ritzy Marina gives way to Bohemian energy at the Venice Boardwalk, while Santa Monica and its Pier,

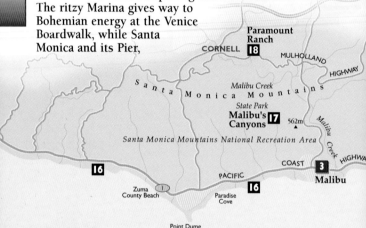

Promenade and Palisades Park offer laid-back beach-town vibes. Farther north, visitors ogle Malibu's movie-star colony and miles of pricey waterfront real estate interspersed with some magnificent public beaches ranging from crowded surf spots to deserted coves. The Santa Monica Mountains loom over Malibu, a vast rural sanctuary on the edge of the city. Whales and dolphins frolic offshore. Although some 15 or 20 million people live within hailing distance of Santa Monica Bay, it remains an inviting place.

This western edge of L.A. consists of small, primarily wealthy towns: – Malibu, Pacific Palisades, Santa Monica, Venice and Marina del Rey northwest of the airport (the focus here), and a tight cluster of other towns to the south. Some are independent cities, others are tentacles of the vast L.A. octopus; together they form an extensive urban waterfront, one unlike any other place on earth. Here you'll find surfers with dreadlocks and aspiring movie stars, jugglers with chain saws and guitarists singing the blues. On L.A.'s wild and wacky beaches, the circus is in town every day.

Page 49: Easy riders on a fun wave at Malibu's Surfrider Beach

At Your Leisure

★ Don't Miss

From the mellow towns of the South Bay to the wild shores of northern Malibu, visitors find that surf, sun and seaside fun define a day on L.A.'s urban beaches.

The Beaches in a Day

8:00 am

Enjoy breakfast in Venice or Santa Monica (Back to the Beach, ➤ 185, is a great spot), then drive northwest on the Pacific Coast Highway. You'll pass **14** **Will Rogers State Beach** (➤ 67; take a quick jag up Sunset Boulevard for a look at the **13** **Self-Realization Fellowship Lake Shrine**, ➤ 67). Continue on to Malibu. Lined with super-expensive waterfront housing on your left and the Santa Monica Mountains on your right, the Pacific Coast Highway (PCH) offers a scenic cruise into this starstruck beach town. Weekdays, the rush-hour traffic headed the other way serves to remind of the price people pay to live in paradise.

9:30 am

Stop at Malibu Surfrider Beach just north of the (now closed) Malibu Pier for a walk along the California surf scene. Stroll around the point to glimpse the **3** **Malibu Lagoon** (above) and the **3** **Malibu Colony** (➤ 61–62). Take a little time to walk up the Colony beach (stay below the high tide line and you won't be trespassing) and you just might see a few movie or TV stars catching some early rays.

11:00 am

Enjoy a tour of the **Adamson House and Museum** (➤ 61, left). The tile decoration is stunning, and the museum offers an intriguing look at life on the old Spanish *ranchos* of Malibu.

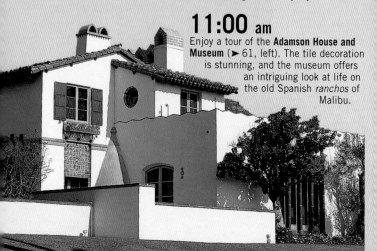

12:00 noon

Stop for lunch locally (try La Salsa, just south of the Malibu Pier, for good inexpensive Mexican fast food, ➤ 62), and head to one of the gorgeous **beaches** farther northwest (➤ 68): La Piedra, El Matador, El Pescador and Nicholas Canyon beaches are especially appealing. Drive up one of the canyons, spend a couple of hours on the beach or explore the mountains.

3:00 pm

Head back to Venice or Santa Monica. Stroll **Palisades Park** (➤ 182), **2 Santa Monica Pier** (➤ 58), and/or **1 Venice Boardwalk** (➤ 54–56, above). Enjoy a cycle ride or an inline skate tour along the beach. If art's your thing, head up to **9 Bergamot Station** (➤ 65) and check out Santa Monica's lively gallery scene.

5:30 pm

Savor a sunset cocktail with a view on the Santa Monica Pier (the Mexican place at pier's end has good margaritas), on the boardwalk or in one of the restaurants on Ocean Avenue.

6:30 pm

Dine at one of the fine restaurants on **11 Montana Avenue** (➤ 66), **7 Main Street** (➤ 64 and 70–71) or elsewhere in Santa Monica or Venice. After dinner, stroll Santa Monica's Third Street Promenade (left and right) – it's a lively scene.

❶ Venice Beach and Boardwalk

The Venice Beach Boardwalk has been a honky-tonk beachfront hangout since it opened nearly 100 years ago. Over the decades it has seen good times and bad, but has always attracted a spirited, pleasure-seeking crowd. Today, that crowd unselfconsciously puts on a show: Visitors and locals alike play roles in one of the most entertaining public spectacles in all of Southern California.

The history of Venice stretches back to 1904, when a "vision-ary" real-estate entrepreneur named Abbot Kinney took control of 160 acres of marshy beachfront land south of Santa Monica, and decided to create a town modeled after the great Renaissance city-state of Venice, Italy. Kinney drained the marshes and created an 18-mile network of working canals. He imported a few authentic gondoliers, built a pier, added theaters, planned restaurants and cafés, and erected a fancy hotel designed after St. Mark's Basilica in Venice. He threw a Grand Opening party on July 4, 1905, and sold many an overpriced canal-front lot; but then most of his investors built bungalows instead of mansions, and his vision of palazzos

A trompe l'oeil climber scales a Venice wall

Wheelers of all sorts rule the Cycle Path

A Walk Through the Venice Canals

The watery remnants of Abbot Kinney's grand Venetian vision, ironically enough, have emerged in this millennium as a new version of that vision, which is to say, expensive residences fronting Venice canals. There are only a few canals left, in a small enclave just south of South Venice Boulevard; and many of the decades-old homes here are relatively modest. However, there's no denying that this bucolic neighborhood has undergone a renaissance, powered by skyrocketing real-estate values and the inventive flair of some imaginative architects.

Focus on the homes along Dell Avenue. Roam up and down the Courts, enjoy views from the bridges and admire the ducks and boats in the canals. It is a lovely, pleasantly tranquil scene, a wonderful assemblage of old houses mingled with the occasional ultra-contemporary architectural marvel. You can stroll the district in an hour, then head back to the beach.

lining the canals never came to pass. Subsequently, when Venice visitors demanded cheaper thrills, Kinney obliged, enhancing his fiefdom with amusement park rides, a casino, arcades and other carny attractions.

In the 1920s, pollution from oil derricks to the south began to wreak havoc in the canals, and soon, although the Boardwalk continued to thrive, many of the canals were filled in and the city began a long, slow slide into decay. For decades, the few remaining canals festered and Venice became a maligned, grubby little town.

In the late 1950s and 1960s, artists began moving into the area, and it took on some Bohemian cachet. The money always follows the artists, and so it went in Venice. In the last 30 years, with ritzy Marina del Rey to the south and pretty Santa Monica to the north, Venice has been transformed. Today, real estate along the Boardwalk is outrageously expensive, and the neighborhoods clustered around the last of the canals (now dredged and cleaned) have emerged as expensive residential enclaves.

Venice can be pricey, yes, but exclusive, no. On a hot summer day, just about anything goes here, from Hare Krishnas chanting to Rastafarians juggling, to street vendors plying their wares, most of it legal. A trip through this informal performance-art spectacle is a must for any visitor curious about L.A.'s cultural *zeitgeist*.

Modern-day Venetians in love

VENICE BEACH AND BOARDWALK: INSIDE INFO

Top tips Don't hang out on or near the Venice Boardwalk **at night**. After dark the area can be scary and dangerous.

• L.A.'s beaches are often **overcast** until midday, especially in spring and early summer. If you want guaranteed sunshine, do your inland stuff in the morning and hit the beach in the afternoon (and wear **sunscreen**; even with a cooling breeze off the ocean that California sun can fry your skin).

• Don't be surprised if the **water feels cool**, even cold; it rarely reaches 70 degrees Fahrenheit before late summer.

• If you're **driving** come early, especially in summer, and especially on weekends. The parking lots fill up fast!

If you'd rather see it on skates or a cycle, you'll find them for rent all up and down the Boardwalk. On foot or on wheels, you'll encounter a constant stream of zany characters. Wheelers and walkers are separated, so you won't have to worry about being flattened by cyclists, bladers or skateboarders. There are plenty of restrooms along the way, where you can change if you want to swim, or have a go at surfing on one of the soft-top (safer) surfboards or boogie boards for rent at various stands along the Boardwalk.

Check out the last colonnaded remnants of Kinney's vision of Venice on and off the Boardwalk on **Windward Avenue**. On the beach south of Windward, musclemen flex their pecs, pumping heavy iron in the **Muscle Beach** outdoor weight-lifting center. Among the houses lining the Boardwalk between Windward Avenue and Washington Boulevard to the south are several designed by architectural superstars such as Frank Gehry and Antoine Predock.

Slip over to Main Street for a stroll, head east on Venice Boulevard and right on Dell Avenue for a tour of the **Venice Canals** (► 55) or walk south from Washington onto the quieter sands of the Marina Peninsula.

TAKING A BREAK

Figtree's Café, on the Boardwalk (429 Ocean Front Walk, tel: 310/392-4937, daily 9–6, inexpensive–moderate) offers everything from great French toast and homemade muffins for breakfast to pasta and burritos for lunch.

A one-stop shopping emporium in Venice Beach

➕ 202 D2
Santa Monica Visitors Bureau and
Santa Monica Convention
& Visitors Bureau
(► 35)

2 Santa Monica Beach and Pier

A hundred years after its 1874 debut, the Santa Monica Pier was in danger of being swallowed up by history – and the ocean. In the winter of 1982 a series of powerful storms knocked half of the Pier into the ocean; what remained was seriously damaged and in danger of collapse. Up on top, with gangsters and thugs duking it out with the cops on a nightly basis, the atmosphere became unsavory at best and people stayed away.

The beach and pier, a perfect surfside combo

Fortunately, "Save the Pier" citizens groups persuaded the powers that be to give the Pier another chance. It was restored, rebuilt and tidied up, with a new substation of the local police installed to keep an eye on the baddies. The wonderful **old sign** arching over the entrance to the Pier at the foot of Colorado Boulevard once again beckons the fun-seeking multitudes, as it has done for the past 50 years.

In the 1990s the Pier reemerged as a hot destination for tourists and locals alike, especially on Thursday nights in summer, when twilight concerts featuring swing bands and other musical stylists draw crowds of revelers and dancers. Call (310) 458-8900 for the latest information on who's playing where.

Santa Monica Pier

For a taste of old-time beach-front resort atmosphere, the Pier is the place to go. The recent changes have not undermined its carnival-like ambience, generated by fast-food stands, arcades, curio shops, drinking and dining spots, amusement park rides and one fine carousel. The

Stepping Out

If you're up for a walk in non-beach territory, go up or down the **Adelaide Steps** on Fourth Street – the view from either top or bottom is awesome (▶ 183).

beautifully restored **Looff Carousel**, built in 1922, features 44 handcarved wooden horses. With calliope music setting the mood, you can take a rollicking 50-cent ride into history.

Pacific Ocean Park, a fantastic, shambling giant of an amusement park pier just down the beach, competed with the Santa Monica Pier for decades, until it was demolished in the 1970s. In a nod to remembered glories, the Santa Monica Pier's amusement park section is named **Pacific Park**. It offers a scaled-down sampling of the rides, including the roller coaster and a Ferris wheel, that once drew crowds to the Park. Also here is the Arcadia Club, which features live rock and pop music.

At Pier's end, stoic anglers still drop their lines in search of perch, rockfish or whatever else lurks around the pilings below. Note that the waters here are not very clean, especially after rainfall: nearby storm drains flush whatever comes off the streets into the ocean.

Another crowd-pleaser is the **UCLA Ocean Discovery Center**, tucked in at the foot of the Pier. The center explores the interrelated themes of marine biology and ocean pollution.

The surfboard as a fashion statement

North of the Pier

North of the Pier, the parallel cycle and walking paths skirt the sands of Santa Monica Beach on one side, with a mix of old-time mansions, modest bungalows, beach clubs and architect-designed pads of the *nouveau riche* on the other.

This so-called Gold Coast once boasted a 120-room house owned by William Randolph Hearst, that flamboyant newspaperman, and one of the larger houses still standing once belonged to Peter Lawford, a Kennedy in-law (the house reportedly served as a trysting place for John F. Kennedy and Marilyn Monroe).

SANTA MONICA BEACH AND PIER: INSIDE INFO

Top tip Park in one of the public parking structures on Second or Fourth streets (flanking the Promenade on Third Street), and **walk** to the Pier, rather than fighting the car-crowds going into the beach lots.

South of the Pier

South of the Pier, the beach offers a children's playground, with stone sculptures for climbing. Nearby, volleyball courts feature world-class action, and gymnastic apparatus conjures another bit of historic lore: the original **Muscle Beach** was here. In the 1930s and 1940s, the first "hardbodies" of the modern world strutted their stuff on the Santa Monica sand.

Several swanky new hotels have opened south of the Pier, but the old-time charm lingers. Cyclists, bladers, walkers, skateboarders and joggers jostle for space on the boardwalk and cycle path, while surfers hit the waves, sun-worshippers bake in the sands, and seagulls vie for leftover fast food. The Santa Monica Pier may not be sweet and sanitary like Disneyland, but for those enamored of life on the urban beach, the scene at the Pier can't be beat.

TAKING A BREAK

Ye Olde King's Head Restaurant and Pub (116 Santa Monica Boulevard, tel: 310/451-1402, daily 11 am–2 am, food until 10 pm, high tea Mon–Fri) serves traditional English pub-style food in a traditional English pub atmosphere, with plenty of English beers on tap and in bottles.

✚ 202 D2
Pacific Park
✚ 202 D2 ☎ (310) 260-8744 ⊙ Mon–Thu noon–7, Fri–Sat noon–midnight, Sun noon–11; subject to seasonal changes 🎟 Free; rides inexpensive–moderate

UCLA Ocean Discovery Center
✚ 202 D2 ✉ 1600 Oceanfront Walk ☎ (310) 393-6149; www.odc.ucla.edu
⊙ Tue–Fri 3–6 pm, Sat 11–6, Sun 11–5, in summer; Sat–Sun 11–5, in fall/winter 🎟 Inexpensive

③ Malibu

Native Americans, Spanish
colonists, American ranchers, movie stars
and surfers have all planted their flags on or near
Malibu Point, laying claim to what has become some of the
world's most expensive turf. Malibu Point, the little curve of
beach tucked in between the pier (built in 1945, now closed)
and the lagoon, remains one of California's premier summer
surf breaks – famous as one of a handful of beaches whose
denizens created the surf culture in the 1950s and 1960s.

For centuries, the Chumash (► 14–16) had a settlement at
Malibu Point, which they called *Humaliwo*, "the place where
the surf sounds loudly." First, Spanish explorer Juan Cabrillo
anchored offshore in October 1542. An overland expedition
from Mexico came in 1775, seeking to shore up Spanish
claims. One member of the expedition was José Bartóleme
Tapia. Expedition diaries established that the group camped
in Malibu Creek on Feb. 22, 1776.

Years later, Tapia was granted "rights of concession" (a sort
of property lease) to Rancho Malibu Topanga Sequit. Tapia
Park, a few miles up the road in Malibu Canyon, honors his
memory. The ranch changed hands several times over the
decades and ended up in the hands of the Rindge family.

**Longboard
antics at
Surfrider Beach**

A tiled fountain at the Adamson House

Malibu Origins

Frederick Hastings Rindge, a wealthy poet, philosopher and philanthropist, and his wife, May, purchased the 13,350-acre Malibu Ranch in 1892. They built a big house in Malibu Canyon and created a cattle- and grain-raising operation, expanding the acreage to more than twice what it once was. Then a run of bad luck hit: The original house burned down in 1903, a victim of a Malibu brush fire. (Such fires have been torching expensive Malibu houses ever since.) Two years later Rindge died. His wife struggled to keep the ranch intact, but after a 17-year legal battle the Pacific Coast Highway sliced through her land. Undaunted, at the age of 65 she began construction of a family "castle" on a ridge behind Malibu Point. Mrs. Rindge died in 1941 before the castle was completed, and it was sold to the Franciscans in 1942. It has served as the Serra Retreat since; the monks even rebuilt after another raging fire burned much of it to the ground in 1970.

Adamson House and Malibu Lagoon

Lost in that fire were thousands of irreplaceable Malibu tiles that had been created in the Malibu Pottery, founded by the Rindges in 1927 on Carbon Beach to produce Mediterranean-style tiles. The pottery turned out magnificent work, much of which decorates the **Adamson House** on Malibu Point. This Moorish-Spanish Colonial Revival house, built in 1929 by the Rindge's only daughter, Rhoda Rindge Adamson, features an impressive array of Malibu tiles both inside and out, on walls, floors and ceilings, along with hand-carved teak doors, lead-framed bottle-glass windows and other refinements.

Since 1981, the house and grounds have been open to the public. A gift shop on the grounds sells reproductions of Malibu tiles, and a small museum in the house explores Malibu history. Colorful gardens and sweeping lawns roll down to the edge of the **Malibu Lagoon** (now a bird refuge and state park) on one side, and the surfing beach on the other. The house's docent-guided tour comes highly recommended; the Persian "carpets" made of tile are worth the price of admission, as is the view of the Malibu surf from the living room and veranda.

Malibu Colony

The Malibu Colony started in the late 1920s, when the Rindges sold the beach to Art Jones, who promoted it by leasing lots to movie stars. Residents in the 1930s included such old-time stars as Clara Bow, Ronald Colman, Gloria Swanson, Gary Cooper and Barbara Stanwyck. Today the colony is a gated private enclave, every house is worth millions and movie stars and other very rich people still live there. Stroll up from Surfrider Beach – stay below the high-tide line on the beach and you can't be accused of trespassing.

The Malibu Colony, movie star enclave

Surfing

Ronald Colman played a role in promoting Malibu's other contribution to American culture: surfing. He was great friends with the Hawaiian surfer/promoter Duke Kahanomoku. The Duke taught surfing to Colman and other members of the Santa Monica Swim Club, and soon they had "colonized" the break at Malibu.

TAKING A BREAK

La Salsa (22800 Pacific Coast Highway, Malibu, tel: 310/317-9466, daily 8 am–9:30 pm, inexpensive) offers a great range of Mexican food.

Adamson House and Malibu Lagoon Museum
✚ 202 C2 ✉ 23200 Pacific Coast Highway, PO Box 291, Malibu ☎ (310) 456-8432 🕐 Museum and House: Wed–Sat 11–3. State Park: daily 9–7
💲 Inexpensive; parking free on the Coast Highway or moderate in the parking lot just south of the entrance

MALIBU: INSIDE INFO

Top tip The Pacific Coast Highway **gets crowded** even on weekdays in summer. To avoid traffic try to get on the road to the beach before 11 am and plan on returning late.

At Your Leisure

4 The South Bay

Heading south from Marina del Rey, the southern half of the Santa Monica Bay beachfront consists of a series of small towns, including (from north to south) Playa del Rey, El Segundo, Manhattan Beach, Hermosa Beach, Redondo Beach, Torrance and the Palos Verdes Peninsula, which forms the bay's southern edge. All have their charms, but the most pleasant are **Hermosa Beach** and **Manhattan Beach**, small cities steeped in seaside surf culture. Each has an attractive municipal pier (Manhattan's features a small aquarium), and low-key retail areas with restaurants, bars and stores right off the beach. Parking is often hard to find, so one good way to get here is via the cycle path from Venice and Santa Monica to the north (► 184–186). Farther south, **King's Harbor** at Redondo combines the tacky, fast-food/curio-shop pleasures of an old-time wharf with a yacht harbor; beautiful **Palos Verdes** replicates the over-priced water-front real estate of Malibu, *sans* movie stars. South Bay waters are cleaner than Santa Monica's, so this is a good area to swim or surf.

✚ 202 D1

5 Marina del Rey

Home to several thousand boats and several hundred flight attendants and pilots (LAX is 10 minutes away), Marina del Rey has one claim to fame: the world's largest man-made **yacht harbor**. It also sports an upscale Ritz-Carlton hotel and **Fisherman's Village** (13855 Fiji Way), a pseudo-Cape Cod-style shopping and dining complex. The marina was dug out of a vast wetlands area in the 1960s and helped drag neighboring Venice out of its doldrums by the sheer force of its economic impact. The nicest thing about the marina is the

The South Bay offers uncrowded beaches

boats, best seen when sailing or chugging in and out of the channel connecting the marina with the ocean. To reach the channel, head all the way south on Pacific Avenue or Via Marina to where the peninsula meets the channel; better yet, circle the marina via Washington, Lincoln and Culver boulevards and make your way to the northwest corner of **Playa del Rey**, the quiet, out-of-the-way beach town on the marina's south side.

✚ 202 D2 Marina del Rey Visitor & Convention Bureau (➤ 35)

6 California Heritage Museum

Any museum that features an exhibition called "COWABUNGA – The Santa Monica Bay Surfing Experience 1907–1967" can't be all bad. Other California-inspired topics explored at the CHM include Malibu tiles, Depression glass, Arts and Crafts furniture, Mexican folk art and Hawaiiana. The museum's mission is to inspire collectors with displays of American decorative and fine arts, California-style. Whatever show's on, the building itself is worth a look: The museum is housed in an 1894 Queen Anne-style house (now a historic landmark) designed by renowned architect Sumner P. Hunt for Roy Jones, son of a Santa Monica founding father.

✚ 202 D2 ✉ 2612 Main Street at Ocean Park Boulevard, Santa Monica ☎ (310) 392-8537 ◷ Wed–Sat 11–4, Sun noon–4 💲 Inexpensive; free parking

7 Main Street, Santa Monica

An eclectic shopping and dining artery that parallels the beach, Main Street is noteworthy for a couple of Frank Gehry buildings: the **Edgemar complex** (2435 Main), and the former **Chiat/ Day/Mojo Headquarters**

The Ballerina Clown overlooks Main Street, Santa Monica

building (340 Main) between Brooks and Clubhouse to the south. Bookend a stroll with these two and you will have done Main Street. Chiat/Day/Mojo presents the street with an eccentric, formidable facade (➤ 22): Giant black binoculars by artists Claes Oldenburg and Coosje von Bruggen mark the entry, flanked by a forest of copper pillars on one side and bowed white "ocean liner" decks on the other. At Edgemar, Gehry makes art of the mini-mall. An ice-cream store and a gourmet restaurant, among others, hold down the neo-constructivist fort, once an egg-packing facility. Between the two Gehrys, enjoy assorted oddball stores, the **California Heritage Museum** (➤ left), the usual high-end boutiques, fab restaurants owned by movie stars, and artist Jonathan Borofsky's compelling *Ballerina Clown* statue on the Renaissance Building at Main and Rose.

✚ 202 D2

8 Santa Monica Museum of Flying

A pleasure for airplane buffs and families with children, the Santa Monica Museum of Flying occupies an old hangar on the north side of the Santa Monica Municipal Airport. The converted hangar was once part of Douglas Aircraft. The museum houses over 30 vintage aircraft, including a 1924 Douglas World Cruiser Biplane (the first airplane to circle the earth), World War II fighters and modern jets – all flight ready. The original Douglas Aircraft Boardroom upstairs includes an impressive 22-seat round

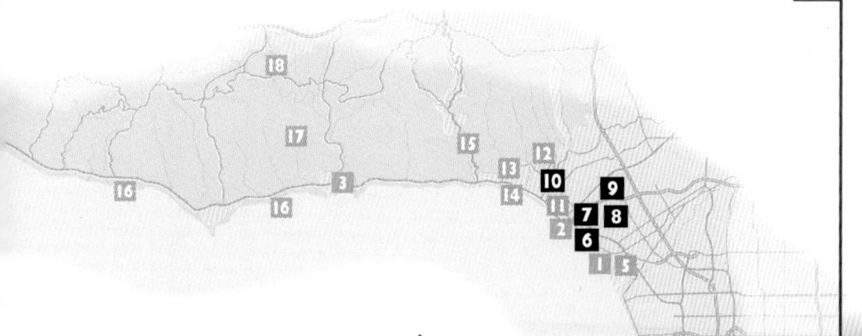

table with an illuminated globe at its center. When you've had enough of the aviation-related exhibits, videos, books and gifts, head upstairs to the sleek DC-3 restaurant overlooking the runway.

202 D2 ✉ 2772 Donald Douglas Loop North, off 28th Street, Santa Monica ☎ (310) 392-8822, www.museumofflying.com ⊕ Wed–Sun 10–5 Suggested donation moderate

9 Bergamot Station/Santa Monica Museum of Art

When architect Fred Fisher converted an old train shed into the gallery complex known as **Bergamot Station** (2525 Michigan Avenue, tel: 310/828-4001; www.bergamot-station.com, open Mon 9–4, Tue–Fri 9–5, Sat 10–5, inexpensive), Santa Monica's art world was transformed, as Bergamot quickly took over as the most dynamic outpost of arty L.A. With 40 galleries and art-related ventures occupying a series of light industry structures in a nondescript section of eastern (away from the beach) Santa Monica, Bergamot has something artistic for everyone. The artists range from unknown to world famous. Top galleries include Robert Berman, Patricia Faure, Rosamund Felsen, Track 16 and a dozen others.

The **Santa Monica Museum of Art** (tel: 310/586-6488; www.smmoa.org, Tue–Sat 11–6, Sun noon–5, inexpensive), occupying one of the buildings of the Bergamot complex, showcases local artists and hosts lively special events, including Friday night Salons featuring artists discussing their work.

198 A1

10 Uplifters' Club and Rustic Canyon Recreation Center

Harry Haldeman helped found the club in 1913, when he and a group of pals bought 120 acres of woods in Rustic Canyon (across Sunset and below the Will Rogers ranch). Decades later, his grandson H.R. Haldeman masterminded Nixon's Watergate fiasco.

Another famous tag is Frank L. Baum, who penned *The Wizard of Oz* and also named "The Lofty and Exalted Order of Uplifters," so-called because their mission was to "uplift art and promote good fellowship."

Vintage aircraft at the Santa Monica Museum of Flying

They built a Spanish-style clubhouse and several cabins in their private forest, where members such as Walt Disney, Harold Lloyd and Darryl F. Zanuck uplifted many a glass right through Prohibition.

Today the clubhouse anchors the 8-acre Rustic Canyon Recreation Center, a lovely spot for a picnic or a walk. The neighborhood features examples from every period of 20th-century residential architecture. Don't get too intrusive: celebrities abound, and they value their privacy.

⊞ 202 D2 ⊠ 600–700 Latimer Road, off Brooktree below Sunset in Rustic Canyon ☎ (310) 454-5734 🆓 Free

🔟 Montana Avenue, Santa Monica

Montana was once a sleepy, mixed retail-residential avenue slicing through the rich north side of Santa Monica. Parking came easy and rents were low for small local businesses. Then, sometime in the 1980s the leafy residential neighborhood around Montana woke up to its own bucolic charms; soon designer coffee shops, antiques stores, yoga studios, gourmet diners and chic boutiques moved in, displacing the old guard and creating a topflight shopping destination. From Seventh Street to 17th Street, high prices and high style prevail. If you like to spend money, this is a good place to indulge; unique, individually owned stores still outnumber the chains. In the middle of it all an old-fashioned neighborhood movie house, the **Aero Theater** (► 74), shows first-run movies on a single screen.

⊞ 202 D2

🔟 Will Rogers State Historic Park

The 187-acre Will Rogers State Historic Park nicely reflects the populist leanings of its former owner and namesake, America's beloved

Will Rogers' home is now a museum filled with cowboy memorabilia

cowboy-philosopher; there's something here for everyone. Rogers and famous aviator Wiley Post were killed in a plane crash in 1935 and the ranch was willed to the state in 1944. Hikers and naturalists explore trails linking the old ranch with the adjacent parklands in the Santa Monica Mountains. Enthusiasts of Western lore and California history find Mission furniture and an eclectic collection of cowboy memorabilia to admire in Rogers' unpretentious ranch house, now a museum. But the biggest draw continues a tradition begun by Rogers: open-to-the-public weekly professional and amateur polo matches on the park's polo field.

🚩 202 D3 ✉ 1501 Will Rogers State Park Road off Sunset Boulevard, Pacific Palisades ☎ (310) 454-8212 🕐 Park: daily 8–7 summer, 8–6 other seasons. House/museum: daily 10:30–5 except major holidays 💲 Free; parking moderate

🔳 Self-Realization Fellowship Lake Shrine

Southern California has always had a reputation for cultivating New Agers, spiritualists and oddball gurus. One of the most popular was Paramahansa Yogananda (1893–1952). Long gone himself, Yogananda still has his followers – his operation is headquartered on Sunset Boulevard in Hollywood. Since 1950 his foundation has owned the Self-Realization Fellowship Lake Shrine, tucked behind a wall of high hedges off Sunset, less than a mile off the PCH in Pacific Palisades. Given the commercialism scarring the nearby intersection, the shrine offers a tranquil little hideaway with gorgeous gardens, a windmill-shaped chapel, a golden dome-topped lotus arch, gazebos and a houseboat (Yogananda's former home) drifting among white swans on a small lake. Walk the trail encircling the lake, sit in the gardens and meditate on the views,

then hit the gift shop. There's also a small museum to learn about Yogananda and his philosophy. On a hill overlooking the lake sits a large temple for the resident monks.

🚩 202 D2 ✉ 17190 Sunset Boulevard, Pacific Palisades ☎ (310) 454-4114 🕐 Tue–Sat 9–5:30, Sun 12:30–4 💲 Free

🔳 Will Rogers State Beach

If you're feeling energetic, leave your car in Rustic Canyon and hike down to Will Rogers State Beach. There you'll find public sands stretching from the northwest edge of Santa

The Self-Realization Fellowship Lake Shrine is a tranquil hideaway

Monica almost all the way to Topanga Canyon. The waters are somewhat polluted at the foot of Rustic Canyon, but otherwise the swimming and lounging are great. Big parking lots, clean public restrooms and fast-food stands make a day at the beach fun and easy; come early in summer, because the lots fill up fast. Rent a bicycle and cycle in: the South Bay Cycle Path (► 184–186) that runs south all the way to Palos Verdes terminates near the northwest end of Will Rogers State Beach, by the private Bel Air Bay Club. The cliffs across the PCH, which frequently slide onto the road

during rainstorms or earthquakes, edge the high-priced suburb of Pacific Palisades.

✚ 202 D2 ✉ Along the Pacific Coast Highway, northwest of Santa Monica, southeast of Malibu

🔢 Topanga Canyon

Native Americans called it "the place where the mountains meet the sea," an apt description. Topanga Canyon Boulevard, connecting the San Fernando Valley to the coast, has unfortunately evolved into a commuter throughway, but Topanga State Park's 10,000-plus acres and miles of trails offer rural adventure within hailing distance of the city. At the foot of Topanga, the state beach's point break provides surfers with some of the best waves south of Malibu. Up the canyon, the primary entrance to the park is at the old Trippet ranch off Entrada Road. The Backbone Trail follows the Santa Monica Mountains' ridge line (spectacular views), then turns toward the ocean to end in Will Rogers State Historic Park. Long a bastion of artists, musicians and old hippies, the canyon wears the aging garb of the Age of Aquarius gracefully, with restaurants such as the **Inn of the Seventh Ray** (128 Old Topanga) serving refined natural foods. The **Topanga Community House** (1440 Topanga Canyon Boulevard), once the scene of impromptu concerts by local residents like The Byrds, Neil Young and Taj Mahal, now offers primarily children's entertainment. In summertime, the nearby **Theatricum Botanicum** (1449 Topanga Canyon Boulevard, tel: 310/455-3723), founded by "The Waltons" actor Will Geer, delivers Shakespeare and other classic and modern plays as well as hosting workshops.

✚ 202 C3 ✉ North on Hwy. 127 (Topanga Canyon Boulevard) off the PCH west of Pacific Palisades, east of Malibu

🔢 Beaches of Northwest Malibu

Once you're past the private movie star residential enclave of Malibu Colony and the build-up around Pepperdine University, heading northwest on the coast highway, Malibu's residential and commercial density thins. Here, you'll find a number of public beaches offering varying degrees of privacy. While **Zuma Beach** northwest of Point Dume is crowded with day-trippers from the San Fernando Valley, the beaches beyond (beginning with **Trancas Beach** and including **El Pescador**, **La Piedra**, **El Matador**, **Nicholas Canyon** and **Leo Carillo**) offer wonderful opportunities for sunning, swimming, beachfront strolling, kayaking, fishing and scuba and skin diving. The waters are a little colder here than in Santa Monica Bay, but they are also cleaner. On or south of Point Dume you'll find numerous public beaches: **Westward Beach**, **Point Dume State Beach**, **Paradise Cove**, **Escondido Beach**, **Dan Blocker State Beach** and others nearer Malibu. To find these gems, watch for the names on road signs or small "coastal access" signs. Bring your own food and drink. Note:

Some of the beaches, especially Zuma, have large, dangerous surf and attendant riptides.

🚼 202 B2

🔟 Malibu Canyons

Between Topanga Canyon and the Los Angeles county line where it meets the ocean, Malibu's coastline offers myriad beaches and seaside diversions. Less traveled but more appealing for those who want to get off the beaten path and drive are the many canyons that wander north and east from the coast through the mountains to the valleys on the other side. The drives take you up into the Malibu Mountains, where pull-offs frequently provide spectacular views of valleys, mountains, the coastline and the Pacific. It's easy to do a loop drive rather than backtrack, since most of the canyon roads link up high in the hills, via **Mulholland Drive** (► 10), which winds along above and through the mountains all the way from Hollywood to the northwestern reaches of Malibu, where it hits the beach near the Los Angeles/Ventura county line.

Some of the more intriguing roads for drives, views, trail access or interesting destinations include Tuna, Las Flores, Malibu, Latigo and Decker canyons. All roads begin at the Pacific Coast Highway.

🚼 202 B3

🔟 Paramount Ranch

The Malibu Mountains contain residential areas, great swatches of parkland and working movie and television studio backlots, the most significant one still in use being the Paramount Ranch. The ranch has been used for cowboy flicks since the 1920s.

Sights include a permanent set called "Western Town," complete with railroad station and tracks, cemetery, general store and saloon. The set has been used in plenty of films and TV series including "Have Gun, Will Travel," "The Rifleman," and more recently, "Dr. Quinn, Medicine Woman." Beyond the movie sets, the Ranch offers picnic grounds and trail hiking.

Top tip: The half-mile long Coyote Canyon Trail is short enough for children to manage and beckons with wildflower meadows and oak forests for picnicking, plus bird's-eye views of Western Town.

🚼 202 B3 ✉ 2813 Cornell Road off Dume-Kanan Road, not far from Mulholland Drive north over the hills from Malibu (access is quicker from the Ventura Freeway on the other side ☎ (818) 597-9192 🕐 Daily 8 am–dusk; sets closed to the public during the week if filming is underway

Jane Seymour as Dr. Quinn, Medicine Woman, at the Paramount Ranch

Where to...
Eat and Drink

Prices
Expect to pay per person for a three-course meal, excluding tax, drinks and service

$ under $15 $$ $15–$25 $$$ over $25

RESTAURANTS

❖❖❖ Chinois on Main $$$

It was only a matter of time before Wolfgang Puck delved into Chinese cuisine. Make reservations well in advance to join the aficionados who clamor for such signature dishes as whole Maine lobster, Cantonese duck, warm sweet curried oysters and grilled squab with pan-fried noodles. Watch the wizards wield their magic from a counter seat.

➕ 202 D2 ⊠ 2709 Main Street, Santa Monica ☎ (310) 392-9025 ⏰ Wed–Fri 11:30–2, Mon–Sat 6–10:30, Sun 5:30–10

❖❖ Geoffrey's $$

The knockout location on a cliff above the Pacific Ocean is reason enough for romantics to come pounding on the door; the creative California cuisine is another. Prime time here is during sunset hours or Sunday brunch, when diners can raise their glasses toward the horizon. Celebrities will be your dining partners for such delights as *ahi* tartare, stuffed rack of lamb and two-pound Maine lobsters.

➕ 202 C2 ⊠ 27400 Pacific Coast Highway, Malibu ☎ (310) 457-1519 ⏰ Mon–Fri noon–10, Sat 10:30–10, Sun 11–10

❖❖❖ Granita $$$

Wolfgang Puck's Malibu restaurant caters to celebrities-by-the-sea with Mediterranean-influenced cuisine. You'll find all the Puck trademarks: open kitchen, wood-burning oven and those infamous designer pizzas. Chef Jennifer Naylor manages to eke out imaginative surprises such as morel mushroom lasagna and miso-glazed *ahi*. Tasty fresh-fruit granita is the big hit for dessert.

➕ 202 C2 ⊠ 23725 W. Malibu Road, Malibu ☎ (310) 456-0488 ⏰ Tue–Fri 6–10:30 pm, Sat–Sun 11–2, 5:30–10:30

❖❖ Michael's $$$

Creative "nouvelle American" cuisine is on offer at this ever-dependable Santa Monica landmark that still boasts one of the most romantic garden settings. New chef Albert Melera has zipped up the menu: seared salmon, scrumptious risottos and sautéed spot prawns, accompanied by a terrific wine list, with delectable desserts to follow.

➕ 202 D2 ⊠ 1147 Third Street, Santa Monica ☎ (310) 451-0843 ⏰ Tue–Fri 11:30–2:30, 6–10:30, Sat 5:30–10

❖❖❖ Ocean Avenue Seafood $$

This lively eatery with an ocean-view patio serves a broad range of quality seafood. You'll find fish selections from all over the world, and the menu changes daily. Oyster lovers can select from a treasure chest of delights, while other dishes might include Hawaiian ahi, Maine lobster, and mainstay crab cakes and clam chowder.

➕ 202 D2 ⊠ 1401 Ocean Avenue, Santa Monica ☎ (310) 394-5669 ⏰ Mon–Sat 11:30–11, Sun 11:30–9:30

❖❖❖ Rockenwagner $$$

Chef Hans Rockenwagner continues his saga as one of the most extraordinary culinary masters in L.A. His inspired artistry blossoms through specialties such as crab soufflé and tiered salmon. Weekend brunches revolve around the now-famous breads and assorted cheeses.

🏠 202 D2 ⊠ 2435 Main Street, Santa Monica 🕿 (310) 399-6504 🕘 Mon–Fri 11:30–2:30, 6–10, Sat–Sun 9–2:30, 5:30–10

～～～ Valentino Restaurant $$$

Get dressed in your best for this pull-out-all-the-stops splurge. Order from a menu of carpaccio or seared *ahi* appetizers, heavenly pastas, veal and seafood entrees, or a seasonal risotto. With 1,000-plus choices, and a 120,000-bottle cellar, choosing the wine may be difficult.

🏠 202 D2 ⊠ 3115 Pico Boulevard, Santa Monica 🕿 (310) 829-4313 🕘 Mon–Thu 5:30–10:30, Fri 11:30–2:30, 5:30–10:30, Sat 5:30–11:30

CAFÉS

Interactive Café

Just around the corner from the Third Street Promenade, the Interactive Café's house blend is a mix of interesting art, excellent espresso and smoothies and a racks of newspapers and magazines.

🏠 202 D2 ⊠ 215 Broadway, Santa Monica 🕿 (310) 395-5009 🕘 Sun–Thu 7 am–1 am, Fri–Sat 7 am–2 am

Newsroom Café $

This is one of the best places in town for the health-conscious seeking smoothies, salads and other vegetarian choices. Celebrity sighting is almost guaranteed.

🏠 202 D2 ⊠ 530 Wilshire Boulevard, Santa Monica 🕿 (310) 319-9100 🕘 Mon–Fri 8 am–10 pm, Sat–Sun 9 am–10 pm

Novel Café $

Antiestablishment hippies and pseudo-intellectuals lounge around this colorful coffeehouse reading, recovering, surfing the net or writing the next *Catcher in the Rye*.

🏠 202 C2 ⊠ 212 Pier Avenue, Santa Monica 🕿 (310) 396-8566 🕘 Daily 24 hours

BARS

Chaya Venice

Join the hordes who flock to this Euro-Asian-style bar/restaurant. Half-price sushi and creative drink concoctions make happy hour even happier.

🏠 202 D2 ⊠ 110 Navy Street, Venice 🕿 (310) 396-1179 🕘 Mon 11:30–2:30, 6–10:30, Tue 11:30–2:30, Wed–Fri 11:30–2:30, 6–midnight; Sun 6–10 pm

Duke's Malibu

Come to this beachfront spot for an authentic taste of Malibu surfer life, complete with *aloha* atmosphere and terrific views. Sip on a cocktail and watch the waves crash.

🏠 202 D2 ⊠ 21150 Pacific Coast Highway, Malibu 🕿 (310) 317-0777 🕘 Mon 5–9 pm, Tue–Thu 11:30–9, Fri–Sat 11:30–10, Sun 10–9

Hotel Casa Del Mar

A cocktail on the elegant ocean-view veranda of this restored 1929 landmark on the beach will lull you back to L.A.'s Golden Era.

🏠 202 D2 ⊠ 1910 Ocean Front Walk, Santa Monica 🕿 (310) 581-5533 🕘 Daily 6:30 am–10:30 pm

The Library Alehouse

Choose from over two dozen microbrews on tap and another dozen bottled beers in an L.A. Craftsman-style library environment that drips with English-pub tradition. Finger food, light meals and snacks are also on offer.

🏠 202 D2 ⊠ 2911 Main Street, Santa Monica 🕿 (310) 314-4855 🕘 Fri–Sat 11:30–2, Sun–Thu 11:30–midnight

Ye Old King's Head

Anglophiles can't get enough of this friendly pub where you can down a pint, throw some darts and order up bangers and mash.

🏠 202 D2 ⊠ 116 Santa Monica Boulevard, Santa Monica 🕿 (310) 451-1402 🕘 Sun–Thu 11–10, Fri–Sat 11–11

Where to... Shop

The beach area affords a wonderfully casual shopping experience complete with ocean breezes and salty air. Santa Monica Place and the adjacent Third Street Promenade combine mall action with a pedestrians-only, open-air stretch of eclectic stores and chains. Main Street nearby features its own brand of uniqueness with specialty stores galore, while Montana Avenue (between Seventh and 17th streets) is a hidden enclave of upscale boutiques. Additional choices include Marina del Rey's harborfront Fisherman's Village, funky Venice Beach and decidedly non-funky Malibu.

You'll find branches of both Macy's and Robinsons-May department stores in **Santa Monica Place** (Broadway at Second Street).

Third Street Promenade (between Broadway and Arizona Avenue) is a primary lure for hip shoppers.

Fred Segal (500 Broadway), one of L.A.'s beloved merchants, offers clothing, hats and a dizzying array of interesting items.

Within the **Segal complex** are: **Zero Minus Plus**, with fine tableware and stationery; **Life Size at Fred Segal**, with kid-size versions of adults' designer duds; and **Fred Segal Essentials & Scentiments**, with high-quality bath and body products, aromatherapy candles and custom-blended fragrances.

Pass up the big-name booksellers for **Midnight Special** (1318 Third Street Promenade), an independent shop crammed with everything from poetry to politics, literature and literary journals, plus an extensive magazine section.

Hennessy & Ingalls Art and Architecture offers thousands of volumes, magazines and journals devoted to those topics.

Art, architectural and photography books, as well as out-of-print volumes and exhibition catalogs, are the focus of **Arcana Books on the Arts** (1229 Third Street Promenade).

A fine selection of vintage wear, including Hawaiian shirts, Harley jackets, gowns and poodle skirts is stocked at **Muskrat Clothing** (1248 Third Street Promenade).

Zip by L.A.'s fashion police dressed in punky, edgy club- and street-wear from **Na Na** (1245 Third Street Promenade).

Puzzles galore, along with action figures and other toys are available at **The Puzzle Zoo** (1413 Third Street Promenade).

Broadway Deli (1457 Third Street Promenade) has hundreds of wines from California and abroad, as well as one of L.A.'s largest selections of grappa, along with salads, cheeses and many other fixings for a fine picnic.

Bergamot Station (➤ 65) is the hub for many of L.A.'s contemporary art scene and also home to the **Santa Monica Museum of Art**. You'll find exceptional collections of paintings, prints, photography, sculpture, glasswork, jewelry, art furniture and other media spread throughout approximately 30 galleries under one roof. Among the residents are the Rosamund Felsen Gallery, Shoshona Wayne Gallery, Peter Fetterman Photographic Works of Art, Patricia Faure Gallery, Sculpture To Wear and the Gallery of Functional Art. Most are open Tuesdays through Saturdays.

Antiques hounds will want to browse the **Santa Monica Antiques Market** (1607 Lincoln Boulevard, open daily) where about 100 merchants sell vintage, collectible and antique goods in a warehouse setting. The quality offerings include furniture, clothing, costume jewelry, accessories, sporting equipment, linens and lighting from pre-Victorian through the 1950s.

If you're in town during the fourth (and fifth) Sunday of the month, you'll find hundreds of vendors at the **Santa Monica Outdoor Antiques and Collectibles Market** (Santa Monica Airport). Furniture, clothing, estate jewelry and vintage items are yours for the bargaining. Admission is charged, but parking is free.

Cutting-edge eyewear, vintage styles and a range of sports goggles are offered at **Eyes on Main** (3110 Main Street).

C.P. Shades (2937 Main Street) is a prime retailer for California-casual sportswear.

Patagonia (2936 Main Street) will prepare you for outdoor adventures with quality active wear, beach wear and its trendy signature surfboards.

Even if you're not dining at the restaurant, stop by **Rockenwagner**

(▶ 70) for exceptional breads and other German-style treats.

Max Studio (2712 Main Street) will adorn you with L.A. designer Leon Max's elegant garb.

Movie addicts should visit **Vidiots** (302 Pico Boulevard), a tiny place but with a vast and formidable collection of rare and foreign movies, scripts and movie-related books.

MONTANA AVENUE

Handmade arts, crafts and antique jewelry are highlighted at **Brenda Cain** (No. 1211).

You'll find high-quality antiques at **Lillian Lageyre** (No. 1231) and unique furnishings and home accessories at **The Blue House** (No. 1402).

If you like knitting, **L'Atelier** (No. 1111) will thrill you with its top-of-the-line imported yarns and chic patterns.

Room With A View (No. 1600) is noted for fine bed linens, but

you'll also find lovely infant wear and cuddly teddy bears.

New York designer Helena Stuart's **Second Skin** collection of lingerie is nearby (No. 1407).

VENICE

Venice may seem like an unlikely area for quality stores; nonetheless, visitors will find some happy surprises.

Fabulous 1950s furnishings are the claim-to-fame at **Johnny B. Wood** (1409 Abbot Kinney Boulevard).

Neptina, at No. 1329, features showstopper window displays, designer glass and ceramics, along with standout furniture.

Immortalize your L.A. cycling experience with a custom-designed bicycle, Spandex apparel and protective helmets at **Helen's Cycles** (2472 Lincoln Boulevard).

Cycle on down to **Small World Books** (1407 Ocean Front Walk), where you can browse fiction,

literature and mysteries, then read your purchase on the beach.

OTHER AREAS

Farther afield, the **California Map and Travel Center** (3312 Pico Boulevard) is the perfect place to load up on travel guides, maps and atlases, hiking and cycling directories and handy travel accessories.

Just down the street, **Caprice** (3213 Pico Boulevard) will tempt you with some of the city's finest French pastries, truffles and fruit tarts – all freshly made.

Load up on fresh fruits, vegetables, flowers, crafts and other items at one of the local **farmer's markets**: Sundays 9–1, Ocean Park Boulevard and Main Street, Santa Monica; Saturdays 8:30–1 and Wednesdays 9–2, Second Street and Arizona Avenue, Santa Monica; and Fridays 7–11 am, Venice Boulevard and Venice Way, in Venice. Be sure to bring your own shopping bags.

Where to...
Be Entertained

THEATER

Morgan-Wixson Theater
Operettas, contemporary plays, musical comedies, literary events and other performances.

🚇 202 D2 ⊠ 2627 Pico Boulevard, Santa Monica ☎ (310) 828-7519

Santa Monica Playhouse
Musicals, comedies and innovative works, including many family-oriented productions.

🚇 202 D2 ⊠ 1211 4th Street, Santa Monica ☎ (310) 394-9779

Santa Monica Puppet and Magic
Puppeteers and magicians mesmerize all ages at this fascinating place.

🚇 202 D2 ⊠ 1255 2nd Street, Santa Monica ☎ (310) 656-0483

MUSIC

14 Below
Mostly unknown rock and acoustic performers appear nightly.

🚇 202 D2 ⊠ 1348 14th Street, Santa Monica ☎ (310) 451-5040

Gotham Hall
Trendies come here to shoot pool, dance to live music or just sit on a couch looking pretty.

🚇 202 D2 ⊠ 1431 Third Street Promenade, Santa Monica ☎ (310) 294-8865

Harvelle's
There's nothing pretentious about this funky little blues joint, with live sounds and good vibes.

🚇 202 D2 ⊠ 1432 Fourth Street, Santa Monica ☎ (310) 395-1676

Lush
Disco on weekends with local yuppies who hustle on the dance floor of this mini-disco.

🚇 202 D2 ⊠ 2020 Wilshire Boulevard, Santa Monica ☎ (310) 829-1933

McCabe's Guitar Shop
This 1960s icon continues presenting legendary and local folk artists in an intimate back-of-the-store performance space.

🚇 202 D2 ⊠ 3101 W. Pico Boulevard, Santa Monica ☎ (310) 828-4403

Pacific Park
Entertainment is often on hand during peak hours, with dance concerts and a music series during summer months (► 58).

🚇 202 D2 ⊠ 380 Santa Monica Pier, Santa Monica ☎ (310) 260-8744

Temple Bar
Westsiders pack into this popular club to hear resounding world beat, and other hip and hopping sounds.

🚇 202 D2 ⊠ 1026 Wilshire Boulevard, Santa Monica ☎ (310) 393-6611

COMEDY AND CABARET

Comedy Underground
Stand-up comedy acts and featured comedians perform here Wednesday through Saturday.

🚇 202 D2 ⊠ 320 Wilshire Boulevard, Santa Monica ☎ (310) 451-1800

MOVIES

The four-screen **Loews Broadway**, four-screen **Mann Criterion** and **AMC Santa Monica 7** movie theaters are all located on the Third Street Promenade.

Aero Theater
A single-screen cinema (► 66) draws a neighborhood crowd, which often includes celebrities.

🚇 202 D2 ⊠ 1428 Montana Avenue, Santa Monica ☎ (310) 395-4990

The Westside and Beverly Hills

Getting Your Bearings

L.A.'s Westside, including Beverly Hills, is a place defined not so much by geography as by economy: just about everybody who lives in this area is doing quite well, thank you. The neighborhoods include Brentwood, Westwood, Bel Air, Century City, parts of West Los Angeles and the fabled city of "90210 Beverly Hills." The inexact "borders" lie around 26th Street to the west, Olympic Boulevard to the south, Mulholland Drive to the north and La Cienega Boulevard to the east.

The Westside counts among its pleasures the Getty Center, an architectural tour de force on its way to becoming one of the world's most important cultural institutions. Not far from the Getty, visitors can explore the Skirball Cultural Center, another majestic piece of contemporary architecture, designed to celebrate the richness of the Jewish experience. The Holocaust is touched on here but explored more thoroughly and eloquently at the Museum of Tolerance, in another part of Westside.

This well-to-do section of L.A. also offers pleasant walks and intriguing drives. With or without a map to the stars' homes, after window-shopping on Rodeo Drive or strolling the student haunts of Westwood Village and UCLA, you can tour the residential streets of Brentwood, Bel Air and Beverly Hills for a voyeuristic taste of The Good Life, Southern California-style. North of Sunset, take a spin up into loftier precincts for lovely panoramas of the city and peer through banks of immaculate greenery in front of elegant homes, ranging from rustic ramblers to massive mansions, which house the city's privileged classes.

MULHOLLAND DRIVE

Skirball Cultural Center **10**

405

NORTH SAN DIEGO SEPULVEDA BOULEVARD FREEWAY

Getty Center **1**

Page 75:
Shopping,
Beverly
Hills-style:
Rodeo Drive

Below left:
The Getty,
L.A.'s new
Acropolis, rules
the Westside

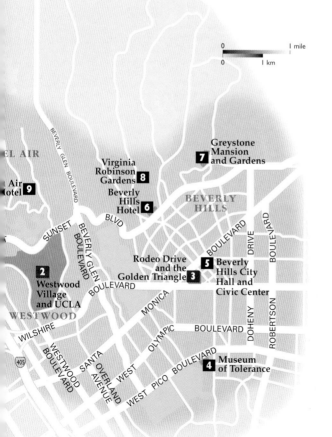

After a morning at the Getty Center, taste the upper crust of the American Dream with a shopping and sightseeing tour of Beverly Hills.

Westside and Beverly Hills in a Day

8:00 am

Breakfast in ❸the **Golden Triangle** (➤ 88–91), soaking up the ambience at Nate and Al's (414 Beverly Boulevard, tel: 310/274-0101, daily 7:30–7, $–$$). Unchanged since opening in 1945, it offers deli breakfasts and servers who act like your mom.

9:00 am

Kill some pre-Getty time exploring a few nearby notable addresses: the Schnabel House at 526 Carmelina, by Frank Gehry; the Sturges House, at 449 Skyway, by the one and only Frank Lloyd Wright; and the modest little house at 12305 Fifth Helena Drive, off Carmelina, where Marilyn Monroe died.

10:00 am

Opening time at the ❶**Getty Center** (➤ 80–84, left and below). Spend two or three hours exploring the collections, buildings, gardens and views. Make sure you've called ahead for a parking reservation.

1:00 pm

Lunch at the Getty Center.

1:30 pm

Drive to **2 Westwood** (► 85–87), park you car and take a stroll through the village and at least a small part of **2 UCLA campus** (► 86–87, below left). Or drive up to the **10 Skirball Cultural Center** (► 96, above), five minutes from the Getty, for an hour well spent in this beautifully designed museum and cultural complex that celebrates Jewish history and life. Or for a different look at Jewish life, drive down to Beverly Hills and spend an hour at the **4 Museum of Tolerance** (► 92).

2:30 pm

Head to **3 Rodeo Drive** (► 88–91, below) and soak in the ambience of one of the world's most chic retail districts. Visit the **Museum of Television and Radio** (► 90) or the **5 Beverly Hills Civic Center** (► 92).

4:30 pm

Stop in for afternoon tea at the elegant Regent Beverly Wilshire Hotel (► 91).

5:00 pm

Explore **Bel Air** and **Beverly Hills** (► 23) by car; if you want to take the celebrity tour, get out your movie star map and start looking for street names and numbers.

6:00 pm

Indulge in a cocktail at the **6 Beverly Hills Hotel** (► 41 and 93, opposite top right) or drive up Stone Canyon and have that cocktail at the **9 Bel Air Hotel** (► 95), surely one of the most beautiful hotels in America, if not the world.

7:00 pm

Stay on at the Bel Air Hotel for dinner at one of L.A.'s most romantic restaurants, the Dining Room, or switch from one fabulous hotel to another and have dinner at the Polo Lounge at the Beverly Hills Hotel. Either way, you'll need a reservation, you'll eat great food, and it is very possible that you'll see a few famous faces.

Ⓘ Getty Center

Opened in 1997, the Getty Center has quickly assumed a richly deserved position as the single most compelling attraction in Los Angeles. Don't miss it! This massive museum, education and art conservation complex proffers the pleasures of great classical art from the fabulously well-endowed Getty Collections (remember that this complex alone cost about $1 billion to construct), inspired contemporary architecture by Richard Meier and drop-dead views from a mountaintop setting just minutes off Sunset Boulevard near Bel Air.

All this and a garden created by Robert Irwin, one of L.A.'s premier contemporary artists, add up to a great way to spend a day or a couple of hours. The Getty campus covers less than a quarter of the 110-acre hilltop site, and the building complex itself is shaped in response to the contours of the two ridges that form the site. The highlight of the landscaping is Robert Irwin's enormous Central Garden, a piece that re-creates a ravine between the museum proper and the nearby Research Institute.

Architect Richard Meier's finest projects – and the Getty ranks high among them – offer a compelling integration of

Opposite: Skylights and glass walls establish a light, airy ambience

Below: Plazas and gardens surround the buildings

Museum-going in L.A. can be a casual affair

classical proportion and contemporary style. Composed primarily of off-white marble and white metal panels, the Getty's low-rise buildings attain a pleasingly rich, dense complexity. The heart of the center is the museum itself, consisting of 54 galleries contained in five two-story pavilions around a central courtyard. Linked by bridges and open passageways, the gallery buildings are accessed from a cylindrical entry pavilion. These museum structures are clad in Italian travertine marble to distinguish them from the nearby non-museum buildings, which are finished in white aluminum and clear glass, and they house offices and education and conservation facilities.

The bottomless well of the Getty endowment will in time elevate the museum's collections to a place among the world's finest. Meanwhile, you can trip through the galleries at whatever speed feels comfortable, lingering on the masterpieces and skimming the rest at your chosen pace. Take 10 minutes to view the **orientation film** in the entry gallery; it'll help you focus on what you want to see.

The holdings include the work of 1,145 artists ranging from antiquity to the present day, grouped in collections representing pre-20th-century European paintings, drawings, illuminated manuscripts, sculpture, decorative arts and American and European photographs, all arranged chronologically. The museum's expansive chronological range is its greatest strength: While the famous masterpieces are admittedly few, almost every period of Western history has been represented in some way, shape or form. If you have only one hour to spend here, the museum offers printed guides for those in a hurry.

Among the must-see (and so usually crowded) "stars" of the collection are Van Gogh's **Irises** (1889) and Belgian James Ensor's raucously teeming, pre-Expressionist **Christ's Entry into Brussels** (1889). For those drawn to masterpiece-makers, the collection offers 16 Rembrandts, 19 Rubens, an intriguing selection of Degas' drawings and photographs, and works by Millet,

Raphael and others. The photography includes over 100 pieces by Man Ray and works by David Hockney, Moholy-Nagy, Tina Modotti, Walker Evans and Lucas Samaras, highlights of an impressive collection spanning the 19th and 20th centuries.

A somewhat provocative design decision led to the installation of **"period" rooms** to house "period" works. As a result, you'll find yourself passing from the cool contemporary ambience of Meier's pale marble courtyards and passageways into galleries

How to Get There
Little or no parking can be found in nearby streets. It is highly recommended that you come by taxi or public transportation on MTA bus 561 or Santa Monica bus 14.

decorated with richly colored walls, heavy moldings and other rococo embellishments, evoking a kind of postmodern eclecticism perfectly attuned to the anything-goes design scene of Los Angeles.

The Center sits like an Acropolis, a culture palace luminously aglow in the California sun. Yet as anyone in Southern California will gleefully tell you, early fears of the Getty ending up an isolated, little-visited elitist monument to dead art and deader artists have proven unfounded. The place is a smash hit with residents and visitors alike.

The Central Garden

Artist Robert Irwin created the Getty's Central Garden,

Van Gogh's *Irises* is perhaps the Getty's most famous single work of art

the heart of which consists of a tree-lined walkway descending through layers of artfully planted gardens.

The walkway crosses a stream winding downhill amid a diverse assortment of grasses and other plantings, with arbors draped with bougainvillea that establish intimate seating areas around a small plaza. Below the plaza, waterfalls splash in a pool ringed with beds planted for color and reflectivity.

The Central Garden neatly bridges the aesthetic space between Meier's classically modern buildings and the rough, chaparral-covered terrain of the site.

You can see a thrilling contrast here between the garden's intimate, colorful plantings and the panoramic views of Greater L.A. and the Pacific. Hope for a fog- and smog-free day when you visit.

TAKING A BREAK

There are various options at the Center: **The Restaurant** (reservations recommended), the **Garden Terrace Café** and **The Café**. **Coffee carts** offer snacks and there are **picnic tables** if you bring your own lunch.

✚ 198 A3 ✉ 1200 Getty Drive, near the intersection of the San Diego Freeway (405) and Sunset Boulevard ☎ (310) 440-7300 for all information, parking and restaurant reservations; www.Getty.com 🕐 Tue–Wed 10–7, Thu–Fri 10–9, Sat–Sun 10–6; closed Mon and major holidays
💵 Free. Reservations required for parking (inexpensive) on weekdays until 4 pm

GETTY CENTER: INSIDE INFO

Top tips Take advantage of the Getty's well-trained staff and docents by taking **one of the several tours** offered. One-hour gallery tours are offered three times daily in English and once in Spanish. Meet by the stairs in the entrance hall. Architecture tours take place continuously every day (30 minutes). Meet to the left of the museum entrance doors. One-hour garden tours are organized daily. Sign up at the information desk in the entrance hall.

• **Bring sunglasses!** You don't often think of a museum as a place requiring them, but you'll probably spend a lot of time outside here, admiring the buildings, gardens and views. The endless expanses of white marble and white-painted metal make for a blinding experience if you don't have shades.

2 Westwood Village and UCLA

In spite of a plethora of massive towers thrown up nearby over the past 30 years, Westwood Village maintains an enticingly low-key "village" ambience. Bordered on the south by Wilshire Boulevard and on the north by the UCLA campus, it offers a lively array of eateries, stores and student-oriented businesses, and a couple of stand-out theaters from the glory days of movie-house design.

Left: Rembrandt's *An Old Man*, from 1630, is another highlight of the collection

Disentangle yourself from the brutal traffic along and around Wilshire by parking in a lot, and explore the low-rise Village streets and the UCLA campus on foot. Dating from the 1920s, the Spanish Revival-style Village was planned as a shopping district, and remains one, more or less: The main drag, Broxton Avenue, is lined with restaurants, movie theaters and retail stores. What lends Broxton visual distinction are three theaters: the **Fox Westwood Village**, at 961 Broxton, with its 1931 Spanish Revival glories still intact, and the neon-spired 1937 **Bruin** across the street at 948, along with the landmark **Dome**, circa 1929, at 1099 Westwood Boulevard. The Moderne-style Dome originally housed the offices of Janss Investment Corporation, responsible for transforming part of the original 3,300-acre Rancho San Jose de Buenos Aires into Westwood Village.

After a disagreement with the L.A. County Museum of Art, billionaire oilman Armand Hammer moved the bulk of his

Above: A bust of oil tycoon Armand Hammer at his namesake museum

Left: Vintage movie houses lend Westwood Village low-keyed charm

art collection to his own museum, located on the first floor of his **Occidental Petroleum Company** office tower on Wilshire. The reception area and several galleries devoted to changing exhibitions are contained in the tower, with other exhibition galleries housed in a windowless, horizontally striped extension of the tower that nudges north into Westwood Village.

Since UCLA took over the operation of the museum in 1994, the curated shows have become more contemporary in focus. Some critics have argued that Hammer's collection consists primarily of lesser works by greater artists, but there are a number of real masterpieces here, like Van Gogh's *Hospital at St. Remy* and John Singer Sargent's *Dr. Pozzi at Home*.

South of Wilshire, behind the Avco Cinema, the miniscule **Westwood Memorial Park** shelters the grave of Armand Hammer along with an impressive array of the famous dead, including Peter Lorre, Natalie Wood, drummer Buddy Rich and the immortal Marilyn Monroe.

The **University of California at Los Angeles** arrived in its present-day Westwood location in 1925. Architect George Kelham masterplanned the original campus, inspired by northern Italian Romanesque architecture. The original grassy central quadrangle remains the heart of the campus, surrounded by the university's central cluster of early buildings. The best of these originals include **Royce Hall**, constructed in 1929 from a design by architect David Allison, and inspired by a Milanese basilica; **Powell Library**, also from 1929, by George Kelham after the Church of San Zenove in Verona; **Kerckhoff Hall**, a 1931 neo-Gothic beauty housing the Student Union; and the **Fowler Museum of Cultural History**, adjacent to Royce Hall and

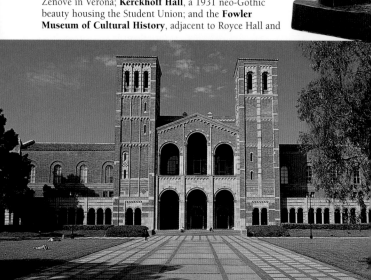

WESTWOOD VILLAGE AND UCLA: INSIDE INFO

Top tip An especially noteworthy part of Armand Hammer's collection at the Occidental Petroleum offices in Westwood is in the **Grunwald Center for the Graphic Arts**, home to some 35,000 drawings, prints and photos.

Hidden gems UCLA **Film and Television Archive** (Melnitz Hall, on UCLA; by appointment at Powell Library, or tel: (310) 206-5388, Mon–Fri 9–5 for access, free). This vast archive contains classic, foreign and art films, TV shows from the medium's early days to present day, and journalism footage from local and state news, including newsreels dating back to the turn of the 20th century.
• Another great alfresco destination is the **UCLA Hanna Carter Japanese Garden** off the UCLA campus (325 Westwood Plaza, tel: 310/794-6241, Tue, Wed, Fri 10–3, free; by appointment only). The garden is an inspired exercise in Zen tranquility.

home to a vast collection of artifacts, including masks from every part of the globe, a 10,000-piece textile collection and extensive artworks from Africa and Polynesia. The nearby **Athletic Hall of Fame** houses a different sort of artifact: the countless awards won by UCLA teams over the years. Of special note is the tribute to John Wooden, the UCLA basketball coach recognized as the greatest in the history of the sport.

The verdant splendors of UCLA call for walking. Get a map and self-guided tour brochure from one of the information kiosks and take a walk around. Close to Westwood Village, the **Mathias Botanical Garden** (open daily, free) conjures a country glade on the east side of campus, with lilies, fern grottoes and redwood trees. Abutting the Wight Art Gallery in the northeast campus, the five-acre **Franklin Murphy Sculpture Garden** offers the best selection of sculpture in L.A., with more than 70 pieces by Rodin, Joan Miró, Jean Arp and Deborah Butterfield, among others. A free tour can be reserved (tel: 310/443-7041).

TAKING A BREAK

Though you may hate to give up your Westwood parking spot, get in your car and head down to **The Apple Pan** (10801 Pico Boulevard, just east of Westwood Boulevard, tel: 310/475-3585, Tue–Thu and Sun 11 am–midnight, Fri–Sat 11 am–1 am, closed Mon, $, no credit cards) for a classic L.A. burger. Save room for a piece of homemade apple pie.

Top: Marilyn's grave at Westwood Memorial Park

Center: A powerful piece from the UCLA Sculpture Garden

Left: Royce Hall: Gothic grandeur at UCLA

🔲 198 B3 Westside Village
UCLA
🅖 Guided UCLA campus walking tours can be booked (reservations required) ☎ (310) 825-4321 or 825-8764 🅤 Inexpensive; free Thu 6–9 pm. Parking inexpensive

UCLA Hammer Museum
✉ 10899 Wilshire Boulevard ☎ (310) 443-7000, www.hammer.ucla.edu
🅖 Tue–Sat 11–7, Thu 11–9, Sun 11–5. The Grunwald collections can be seen by appointment only (tel: 310/443-7078)

③ Rodeo Drive and the Golden Triangle

Even if you don't like to shop, you have to do Rodeo Drive, if only to gawk at the Bentleys and Benzes lining up for parking spaces or the tastefully executed monuments to excess that line the streets.

First, get located. The Golden Triangle is a wedge-shaped commercial district bordered by Wilshire Boulevard to the south, Santa Monica Boulevard to the west and Rexford Drive to the east. Along with the crème de la retail crème, the 20 blocks of the Triangle contain a few architecturally significant historic and modern buildings, a couple of ultra-chic restaurants, a classy hotel or two and the offices and salons of the high-priced service industries that cater to the rich and famous: psychiatrists, cosmetic surgeons, agents and celebrity hairstylists.

Left: A plaque from Tiffany on Rodeo

Below: Rodeo Drive seen across Wilshire Boulevard

Right: Shoppers descend Rodeo Drive's Spanish Steps

Below: A doorman in top hat and shades – only on Rodeo

The primary activity here is shopping if you can afford it, and window-shopping if you can't. The excitement starts at **Two Rodeo**, a kind of hyper-upscale mini-mall at the foot of Rodeo between Wilshire Boulevard and Dayton Way. Along with top-of-the-line stores – **Tiffany & Co.**, **Cartier**, **Christian Dior** and other famous names – Two Rodeo is distinguished by the **Spanish Steps** linking Wilshire with Via Rodeo, a cobblestone, pedestrians-only passage that dates from Beverly Hills' founding in 1914.

Each of Two Rodeo's two- and three-story buildings have been designed to stand out individually, evoking not only different styles but different historic moments. Two Rodeo opened in 1990 and has a slightly unreal, sanitized theme-park ambience. Nevertheless, it makes for a pleasant interlude while slogging the car-clogged streets. The other "mall" on Rodeo lies up the street at No. 421, home of the **Rodeo Collection**. Lording it over the Rodeo sidewalks between the two "malls" are several dozen of the most expensive and well-known temples of consumerism on the planet, including **Van Cleef & Arpels** (300), another **Cartier** (370), **Louis Vuitton** (307), **Polo/ Ralph Lauren** (444) and **Giorgio Beverly Hills** (327).

While the stores along high-rent Rodeo all sport recognizable names, many of the side streets offer less pricey, more adventurous action. Stroll along **Little Santa Monica Boulevard** for specialty shops, and also check out the hipper-looking row of retailers on **Brighton Way**. Then drop in for tea at the **Regent Beverly Wilshire** (➤ opposite) and plot another walk through the Triangle.

You can backtrack up Rodeo to **322 Anderton Court**, for example, to see what Frank Lloyd Wright did in the realm of retail architecture. With a ramp winding up around a metal mast, it smacks of a warm-up for the Guggenheim in New York, and at the same time conjures a kind of nautical Streamline Moderne look.

Farther afield, the **Beverly Hills City Hall** and adjacent **Civic Center** (➤ 92–93) hold the fort on Rexford, close to a post office housed in an Italian Renaissance-style building at 9300 Santa Monica Boulevard. Even gas stations get the treatment here: Check out the Unocal station at 427 N. Crescent, a flashback to the golden age of gas in the 1950s and 1960s. At one corner of the Triangle, the intersection of Wilshire and Santa Monica, the **Electric Fountain** offers a circular frieze depicting scenes from early California history, beneath a statue symbolizing a Native American rain prayer. Look for the sleek marble and glass building at 9830 Wilshire. This ode to the power of the Hollywood agent was designed by I.M. Pei for the Creative Artists Agency in 1989.

A nice counterpoint to Pei's contemporary cool can be found at 507 N. Rodeo: the **O'Neill House**, a neo-art nouveau 1986 home by architect Don Ramos. Another fairy-tale house can be found at 516 N. Walden Drive at Carmelina. Called the **Witch's House**, the privately owned Spadena House served as the headquarters building for a Culver City movie studio in the 1920s. Its name was inspired by the steeply pitched roof, jagged fences, gnarled windows and broomstick entrance.

Back in the heart of the Triangle, the **Museum of Television & Radio** draws visitors into an assemblage of the soothingly bright, angular white spaces that signify the work of architect Richard Meier. This small museum, a block from Rodeo, opened in 1996 as a branch of the original museum in New York. Along with special exhibitions devoted to topics like "The Sounds of Silents" (silent films restored with full

Top: The Electric Fountain features an historic frieze

Above: The statue depicts a Native American rain prayer

RODEO DRIVE AND THE GOLDEN TRIANGLE: INSIDE INFO

Top tip Admirers of architect Richard Meier's work can see another example at the **Gagosian Gallery**, 456 N. Camden Drive, a spartan, garage-like volume that shows the work of modern-day art stars, among them Cindy Sherman, David Salle and Eric Fischl.

orchestration), "Hello, Goodbye" (three months of pilots, premieres and final programs from series television archives) and "The Role of the Media in Creating the News," the collections feature over 100,000 programs: films, TV and radio shows, including documentaries, commercials and newscasts.

TAKING A BREAK

Try afternoon tea at the **Regent Beverly Wilshire** hotel across Wilshire Boulevard from the Golden Triangle. Rest your feet in a richly elegant lobby, perhaps spot a star at a nearby table, enjoy fine tea and upscale snacks.

🖽 199 D3 Rodeo Drive and The Golden Triangle
Museum of Television & Radio
✉ 465 N. Beverly Drive, Beverly Hills 90210 ☎ (310) 786-1000;
www.mtr.org 🕒 Wed–Sun noon–5, Thu noon–9 💲 Free; contributions
welcome

A dream come true for TV and radio history buffs: the Museum of Television & Radio

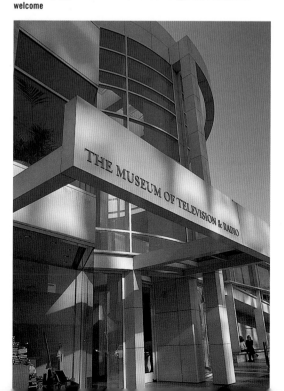

At Your Leisure

4 Museum of Tolerance

The always difficult, painful subject of the Holocaust has been handled with sensitivity and resourcefulness at this powerful museum, associated with the Simon Wiesenthal Center. One of its strong suits is the state-of-the-art technology employed in making the exhibits highly interactive. Along with the powerful exploration of the plight of the Jewish people in Nazi Germany, the museum examines the ways different political, religious and social systems contri-bute to racism, prejudice and other forms of intoler-ance. The enormous four-level complex includes a permanent exhi-bition level; a multimedia learning center containing documents, photographs, artifacts, testimonies and maps (all easily accessed from workstations); an archival exhibit with Holocaust materials; gallery space for temporary exhibitions; and theaters, shops, cafeterias and court-yards. The **Tolerancenter** offers several clever interactive exhibits focusing on different aspects of prej-udice, including The Point of View Diner, a 1950s-style diner with video jukeboxes exploring various contro-versial subjects. The **Holocaust Center** is also interactive and can be painfully moving: Each visitor is issued a photo passport of a Nazi-era child, and as you tour the exhibit, the passports are updated. After you've seen and heard the story of the Nazis and the resulting Holocaust, you learn the fate of the child whose passport photograph you've been carrying.

➕ 199 D2 ✉ 9786 West Pico Boulevard (between Overland Avenue and Beverly Drive) ☎ (310) 553-9036, www.museumoftolerance.com
🕐 Mon–Thu 11:30–4 (last entry), Fri 11:30 am–1 pm (last entry) Nov–Mar; Fri 11:30–3 (last entry), rest of year. Closed Jewish holidays 🎫 Moderate

A neo-baroque dome crowns the Spanish-style Beverly Hills City Hall

5 Beverly Hills City Hall and Civic Center

Beverly Hills' ornate City Hall dates from 1932, which goes to show that this particular neighborhood was not exactly suffering even in the middle of the Great Depression. Architect William Gage's mid-rise confection features a classic civic form: low base signifying government, high tower signifying business. The look is pure Southern California eclectic; the overall style is Spanish Revival with art-deco touches, while the tower evokes Moderne design and the dome on top is colorfully detailed in a neo-baroque mode. Next door, architect Charles Moore used the retro tactics of postmodernism to excellent effect here, in the expan-sion of City Hall known as the Beverly Hills Civic Center. Built in the 1980s, the Civic Center exhibits an appealing Spanish flavor, richly seasoned with art-deco influences. The whole composition, including a large new public library, fire and police departments and a parking garage, has been artfully arranged around elegantly landscaped courtyards.

🔢 199 D3 ✉ 444 & 455 N. Rexford Drive, Beverly Hills ☎ (310) 285-1000 ⏰ First floor daily 7:30–5:30, library Mon–Thu 10–9, Fri & Sat 10–6, Sun noon–6

🄆 Beverly Hills Hotel

The legendary "Pink Palace" opened in 1912 when developer Burton Green constructed the Mission Revival-style hotel to attract wealthy visitors to the new town of Beverly Hills, population 500. With its ideal location on Sunset Boulevard at the foot of the northern hills and canyons, the 12-acre property soon claimed its place as the social nexus of the movie industry and symbol of the glamorous life lived by the stars. The classic pink and green hotel was purchased by the Sultan of Brunei in 1987; he invested a bit more than $100 million in a complete makeover in 1995, bringing the old queen up to contemporary standards without sacrificing an iota of her low-keyed, high-toned style. The **Polo Lounge** remains at the center of deal- and scene-making in Hollywood, while the hotel's 21 bungalows, nestled among immaculately tended gardens, are still the hideaways of choice for visiting celebrities. Just about every famous name in Hollywood history made history here, for better or worse, from Marilyn Monroe to John Belushi. Partake of the excellent fare at the Polo Lounge, and witness Hollywood at work while you eat;

The Beverly Hills Hotel still reigns over Hollywood society

Hillside: the 46,000-square-foot, 55-room house is in a classic English Tudor style. In the late 1920s oilman Edward S. Doheny built the house on a 415-acre tract north of Sunset, thus claiming title to the largest family estate in Beverly Hills. Most of the land was sold off in the 1950s, but the 18 acres of wonderfully landscaped gardens that remain with the house have been transformed into a very appealing public park.

The house is not open to visitors, but you can get close enough to admire the intricacies of the chimneys and the fine limestone facades, and you can peek in the windows. The formal and informal gardens circling the house are worth exploring; along with koi ponds, a swimming pool and expansive lawns, there are splendid views of the house and grounds in the foreground and the city in the distance.

🚩 199 D3 ✉ 905 Loma Vista Drive (off Doheny Drive), Beverly Hills ☎ (310) 550-4796 ⓖ Gardens daily 10–6 🎫 Free

have a milk shake or sandwich downstairs at the cozy little Fountain Coffee Shop. You might find yourself (literally) rubbing elbows with some-one you've seen in the movies.

🚩 198 C3 ✉ 9641 Sunset Boulevard (at Rodeo Drive), Beverly Hills ☎ (310) 276-2251 or (800) 283-8885; www.thebeverlyhillshotel.com

🔲 Greystone Mansion and Gardens

The massive, rambling Greystone Mansion looks as if it might have been airlifted from the English countryside and planted on a Beverly

The Greystone Mansion, a bastion of Tudor grace in Beverly Hills

garden tours. The **gardens** are glorious, with five distinct zones: the Italian Terrace Garden, the Formal Mall Garden, the Rose Garden, the Kitchen Garden and the magnificent Tropical Palm Garden. Dominated by hundreds of Australian king palms, the palm garden is the largest collection of its kind in the country. Garden-lovers, remember. No matter what time of year you're in L.A., something will be in bloom at this or any other garden you visit.

✚ 198 C3 ✉ 1008 Elden Way, Beverly Hills ☎ (310) 276-5367 🕐 By appointment for tours only, Tue–Thu 10 am and 1 pm, Fri 10 am 💷 Moderate

The lush and elegant Virginia Robinson Gardens

Roses bloom year-round in L.A.'s temperate climate

8 Virginia Robinson Gardens

Nestled at the end of a cul-de-sac in a quiet residential neighborhood near the Beverly Hills Hotel, the Virginia Robinson Gardens rank high on the list of under-visited parks in the L.A. area, to the great good luck of those who take the time to make their reservations in advance.

Designed in 1911 in classic beaux arts style by architect Nathaniel Dryden (landscape design by Charles Gibbs Adams), the house and six-acre estate was built for the heiress to the Robinson department store empire. Mrs. Robinson willed the property to Los Angeles County; the Department of Parks and Recreation manages the site, offering tours by appointment only.

While the house is not open to the public, the 1924 **Renaissance Pool Pavilion** serves as the starting point for the 75-minute docent-guided

9 Bel Air Hotel

Tucked into a lush, wooded canyon in the hilly upper reaches of Bel Air, the secluded, mission-style Bel Air Hotel surely ranks as the loveliest, most charming hotel in Los Angeles. Even if you can't afford an overnight stay (rates range from $445 up to $3,000 per night), a visit for a cocktail or tea on the Terrace, or better yet, brunch by the Swan Pool or dinner in the hotel Dining Room comes highly recommended. With its Sunset Boulevard address the Beverly Hills Hotel has always gotten more attention, but many well-heeled visitors and celebrities find the quieter, more intimate Bel Air a better choice. Set in verdant grounds with thousands of flowers, laced with

dominate museums devoted to Jewish culture, is handled delicately in the larger context of Jewish history. The exploration of Jewish assimilation into contemporary American life is fascinating, reminding visitors of how immensely significant has been that culture's influence on America's democratic values and self-image.

The Center has something for everyone: The mock archaeological digs and the hands-on activities in the **Discovery Center** will fascinate kids. The **Tapler Courtyard** serves as a wonderful setting for outdoor concerts, while the auditorium offers a regular series of lectures, films and concerts as well as readings.

Visitors will also enjoy the Center's multicultural museum store, a lively indoor/ outdoor café, provocative temporary exhibitions, a resource center with high-speed Internet access to over 150 related websites and a well-stocked research library.

⊞ 198 A5 ⊠ 2701 North Sepulveda Boulevard ☎ (310) 440-4500; www.skirball.org ⏲ Tue–Sat noon–5, Sun 11–5 💲 Moderate; under 12s free

streams, ponds and fountains making water music at every turn, the hotel is delightfully relaxed and glamorously elegant.

⊞ 198 B3 ⊠ 701 Stone Canyon Road (north off Sunset) ☎ (310) 472-1211 or (800) 648-4097; www.hotelbelair.com

🔟 Skirball Cultural Center

Canadian architect Moshe Safie crafted this spacious, light-saturated cultural complex devoted to Jewish life in America. Located on a 15-acre site at the crest of Sepulveda Pass in the Santa Monica Mountains (a couple of miles from the Getty), the Skirball covers a lot of ground, both physically and culturally. At the heart of the Center lies the museum dedicated to exploring "Visions and Values: Jewish Life from Antiquity to America." Here, 12 galleries organized in chronological order take visitors on a journey from the origins of Judaism through life in the Old World, immigration and assimilation into modern society. The Holocaust, a topic that tends to

Ancient Jewish history is re-created at the Skirball Cultural Center

Where to... Eat and Drink

Prices
Expect to pay per person for a three-course meal, excluding tax, drinks and service
$ under $15 $$ $15–$25 $$$ over $25

RESTAURANTS

The Belvedere $$
Set inside the ritzy Peninsula Beverly Hills Hotel (▶ 41), the Belvedere offers meals throughout the day, but it's the dinner menu that's really stellar. The daily changing menu, comprising small bites, small and large plates and Chef Bill Bracken's suggestions, are a melange of Californian, Asian and French creations – all exquisitely presented and perfectly executed. Expect to see plenty of celebrities.

✚ 198 C2 ☒ 9882 Little Santa Monica Boulevard, Beverly Hills ☎ (310) 788-2306 ⏰ Daily 6:30–11, 11:30–2:30, 6–10:30

La Cachette Restaurant $$
This charming hideaway offers a delightful dining experience to all who seek it out. Owner-chef Jean-Francois Meteigner welcomes guests to his oasis of calm, then treats them to nouvelle French creations such as sautéed squab, farm-raised venison, pan-roasted salmon and cabbage-wrapped *foie gras*. *Tarte Tatin* is the biggest of the hits on the dessert list.

✚ 198 C2 ☒ 10506 Santa Monica Boulevard, Century City ☎ (310) 470-4992 ⏰ Mon–Fri 11–2:30, 6–9, Sat 11:30–2:30, 5:30–10:30, Sun 6–9:30

Crustacean $$$
Now one of the top restaurants in Beverly Hills, patrons can't get enough of the Vietnamese/French delights, which include a "secret" menu of closely guarded family recipes, along with the specialty – whole roasted Dungeness crabs and reputedly addictive garlic noodles.

✚ 199 D3 ☒ 9646 S. Santa Monica Boulevard, Beverly Hills ☎ (310) 205-8990 ⏰ Mon–Thu 11:30–2:30, 5:30–10:30, Fri–Sat 11:30–2:30, 5:30–11:30

The Dining Room $$$
You'll dine like royalty (and pay the price) at this opulent fine dining room in the Regent Beverly Wilshire Hotel. The classy surroundings offer a first-class dining experience for a more mature clientele. Top-rated food and service are the hallmarks of this excellent establishment where American/Continental cuisine is beautifully presented. The heavenly Grand Marnier chocolate soufflé is a "must" for dessert. Dancing and live jazz Friday nights.

✚ 199 D2 ☒ 9500 Wilshire Boulevard, Beverly Hills ☎ (310) 275-5200 ⏰ Mon–Sat 6:30–2:30, 6:30–10, Sun 7–noon

Four Oaks $$$
Nestled in the canyon between Sunset Boulevard and Mulholland Drive, the Four Oaks is famous with celebrities seeking a discreet location to "pop the question" to their beloved of the moment. The romantic setting is reminiscent of Provence, with a cozy dining room, the more popular tree-canopied patio and flawless service throughout. The seasonally changing menu flaunts the sublime California-French cuisine by chef Peter Roelant.

✚ 198 B4 ☒ 2181 N. Beverly Glen, Bel Air ☎ (310) 470-2265 ⏰ Tue–Sat 11:30–2, 6–10, Sun 10:30–2, 6–10

Junior's Restaurant $

If you're craving authentic Jewish deli, Junior's offers some of the finest "tastes-like-someone's-mother-made-it" recipes. The *matzoh* ball soup and delectably creamy *blintzes* are the high points, along with generous corned-beef and pastrami sandwiches, smoked fish platters and the usual lengthy menu of goodies morning, noon or night.

🕇 198 C1 ⊠ 2379 Westwood Boulevard, West L.A. ☎ (310) 475-5771 🕘 Mon–Thu 6:30 am–11 pm, Fri 6:30 am–midnight, Sat 7 am–midnight, Sun 7 am–11 pm

Lawry's The Prime Rib $$

Lawry's draws locals and tourists for what is possibly the most magnificent and succulent prime rib on the face of the earth, accompanied by whipped-cream horseradish and Yorkshire pudding. You can also choose savory steaks or fresh seafood and such comforting side dishes as creamed spinach and mashed potatoes.

🕇 199 E2 ⊠ 100 N. La Cienega Boulevard, Beverly Hills ☎ (310) 652-2827 🕘 Mon–Thu 5–10 pm, Fri 5–11, Sat 4:30–11, Sun 4–10

Lunaria $

Aside from being one of the coolest jazz clubs on the Westside, Lunaria serves delectable French bistro fare. The atmosphere is something like "Hollywood Supper Club meets the South of France," with watercolors, a marble-top bar and an exhibition kitchen behind glass. If you're craving authentic "steak frites," this is the place to come. Other entrees consist of magnificent preparations of lamb and chicken, along with equally fabulous daily specials.

🕇 198 C2 ⊠ 10351 Santa Monica Boulevard, Century City ☎ (310) 282-8870 🕘 Mon 11–2:30, Tue–Thu 11–2:30, 5:30–10, Fri 11–2:30, 5:30–11, Sat 5:30–11 pm

Matsuhisa $$$

It's incredibly expensive but you'll experience Japanese food at its very best. The sushi practically defies description and includes artistically pre-pared renderings of the freshest squid, salmon and sea scallops, all with an international twist. The 25-page menu of cooked seafood is mind-boggling, and you might want to opt for one of the daily specials.

🕇 199 E2 ⊠ 129 N. La Cienega Boulevard, Beverly Hills ☎ (310) 659-9639 🕘 Mon–Fri 11:45–2:15, 5:45–10:15, Sat–Sun 5:45–10:15

Spago Beverly Hills $$$

Reservations are not easy to come by, but once in you'll be lifted into gastronomic heaven. Delicious preparations of lobster, veal, filet mignon and others are on the menu, along with Wolfgang Puck's famous signature pizzas. Master sommelier Michael Bonaccorsi will judiciously select your wine.

🕇 199 D2 ⊠ 176 N. Canon Drive, Beverly Hills ☎ (310) 385-0880 🕘 Mon–Thu, Sun 11–2:15, 5:30–10:30, Fri–Sat 11–2:15, 5:30–midnight

Trader Vic's $$$

Trader Vic's, commanding a prime corner within the Beverly Hilton Hotel, has long been a favorite with locals. Known for its South Seas atmosphere and kitschy decor, dining here is somewhat akin to being at a *luau*. Prepare for tikis, dim lights and umbrellas in the cocktails (rum drinks, in dozens of combinations, are the specialty of the house). The food has departed from the old pineapple chicken, and entered a more contemporary Pan-Asian era with barbecued and wood-fired meat and seafood, as well as interesting stir-fries.

🕇 198 C2 ⊠ 9876 Wilshire Boulevard, Beverly Hills ☎ (310) 276-6345 🕘 Mon–Thu, Sun 5–midnight, Fri–Sat 5 pm–1 am

CAFÉS

A Votre Santé $

This establishment offers two Westside locations where you can recharge with health-oriented tidbits such as stir-fried veggies, turkey burgers, tofu scrambles, muffins and other bakery items.

✚ 199 D2 ⊠ 242 S. Beverly Drive, Beverly Hills ☎ (310) 860-9441 ⏰ Mon–Sat 11–10, Sun 11–9
✚ 198 A2 ⊠ 13016 San Vicente Boulevard, Brentwood ☎ (310) 451-1813 ⏰ Mon–Sat 11–10, Sun 11–9

Barney Greengrass $

Atop Barney's Beverly Hills department store, this is a pricey pit stop for clientele who need a break. Smoked fish, chopped liver, and bagels and cream cheese are among the deli fare. The view is tossed in for free.

✚ 199 D2 ⊠ 9570 Wilshire Boulevard, Beverly Hills ☎ (310) 777-5877 ⏰ Mon–Wed 8:30–6, Thu–Fri 8:30–7, Sat 9–7, Sun 9–6

Brighton Coffee Shop $

Forget café, this is a real 1950s coffee shop, improbably plunked in the middle of trendy Beverly Hills. Savor the taste of nostalgic

Americana with a meatloaf or tuna sandwich and a slice of pie and other past-era favorites.

✚ 199 D3 ⊠ 9600 Brighton Way, Beverly Hills ☎ (310) 276-7732 ⏰ Mon–Sat 7–5, Sun 10–3

New York Bagel $

After a jog or workout, Brentwood residents stop in for fresh bagels and all the trimmings, as well as egg dishes and a variety of other deli delights.

✚ 198 A2 ⊠ 11640 San Vicente Boulevard, Brentwood ☎ (310) 820-1050 ⏰ Daily 7–7

BARS

Bel-Air Bar & Grill

After a day at the Getty Center or Skirball Cultural Center, drop in for a drink at this secluded wood-paneled bar with a lovely garden patio.

✚ 198 A3 ⊠ 662 N. Sepulveda Boulevard, Bel Air ☎ (310) 440-5544 ⏰ Mon–Fri 11:30–3, 5:30–10

Beverly Wilshire Bar

A classy crowd gathers for drinks at the Regent Beverly Wilshire Hotel's sublimely schmoozey bar where tasty treats and live piano music are served up at no extra charge.

✚ 199 D2 ⊠ 9500 Wilshire Boulevard, Beverly Hills ☎ (310) 275-5200 ⏰ Daily 11 am–1 am

Liquid Kitty

Locals gather for drink specialties and – when the music's cranked up – screaming conversations, in this dark and crowded nightspot.

✚ 198 B1 ⊠ 11780 W. Pico Boulevard, West L.A. ☎ (310) 473-3707 ⏰ Mon–Fri 6 pm–2 am, Sat–Sun 8 pm–2 am

Peninsula Hotel Bar

This deliciously dark and elegant ultra-chic hotel bar is a favorite respite for celebrities, their agents and other industry types. Look the part and you'll be welcomed.

✚ 199 C2 ⊠ 9882 Little Santa Monica Boulevard, Beverly Hills

☎ (310) 551-2888 ⏰ Mon–Sat 1 pm–1 am, Sun 3 pm–midnight

Polo Lounge

You can recapture a smidgen of Hollywood's golden era, as you recline with costly wine or cocktails at this legendary watering hole.

✚ 198 C3 ⊠ 9641 Sunset Boulevard, Beverly Hills ☎ (310) 276-2251 ⏰ Daily 7 am–2 am

Q's Billiard Club

A youngish crowd frequents this upscale pool hall with tons of billiards tables and other games.

✚ 198 B1 ⊠ 11835 Wilshire Boulevard, West L.A. ☎ (310) 477-7550 ⏰ Mon–Fri 11:30 am–1:30 am, Sat–Sun noon–1:30 am

Tengu

A cool Japanese hot spot, with flaming drinks, fruit-infused *sakes* and *sushi* to soak it up with.

✚ 199 B2 ⊠ 10853 Lindbrook Drive, Westwood ☎ (310) 209-0071 ⏰ Mon–Fri 11:30–2, 5:30–11

Where to... Shop

Fatten your wallet, up the plastic and jump in the limo for an all-out shopping extravaganza. Most people head straight for Beverly Hills and Rodeo Drive, the world's most famous shopping thoroughfare, with other highbrow retailers on the adjacent streets. Student-oriented Westwood Village and upscale Brentwood (along San Vicente Boulevard) offer additional shopping experiences, or you can tackle the select Century City Shopping Center & Marketplace (Santa Monica Boulevard, at Avenue of the Stars, in Century City) and unpretentious Westside Pavilion (Pico and Westwood boulevards, West L.A.).

Antiques and art hounds may not find bargains but will certainly find top-of-the-line merchandise carefully shipped in from around the world. The Getty Center has one of the best museum stores, with a magnificent array of books, cards, fine art, toys and other items. Even if you're on a tight budget, you can bag a sack of produce with the rich and famous at the Beverly Hills farmers market.

RODEO DRIVE/BEVERLY HILLS

Rodeo Drive – the center of the shopping universe, filled with ritzy designer boutiques, jewelers and salons – is where you'll encounter chauffeur-driven limos and Rolls Royces, depositing celebrities outside their favorite couturier or stylist's door. Take a deep breath and begin your trek where Rodeo Drive meets Wilshire Boulevard. **Two Rodeo Drive**, considered one of the most expensive retail complexes ever constructed, houses branches of Tiffany & Co., Charles Jourdan, Valentino, Christian Dior and Cartier. Here Gianfranco Ferre offers the Milanese designer's fashions for men and women including his gorgeously detailed women's blouses, and century-old Sulka provides men with premiere conservative clothing and movie-mogul pajamas.

Prominent tenants at **One Rodeo Drive**, across the street, include Bulgari Jewels, Denmark Jewelers and the refined smoker's best friend, Alfred Dunhill of London. **Ermenegildo Zegna** (301 N. Rodeo Drive), a quality Italian fabric-maker since 1910, incorporates its luxurious goods into beautifully tailored clothing for both men and women.

Amphora Art & Antiques (308 N. Rodeo Drive) will send you home with fabulous paintings, bronzes and heavy antique silver. The finest antique and estate jewels are showcased at **David Orgell** (320 N. Rodeo Drive), while **Frances Klein** (310 N. Rodeo Drive) specializes in astounding art-deco and art-nouveau jewels – many designed by Tiffany, Bulgari and other famed names. You're practically guaranteed an approving nod from L.A.'s fashion police, garbed or accessorized by the hip Milanese-boutique **Prada** (343 N. Rodeo Drive).

Fendi (355 N. Rodeo Drive), a Roman family-owned business since the 1920s, stocks signature handbags, luggage, watches, women's clothing and furs. Quirkier accessories are the celebrated items at **Moschino** (362 N. Rodeo Drive). **Harry Winston** (371 N. Rodeo Drive), provider of celebrity jewels on Oscar night, could make anyone feel like a star in his necklaces, earrings and rings. At sleek-boutique **Chanel** (400 N. Rodeo Drive) women will find traditional Chanel suits, accessories, fragrances and makeup. Designer **Giorgio Armani** (436 N. Rodeo Drive) provides elegant surroundings for acclaimed clothing and accessories.

Both **Gucci** (347 N. Rodeo Drive) and **Hermès** (434 N. Rodeo Drive) are world-famed for purses, leather goods and their signature silk scarves.

You'll feel like Cinderella at **Ferragamo** (357 N. Rodeo Drive), noted for its finely crafted sandals, stilettos, pumps and other footwear. Expensive and durable hosiery, ranging from sheer to opaque, is the specialty at **The Wolford Boutique** (445 N. Rodeo Drive). **Frette** (449 N. Rodeo Drive) will spoil you forever with their worth-every-cent luxurious Italian sheets – the same you'd sleep on in the world's most elegant hotels.

Branches of the finest elite department stores line the stretch zof Wilshire Boulevard, near Rodeo Drive. Referred to as "Department Store Row," shoppers can whisk among a delicious assortment of under-one-roof retail outlets. **Barney's of Beverly Hills** (9570 Wilshire Boulevard) – West Coast cousin of Barney's New York – is the most impressive, with bleached-oak floors, winding staircases and an enormous skylight for that natural look. But don't look too natural, because this is a store for the young and thin, with five levels of hip designer labels and a popular collection of Vera Wang bridal gowns.

Texas-based **Neiman Marcus** (9700 Wilshire Boulevard) carries a more typical and exclusive range of goods including high-end fashions for men, women and children, cosmetics, lingerie, shoes and housewares. You can rejuvenate with a martini in the fourth-floor men's department or a spa treatment at the Estee Lauder Day Spa in the basement.

Famous **Saks Fifth Avenue** (9600 Wilshire Boulevard) carries both American and European designer fashions, fine jewelry, millinery and cosmetics. Find that perfect frou-frou bridesmaid's gown or prom dress at reasonably priced **Jessica McClintock** (9517 Wilshire Boulevard), or timeless (and expensive) tailored men's and women's wear at **Faconnable** (9680 Wilshire Boulevard).

If you have deep pockets and itchy fingers, and you haven't yet found the perfect souvenir, try the auction houses. Both **Christie's** (360 N. Camden Drive) and **Sotheby's** (9665 Wilshire Boulevard) conduct auctions throughout the year where you can bid for such items as an original Picasso, vintage automobile or a bottle of fine wine.

Hundreds of cheeses yielded from cows, goats and sheep from all over the world are available at **The Cheese Store of Beverly Hills** (419 N. Beverly Drive).

Look no further than **Caviarteria** (158 S. Beverly Drive) for that favorite Russian beluga, as well as tasty foie gras, as Scottish salmon and other exotic treats. Stock up on fresh-roasted coffee beans and Swiss water-process decaf at **Graffeo Coffee Roasting Company** (315 N. Beverly Drive).

Handmade chocolates and melt-in-your-mouth truffles are just some of the sweet-tooth fare to be found at **Edelweiss Chocolates** (444 N. Canon Drive), in business since the 1940s.

You'll be awed by the classic and foreign film collection at **VideoCenter** (145 S. Beverly Drive). **Al's News** (216 S. Beverly Drive), with periodicals geared toward screenwriters and playwrights, is the newsstand to hit if you've got the bug to write your own classic.

Those with simpler tastes might want to pick ripe produce, a bouquet of blossoms and other goods at the **farmers market** in **Beverly Hills** (Sundays, 200 N. Canon Drive, 9–1), or in **Westwood** (Westwood Boulevard and Weyburn Avenue, Thu 2–7).

Where to...
Be Entertained

THEATER

Geffen Playhouse
Celebrated actors perform contemporary off-Broadway-type plays, one-person shows and other works.
✚ 198 B2 ⌗ 10886 Le Conte Avenue ☎ (310) 208-6500

Odyssey Theater Ensemble
Odyssey continually draws raves for its well-executed avant-garde and contemporary plays.
✚ 198 B1 ⌗ 2055 S. Sepulveda Boulevard ☎ (310) 477-2055

MUSIC AND DANCE

Chamber Music in Historic Sights
From October through May, Mount St. Mary's College hosts a series of top-class chamber music ensembles in such diverse historical settings as churches, railroad depots, auto showrooms and other L.A. venues.
☎ (310) 954-4300

Coconut Club
The Beverly Hilton Hotel's Las Vegas-style nightclub draws an older crowd for dinner shows and dancing.
✚ 198 C2 ⌗ 9876 Wilshire Boulevard ☎ (310) 274-7777

Lunaria
Terrific live jazz and blues acts play for the hip clientele who kick back or jive with the sounds in this cozy and classy club.
✚ 198 C2 ⌗ 10351 Santa Monica Boulevard, Century City ☎ (310) 282-8870

Skirball Cultural Center
This museum and cultural enclave presents a full schedule of concerts and performances, film series and lectures. Primary focus is on Jewish culture, although other ethnic groups are showcased (► 96).
✚ 198 A5 ⌗ 2701 N. Sepulveda Boulevard ☎ (310) 440-4500

UCLA Center for the Arts
There's always something happening on this busy campus: concerts, theater, dance, opera and other performances. Venues include the scrumptious 1919 Royce Hall and other hallowed halls.
✚ 198 B3 ⌗ 405 N. Hilgard Avenue ☎ (310) 825-2101

MOVIES

Landmark Cecchi Gori Fine Arts
An oldy-but-goody where mainstream and art films are screened in a decorative environment.
✚ 199 E2 ⌗ 8556 Wilshire Boulevard ☎ (310) 652-1330

Laemmle's Royal Theatre
Independent and foreign films are usually on the bill here.
✚ 198 B1 ⌗ 11523 Santa Monica Boulevard ☎ (310) 477-5581

Mann's Bruin
You can't miss the wrap-around marquee at this 1930s Westwood icon, now showing first-run flicks.
✚ 199 B2 ⌗ 925 Broxton Avenue ☎ (310) 208-8998

Mann's Village
Primarily first-run titles are shown in this popular movie theater where the exterior dates from the 1920s and the modernized interior still affords viewers balcony seating.
✚ 199 B2 ⌗ 961 Broxton Avenue ☎ (310) 208-5576

Nuart Theatre
This excellent revival house offers independent movies, classics, cult numbers and documentaries.
✚ 198 C1 ⌗ 11272 Santa Monica Boulevard ☎ (310) 478-6379

Hollywood, Midtown and Universal Studios

Getting Your Bearings

Northwest of Downtown and east of the wealthy suburbs lies Hollywood. Tinseltown's iconic status as the heart of the movie industry has survived the near disappearance of actual filmmaking. But the movies have never been about reality, and so it makes perfect sense that Hollywood has become a film-world fantasy, sustained by a few icons – the Hollywood Sign, the Chinese Theatre, the Walk of Fame.

The glory days may be gone, but Hollywood still bears traces of its glamorous heritage. There are many attractions worth exploring, including, in North Hollywood, that place where cinematic fantasy and amusement park become one: Universal Studios. Nearby, the chaparral-clad hills of Griffith Park offer endless acres of natural refuge and at least one legendary movie location.

★ Don't Miss

❶ L.A. County Museum of Art ➤ 108

❷ La Brea Tar Pits ➤ 113

❸ Mann's Chinese Theatre and the Walk of Fame ➤ 115

❹ Griffith Park and Observatory ➤ 118

❺ The Hollywood Sign ➤ 119

❻ Universal Studios Hollywood and CityWalk ➤ 120

Moving south from Hollywood down La Brea, Fairfax or La Cienega, you meet Midtown, also known as Mid-Wilshire. Here, a strip of once-grand retail real estate bordering the elegant community of Hancock Park was dubbed the "Miracle Mile."

This stretch of Wilshire offers few miracles today, but just steps west you'll find L.A.'s densest concentration of museums.

Anchored by the brilliant L.A. County Museum of Art (LACMA) with its extensive collections, Museum Row has something for just about everybody, from a facility devoted to that L.A. icon, the automobile, to the amazing La Brea Tar Pits, primal pools of prehistoric ooze absolutely stuffed with the well-preserved bones of creatures from Hollywood's Ice Age.

At Your Leisure

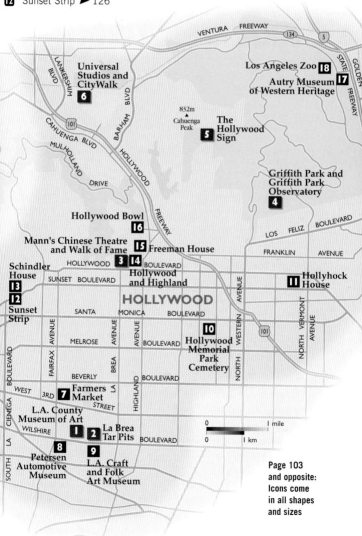

VENTURA FREEWAY · 134 · 5

LANKERSHIM BLVD

Universal Studios and CityWalk 6

Los Angeles Zoo **18**

STATE

GOLDEN FREEWAY

Autry Museum of Western Heritage 17

CAHUENGA BLVD

101

MULHOLLAND DRIVE

BARHAM BLVD

HOLLYWOOD

832m
▲
Cahuenga Peak

The Hollywood Sign 5

Griffith Park and Griffith Park Observatory 4

LOS FELIZ BOULEVARD

Hollywood Bowl 16

FREEWAY

Mann's Chinese Theatre and Walk of Fame 3 **Freeman House 15**

FRANKLIN AVENUE

Schindler House 13

Sunset Strip 12

HOLLYWOOD **3** **14** BOULEVARD

SUNSET BOULEVARD

Hollywood and Highland

HOLLYWOOD

AVENUE

Hollyhock House 11

NORTH VERMONT AVENUE

SANTA MONICA BOULEVARD

NORTH WESTERN

101

MELROSE AVENUE

AVENUE

BOULEVARD

Hollywood Memorial Park Cemetery 10

LA CIENEGA BOULEVARD

FAIRFAX AVENUE

BREA AVENUE

BEVERLY BOULEVARD

NORTH

WEST 3RD **7** **Farmers Market**

HIGHLAND

STREET

L.A. County Museum of Art 1 **2 La Brea Tar Pits**

WILSHIRE

BOULEVARD

SOUTH

Petersen Automotive Museum 8 **9 L.A. Craft and Folk Art Museum**

0 · 1 mile

0 · 1 km

Page 103
and opposite:
Icons come
in all shapes
and sizes

Fabulous museums, fantasy film studios and the storied history and lore of Hollywood make this section of L.A. especially attractive for film and art buffs.

Hollywood, Midtown and Universal Studios in Two Days

Day One

Morning

Breakfast at Kokomo's (Farmers Market, 6333 W. Third Street at Fairfax, Mon–Sat 9–6:30, Sun 10–5, $–$$), famous for power breakfasts for showbiz execs and celebs, or another open-air café in the **7 Farmers Market** (► 124). Take a spin east on Third Street and then down La Brea to Wilshire Boulevard to admire the art-deco beauties that once graced the Miracle Mile. Of special note are the Security Pacific Building at 5209, the Wilson Building at 5217, the former Dark Room at 5370 and the El Rey Theater at 5519. Explore Museum Row, then do the museums. Visit **1 L.A.County Museum of Art** (► 108–112, right) and the adjacent **2 La Brea Tar Pits** (► 113–114), but make time for the **8 Petersen Automotive Museum** (► 124).

Lunch

Have a quick lunch at LACMA's outdoor café, or have a hot dog at the funky L.A. landmark hot dog stand Pink's Famous Chili Dogs (► 132). Prepare to wait: There are lines round the corner most any time of the day or night.

Afternoon

Walk and shop **Melrose Avenue** (► 133). Park and walk **12 Sunset Strip** (► 126, 134), after a side-trip to see **13 Schindler House** (► 127) on N. Kings Road. Drive by the **Capitol Records Tower** (► 117, left), **15 Freeman House** (► 128) and the **16 Hollywood Bowl** (► 128). Stroll the Bowl grounds and visit the museum. Then take a drive through **4 Griffith Park** (► 118) and stop for a walk in one of the gardens, the bird sanctuary or Fern Dell.

Evening

Have drinks at the Bar Marmont (➤ 132) for potential celebrity sighting. Then go to Hollywood for dinner. For star-gazing while dining, try Morton's on Melrose, or a restaurant at one of the hip new hotels; the Fenix in the Argyle on Sunset (➤ 42).

For a gourmet splurge, dine at L'Orangerie (➤ 131) on N. La Cienega or Patina (➤ 131) on Melrose.

Day Two

Morning

Breakfast in your hotel or in the sidewalk café at the Hollywood Roosevelt Hotel on Hollywood Boulevard (➤ 42). Spend the morning on Hollywood Boulevard exploring **8 Mann's Chinese Theatre** and **the Walk of Fame** (➤ 115–117, top and above), the new **14 Hollywood and Highland complex** (➤ 127) and the old movie palaces and other historic sites in the area. Don't miss at least one of the kitschy museums such as Frederick's of Hollywood Lingerie Museum (➤ 117).

Lunch

For a taste of Hollywood history with your meal, eat at the Musso & Frank Grill on Hollywood Boulevard (➤ 131).

Afternoon

Visit Frank Lloyd Wright's **11 Hollyhock House** (➤ 126), stop for a view of the **5 Hollywood Sign** (➤ 119) from Beachwood Avenue, then drive to **6 Universal Studios Hollywood** (➤ 120–123) for a long afternoon.

Evening

Dine and spend the evening at **6 CityWalk** (➤ 122–123).

L.A. County Museum of Art

While the L.A. County Museum of Art has been overshadowed in recent years by the splashy openings of the Museum of Contemporary Art Downtown and the Getty Center on the Westside, the fact of the matter is simple: LACMA's collections are superior and more extensive, in most categories, to the holdings of the newer institutions.

(Note that LACMA has recently hired architect Rem Koolhass to completely masterplan and redesign the museum – watch this space!)

LACMA's three original buildings, including the Ahmanson Building, the Hammer Building and the Bing Center, opened in 1965. They are not among L.A.'s great architectural stand-outs, but gallery renovations, expansions and additions have created an impressive series of buildings housing the museum's 120,000-plus artworks from antiquity to the present day.

Begin with the **Ahmanson Building**, the large, bland structure to the west of the main plaza. On the plaza level is the museum's rich collection of American art. Notable pieces include John Singer Sargent's *Portrait of Mrs. Edward L. Davis and Her Son, Livingston Davis*, Mary Cassatt's *Mother About to Wash Her Sleepy Child* and Winslow Homer's *The Cotton Pickers*. Other rooms on this floor house collections of Western, Federal and Craftsman furniture, art-deco sculpture and other treasures of Americana. The museum's excellent collection of pre-Columbian pieces is also on this level, as is a selection of English art from the 16th and 17th centuries. On the lower level you'll discover an impressive array of Chinese and Korean art, with a striking selection of lacquerware trays, scrolls, stone bowls and jade figures – the pieces cover every era of Asian history dating back some 7,000 years. Outside, the **Gerald B. Cantor Sculpture Garden** offers casts of characters from Rodin's *Gates of Hell* and a massive Rodin statue of French novelist Honoré de Balzac.

Upstairs on the second level of the Ahmanson, you'll discover a wide-ranging collection of European art from the ancient Greeks and Romans through the 19th century. Among the hundreds of masterworks are pieces by Rembrandt (*The Raising of Lazarus, Portrait of Marten Looten*), Hans Holbein (*Portrait of a Young Woman with White Coif*) and the striking *Magdalen with the Smoky Flame* by Georges de la Tour. Have a quick look at the 3,000-year-old Egyptian reliefs on this

floor, then head upstairs to view the Southeast Asian and Islamic Art. Don't miss the sculpted wood-and-copper Buddha figures or the lavish, overscale Tibetan *tanka*, or religious painting, called *Tathagata Amitayus and Acolytes*, an opaque watercolor on cloth dating from the 12th century. The Rajput paintings from the 16th and 17th centuries are also appealing in their richly informative detail.

The Ahmanson's third level houses an astounding collection of textiles and costumes. Highlights include the 16th-century Ardabil Carpet, a silk-and-wool Persian masterpiece and one of only two such carpets in existence.

Armand Hammer, that Occidental Petroleum businessman, got into a spat with LACMA's managers and de-

camped with his collection years ago to open his own museum. The **Hammer Building**, linked to the Ahmanson by a series of galleries, now displays LACMA's collections of Impressionist and post-Impressionist paintings and outstanding drawings, photos and prints. Look for works by Dürer (*Adam and Eve*), Rembrandt (*Christ Presented to the People*), Delacroix (*Strolling Players*), Degas (*Actresses in Their Dressing Rooms*), De Kooning (*Woman*) and Whistler (*Drouet*), among others. LACMA's 6,000-piece photography collection, ensconced in the Hammer Building, includes a generous selection of works by Edward Weston and Alfred Stieglitz, among others.

The museum's fine gift- and bookstore can be found on the plaza level here, along with the visitor information center, the excellent Pentimento Restaurant and galleries devoted to special exhibitions.

With its massive facade looming over Wilshire Boulevard
(thus cutting off the museum's main plaza from the street),
LACMA's early 1980s **Robert O. Anderson Building** has been
critically assaulted on the architectural front. Yet there's no
denying the vitality of its offerings of 20th-century and contemporary art. The first floor is reserved for traveling shows and
special exhibitions, with the bulk of the collection displayed
upstairs on the second and third floors. Here you'll find everything from Blue Period Picasso (*Portrait of Sebastian Juner Vidal*,
from 1903) to David Hockney's joyous *Mulholland Highway: The
Road to the Studio*, from 1980. There are dozens of challenging,
intriguing and simply lovely works to be savored here. On the
challenging front, check out Ed Keinholz's *Back Seat Dodge '38*,
which created quite a furor back in the 1960s as one of the first
pieces of "social protest" art; Sue Coe's *England is a Bitch*, from

1982; Kara Walker's *And Thus… (Present Tense)*; and the eerily
evocative *Central Meridian Garage*, an installation piece created
by Michael McMillen in 1981 and revised in 1994. You'll be
intrigued by the simple weirdness of works by John Baldessari,
Ed Ruscha, Moriko Mori, Mark Tansey and the cerebral, always
strange René Magritte.

Beyond the ironic or confrontational, the LACMA's 20th-
century collection includes countless pieces by those artists,
even in the last, difficult century, whose work is about pure
untrammeled beauty, whatever mode they operate in. Works
by Matisse (*Tea*), Giacometti (three different *Women*, poised

outside the entrance to the galleries), Rothko's *White Center* and Diebenkorn's *Ocean Park Series No. 49*, among dozens of others, make a fabulous array of masterful pictures and sculptures from the last 100 years.

Since opening in the late 1980s, LACMA's **Japanese Pavilion** has emerged as an architectural hybrid, which makes for a strange but satisfying transition from the 1960s Modern ambience of the museum to the grassy parkland surrounding the adjacent La Brea Tar Pits. Designed by the late Bruce Goff, the building's swooping roof lines and exterior decorative elements are unmistakably Asian, as is the evocation of the *shoji* screen achieved by the folded, gridded walls. Inside, soft, natural lighting, a gently sloping ramp, the soothing sound of water flowing and falling and a muted neutral backdrop create a serene ambience for viewing the Asian artworks on display.

David Hockney does Mulholland Drive

For all its exterior extravagance, the Pavilion serves its purpose beautifully. Don't miss the collection of *netsukes* – these small intricately carved objects were used to attach small boxes to the *obi*, or sash, on a kimono. Over the centuries *netsukes* have evolved into one of the more delicately expressive forms of functional art in the world. You'll find the Netsuke Gallery on the plaza level next to the museum store.

The **Bing Center** presents film programs, lectures, Friday evening free jazz concerts, classes, art camps and other programs designed to reach out to the community. Check the schedule to see what or who's playing while in town.

The **Plaza Café**, where you can grab a quick cafeteria-style meal, is tucked into a corner of the Bing Center.

Half a block west of the museum, the old May Company department store has been converted into **LACMA West**. It contains galleries for traveling shows that won't fit into LACMA's limited exhibition space as well as the Boone Children's Gallery, an "experimental" gallery for families and school groups.

Finally, a satellite of L.A.'s under-visited **Southwest Museum** has set up shop here, displaying a fine selection from its impressive collection of Native American textiles, jewelry and decorative artworks.

Asian art goes
L.A. pop:
The Japanese
Pavilion

TAKING A BREAK

The **Pentimento** café on the main plaza at LACMA (closed Wed, $–$$) serves Italian-style food – soups, salads,pizzas and sandwiches. Alternatively you could go to **Kokomo's** at Farmers Market (➤ 124) nearby or **Pink's Famous Chili Dogs** (➤ 132).

🔢 199 E2 ✉ 5905 Wilshire Boulevard, between La Brea and Fairfax (LACMA West, Southwest Museum, corner of Wilshire and Fairfax, one-half block west of main museum) ☎ (323) 857-6000; www.lacma.org 🕓 Mon, Tue, Thu noon–8, Fri noon–9, Sat–Sun 11–8 💷 Adults moderate; seniors and students inexpensive

---

L.A. COUNTY MUSEUM OF ART: INSIDE INFO

Top tips The Friday evening **jazz series** is very popular; there is no reserved seating so come early for good seats.

• Parking is **free** in the museum parking lot off Ogden Drive on Friday nights.

• The **Ticketing and Information Center** is open museum hours and one hour before events.

• **Family programs** on Sundays from 12:30–3:15 offer hands-on art workshops. The price is included in admission for nonmembers.

② La Brea Tar Pits

Right smack in the middle of Los Angeles, powerful saber-tooth cats once roamed, hunting woolly mammoths on Wilshire Boulevard. The proof is in their bones, thousands of which have been interred precisely where the poor critters got stuck, in the dark, primal ooze of La Brea Tar Pits, when they stopped to drink from what must have looked like a cooling pool of water. For fossil enthusiasts of all ages, a trip to the Tar Pits is a guaranteed thriller!

Below:
A mammoth
sinks into
the asphalt

Bottom right:
A Pleistocene
era resident of
Beverly Hills

First, two salient notes: The name is redundant, since La Brea means "the tar" in Spanish; and it is not actually tar but asphalt that has been bubbling forth from the 100-odd pits, randomly situated in the 23-acre park, for an estimated 40,000 years, through the Ice Age of the Pleistocene era. Among the 1 million or more specimens discovered here are the 9,000-year-old bones of a woman (now called La Brea Woman), thousands of bones from *Smilodon californicus*, the saber-tooth cat, along with bones from mammoths, mastodons, long-horned bison, camels, bears, giant rats, ground sloths, vultures, lizards and other species, some extinct, some still around. There are fossilized remains from 59 mammal species and 135 bird species and a total of 660 different species including plants and insects.

These numbers matter, for they establish the significance of the site, but they're not what the experience is about for visitors. You won't find the fenced-in pools pretty to look at (or to smell, for that matter), but the surrounding **Hancock Park** makes for

LA BREA TAR PITS: INSIDE INFO

Top tips **Guided tours** of the Tar Pits take place at 1 pm daily.
• There are guided tours of the **George C. Page Museum** Wed–Sun at 2 pm.
• **Pit 91**, still chock-full of buried fossils, is the scene of a two-month excavation project every summer, so you can watch paleontologists at work from an observation area. (Note how the 28-foot square, 14-foot deep pit has been divided into 3-by-3-foot grids, the better to keep track of the bones.)

pleasant walking and picnicking, and a recent $10 million face-lift to the scene has made things more interesting.

A huge model of a trapped mammoth lurches out of the Lake Pit, grabbing your attention on Wilshire Boulevard.

George C. Page Museum

Open since 1977, the George C. Page Museum, behind the La Brea Tar Pits, puts some science on the bones pulled out of the Pits. Here you can view reconstructed skeletons of giant ground sloths, saber-tooth cats and similar animals. The saber-tooth cat has for long been California's official state fossil.

Below:
A rebuilt mammoth at the George C. Page Museum

Educational exhibits along with a 15-minute film documenting the history of the digs – excavation has been ongoing since 1906 – help to put the whole scene in perspective.

For amateur and budding scientists, the opportunity to watch paleontologists in action in the Paleontology Laboratory, cleaning and classifying the uncovered bones, is a rare treat indeed.

TAKING A BREAK

The best places to go are either **Kokomo's** at the Farmers Market (▶ 124) or **Pink's Famous Chili Dog** stand at La Brea (▶ 133).

✚ 199 F2   ✉ 5801 Wilshire Boulevard, next to LACMA between La Brea and Fairfax   ☎ (323) 934-7243 (George C. Page Museum); www.tarpits.org
🕐 Tue–Sat 10–5 (George C. Page Museum), Tue–Sat 10–5 (Tar Pits)
💲 George C. Page Museum moderate; free first Tue. Tar Pits free

Right: Celebs of all sorts star on the Walk of Fame

3 Mann's Chinese Theatre and the Walk of Fame

The fabulous Sid Grauman (1879–1950), creator of Hollywood's most delightfully vulgar movie palaces, is long gone, but his legacy lives on at the Mann's (formerly Grauman's) Chinese Theatre, as does the legacy of all Hollywood, in the kitschy, richly historic scene on and around Hollywood Boulevard where it crosses Highland Avenue and Vine Street. Don't let the crowds of tourists deter you; this is the heart of Old Hollywood, and well worth a good morning's walkabout. Be sure to check out the latest addition to this part of town, the highly touted new mega-mall – Hollywood and Highland.

Located just west of Highland at 6925 Hollywood, **Mann's Chinese Theatre** has been, for more than 70 years, the main event for tourists seeking the Holy Grail of Hollywood history. Designed by the architects Meyer and Holler under Grauman's direction, with a look inspired by Chinese temples, the theater's dragon reliefs, spiky roof lines and garishly enchanting forms and colors masterfully evoke the exotic East. Beginning with Cecil B. DeMille's "King of Kings" in 1927, every first-night film opening of note took place here, and it has always played a significant role in Hollywood history.

The foot-, hand- and other body-part prints left in cement in the theater's sidewalk by more than 200 movie stars have made permanent the mystique. Legions of fans (some 2 million a year) still flock here to match their hands and feet to the prints of stars as ancient as Douglas

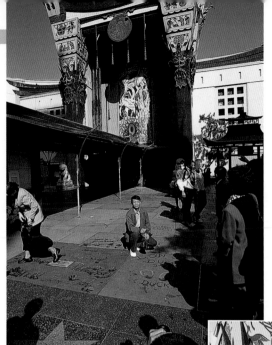

Right: Famous foot- (and other) prints outside the Chinese Theatre

Top: Mann's Chinese Theatre, a Hollywood landmark since 1927

Above: Details lend the theater exotic charm

Fairbanks Sr. and Mary Pickford, the first two invited to leave their impressions, and as contemporary as Meryl Streep, Denzel Washington and Mel Gibson.

According to legend, the tradition began by accident when silent movie star Norma Talmadge serendipitously stepped in wet cement on the opening night of "King of Kings" in 1927.

The **Walk of Fame** provides another opportunity for star-gazing, although some of the obscure characters whose names number among the 2,500 stars embedded in the Hollywood Boulevard sidewalk are far from famous. Established in 1960 by the local chamber of commerce as a way to reinvigorate the fading tourist allure of Tinseltown, the Walk of Fame has always been more gimmick than anything else. It costs the invited "star" or his/her studio or entertainment company about $15,000 to buy a star on the street – a great promotional tool utilized by more than a few entertainment companies to hype new movies or CDs.

The first eight names, unveiled in 1960, lend a sense of what is meant by "far from famous": Olive Borden, Ronald Colman, Louise Fazenda, Preston Foster, Burt Lancaster, Edward Sedgwick, Ernest Torrence and Joanne Woodward. Three or four bona fide stars there, but who are the others? Most of the stars are (or were at one time) household names; a walk down the Walk brings plenty of movie memories into nostalgic focus.

For another angle on the movies, stroll the neighborhood of **Hollywood and Vine**. Take in a few of the historic hotels, movie theaters and other Hollywood Boulevard spots that figure in the Tinseltown myth. Some suggestions: the **Pantages Theater** (➤ 135), at 6233, has a bland exterior but an amazing interior; off the Boulevard at 1817 Ivar Avenue, you'll find the site of the boarding house where Nathanael West holed up while writing his classic Hollywood satire, *The Day of the Locust*; at **Frederick's of Hollywood** (➤ 133), 6608, you can view a lot of delightfully sleazy and famous lingerie.

Check out the **El Capitan Theater**, No. 6834; and the **Egyptian Theater**, No. 6712 (this theater is included in the CityPass offerings (➤ 38), so take in the daily showing of "Forever Hollywood," an insider's look at moviedom history).

The **Hollywood Roosevelt Hotel** (➤ 42) at No. 7000 opened in 1927 as Hollywood's first luxury hotel, and its Cinegrill was the hang-out for W.C. Fields, Ernest Hemingway and F. Scott Fitzgerald; the **Musso & Frank Grill** (➤ 131) at 6667 has been an industry fixture since opening in 1919. Just up from the corner of Hollywood at 1750 Vine, the 1956 **Capitol Records Tower** looks like a stack of records with a turntable on top. The rooftop beacon flashes the word "Hollywood" in Morse code.

Movie Stars' Homes Tour

A classic of kitschy tourism, the Movie Stars' Homes Tour remains a don't miss event. Take a bus tour and let the guide fill you in on the history and all the latest gossip. Tours leave from the Chinese Theatre or your hotel lobby. Otherwise, grab a copy of Movie Stars' Homes Map and navigate yourself. They aren't always up to date, but they're correct enough of the time, and they'll keep you from wandering aimlessly around the streets of Brentwood and Beverly Hills. You might see a star, you might not, but it's great fun to gaze at these huge homes and wonder who goes in and what goes on! But try to respect the privacy of the residents.

TAKING A BREAK

Grand Central Coffee (7000 Hollywood Boulevard, just off the lobby of the Hollywood Roosevelt Hotel; ➤ 42) is good for breakfast and lunch snacks.

🔲 199 F4 **Mann's Chinese Theatre**   ✉ 6925 Hollywood Boulevard   ☎ (323) 464-8111

MANN'S CHINESE THEATRE AND THE WALK OF FAME: INSIDE INFO

Top tips Look out for **unusual prints** outside Mann's Chinese Theatre. Jimmy Durante left a nose-print, Betty Grable her leg-prints and Harpo Marx, of course, left a harp print.
• **Check out the size** of the hand- and footprints in the sidewalk – see if your hand is smaller than Bette Davis' or your foot is bigger than Richard Gere's.

④ Griffith Park and Observatory

Griffith Park is the country's largest city park, although the rugged Hollywood Hills that make up a good portion of it are relatively inaccessible. Named for mining millionaire Griffith J. Griffith, it features 53 miles of trails, glorious gardens, a bird sanctuary, two equestrian centers and every kind of outdoor facility. It is also home to the Los Angeles Zoo, the Autry Museum of Western Heritage and the Greek Theatre.

Since opening in 1935, the Observatory (► below) has been recognized as an L.A. icon, famous for its elegant, copper-domed Moderne design. Regally poised on the slope of Mount Hollywood, it has been used as a set in a number of films, most notably Nicholas Ray's "Rebel Without a Cause," (1955), the movie that made James Dean immortal. Several crucial scenes were shot in and around the Observatory; this bit of movie lore is memorialized on the grounds with a bronze statue of James Dean.

Note: The Griffith Park Observatory closed in 2002 for renovation, which will reestablish this much-loved monument as a state-of-the-art planetarium. The entire facility will be reorganized and updated, with the addition of new facilities underground and a refitting of the planetarium, but the landmark building's dazzling exterior will remain as it is. Re-opening is scheduled for 2004.

Above: James Dean, immortalized in bronze in the grounds of the observatory (below); Scenes in "Rebel Without a Cause" were shot here

✚ 200 C4 ✉ 2800 E. Observatory Road ☎ (323) 664-1191; www.griffithobs.org 🎟 Griffith Park free

5 The Hollywood Sign

Strung across Mount Lee in the Hollywood Hills, the Hollywood sign, with its 50-foot-high letters, is possibly the most famous sign in the world. Contrary to legend, it has been the scene of just one known suicide, by 24-year-old actress Lillian "Peg" Entwhistle in 1932, who leaped to her death from the "H." The sign originally spelled "Hollywoodland" and was put up in 1923 by *Los Angeles Times* publisher Harry Chandler to promote a housing development.

This just may be the most famous sign in the world

In 1949, the "land" was dropped by the Hollywood Chamber of Commerce, which took over management of the sign with the intention of making it a landmark. By 1978 the sign was a wreck. Then celebs stepped in, with various famous folk adopting individual letters. The sign has been well-tended ever since, solidifying its position as L.A.'s supreme pop icon.

The sign has been fenced off so that the public can't get in. The end of Beachwood Drive is as close as you'll get, and it's a long ways off, with infra-red security cameras and a hefty fine waiting for transgressors, of which there are many. Along with a number of college students who've sneaked in to change the sign to their school's names (USC, Cal Tech, UCLA), quite a few pranksters have had their way with it. It has been Dollywood, Holywood, Hollyweed, even Ollywood – thanks to admirers of, respectively, Dolly Parton, evangelist Aimee Semple McPherson, marijuana and Oliver North.

Two good viewpoints of the sign are straight up Beachwood Drive and from the grounds at the Griffith Park Observatory. The best overall view is from the roof deck of the new Hollywood and Highland complex.

✚ 200 B5

6 Universal Studios Hollywood and CityWalk

For those compelled to visit at least one major amusement park while in Los Angeles, Universal Studios may be the best bet. Conveniently close to Hollywood and Downtown, it offers a great mix of amusement-park thrills and movie-making excitement. A word of warning: Like all the big theme parks, this one is expensive and often mobbed, so if you go for the most popular rides, based on the latest hit movies, prepare to spend serious time standing in line.

Sprawling over 415 acres of hilly terrain, Universal Studios has been a working movie backlot since 1915. Over the decades, Universal merged with other companies, expanded and started public studio tours, all the while providing set space for many big hits and great movies: Alfred Hitchcock worked out of Universal, and both George Lucas and Steven Spielberg staged important movies here. In the last five years, Universal Studios has emerged as a major tourist destination,

Visitors tour a set at Universal Studios

less of a working studio and more of a theme park devoted to the art of movie-making.

For film and TV fans the biggest draw continues to be the **Studio Tour**, a guided tram tour through the Universal backlot, narrated by some big-name stars. Each tram, equipped with state-of-the-art sound and video systems, takes you through 35 soundstages, giving a glimpse of what was, what is and what will be in the world of movie-making. There's not much of a chance you'll actually get to see a movie being filmed on this tour, but you'll get a firsthand look at how it's done. Special effects, virtual-reality sets, a special presentation of "Before They Were Stars" on the tram ride and the one and only Bates Motel from Hitchcock's "Psycho" of 1960/2000 are the big highlights of this tour.

Top: Jurassic Park III – The Ride provides realistic dinosaur encounters...

Above: ... Including one with big, bad _T. rex_

For those disinclined to take the tour, take a ride instead. Several of the ones based on hit movies are lots of fun. In **Back to the Future – The Ride**, you'll rock through a race across time and space in a DeLorean car. The movie is dated but the ride remains a thrilling visual rush. **Jurassic Park III – The Ride** features a boat tour through a jungle populated with animatronic dinosaurs, including a couple of _T. rexs_ too realistic for comfort for small children and a heart-stopping 84-foot drop into pitch blackness at the end.

The **ET Adventure** ride is fairly benign, and yes, the ride _is_ the bicycle-passing-the-full-moon scenario from the movie. **Terminator 2: 3D** has its admirers too, while another of the hot ones is a trip through **The Mummy Returns: Chamber of Doom**, based on the second Mummy movie. In some cases, the rides can be far more exciting than the movies, as with **Waterworld** and **Backdraft**. New in 2002 is **Spiderman**

Rocks where you can watch live, death-defying aerial stunts, pyrotechnics and rock 'n' roll as Spiderman fights with his enemies.

The **Wild Wild Wild West** stunt show is good fun, with cowboys tumbling off roofs and clowning around. **The Blues Brothers** put on a 20-minute concert five times a day. The place swarms with characters from TV shows, movies and cartoons. You can have your picture taken in the mouth of the "Jaws" shark, flirting with Marilyn Monroe or flexing with the Warrior Princess Xena, who's wandering around in full gladiatrix garb, trading quips with Hercules. Note that many of the newer attractions are geared toward small children and are well worth the extra time: the **Nickelodeon Blast Zone** with the *Rugrats Magic Show* and *Animal Planet Live!* feature what they want to see.

Terminator 2: 3D "ride" gets right in your face

CityWalk

Universal CityWalk is the pathway that links the Universal Studios theme park (where the big shows and thrill rides live) to the Universal amphitheater and movie theaters (home to one of the biggest movie screens in history). CityWalk is Universal's equivalent of Disney's Downtown Disney (▶ 169), a city "street," lined with stores and restaurants, that is completely removed from urban reality – no crime, no graffiti, no dirt or grit or... well, one could argue "no energy" as well, but people do seem to enjoy themselves.

Here you can find specialty stores selling everything from little red wagons to big blue surfboards and high-priced memorabilia from every possible (Universal) film or TV show from "I Love Lucy" to "Jurassic Park." It's one of the places where you

A snaky scene from Animal Planet Live

can still buy Hollywood trivia – the snow-globe with palm trees or the signed (but spurious) head shots of movie stars. There are bowling alleys, blues bars, movie theaters, two dozen restaurants and one of the largest **IMAX®** theaters.

All of it has been lit with hot neon, cooled with fountains and fueled by a middle-of-the-road rock soundtrack designed to let everybody know what a good time they're having. The best things are the absence of cars and the presence of street performers, who provide a pleasingly personalized counterpoint to the relentless entertainment marketeering. And the crowds of people of all ages roaming around lend the place an urban buzz in spite of its sanitized self. It's expensive and the lines are long, but you and your family can have tons of fun here. It's a good place to wind down after a concert at the **amphitheater** (a vast performance venue with seating for 6,000 for rock 'n' roll or pop concerts, with headliners performing year-round) or a day at Universal Studios.

CityWalk's fantasy version of urban streetlife

TAKING A BREAK

With over 60 restaurants, snack bars and fast-food joints ranging from high-end gourmet to budget fries, Universal's **CityWalk** offers something for everyone. Decide what kind of food you want and you'll almost certainly find it available somewhere in CityWalk.

🚩 199 F5 ✉ Universal Center Drive or Lankershim Boulevard exit, Hollywood Freeway ☎ (818) 662-3801; www.universalstudios.com 🕐 8 am–10 pm summer, 9–7 rest of year 🎫 One-Day Admission (entry to all rides and shows) expensive

---

UNIVERSAL STUDIOS HOLLYWOOD AND CITYWALK: INSIDE INFO

Top tips Universal Studios Hollywood is included in the **Hollywood CityPass**. Take advantage of the free admission (free if you buy the discount CityPass, that is, for a lot less than a family admission to the theme park; ► 38).
• A **Director's Pass** ($79 per person) gets you priority boarding – no waiting in line – for all rides, reserved seating at all shows and a commemorative photo.
• The **VIP Experience** ($125 per person) offers all the above plus a personalized guided tour, special access to production facilities and a private tour of the set for "Providence." The trade-off of increased cost for greater convenience has to be considered at any of the theme parks you might visit.
• **Avoid** summer, holidays and weekends.

At Your Leisure

7 Farmers Market

The Farmers Market first appeared during the Great Depression of the 1930s, when local farmers sold produce off the backs of their trucks. Soon stands replaced the trucks, and a ramshackle clock tower went up. Today the tower reigns over a lively, colorful warren of food stands, curiosity shops, restaurants, antiques stores and souvenir stands. The Market, with its open-air restaurants and a great newsstand on hand, is a top choice for dining or people-watching. Recommended: **Kokomo's** for breakfast and possible CBS celebrity-sightings; CBS Television City is nearby, as are the trendy stores of Third Street and Museum Row.

✚ 199 E3 ✉ 6333 West Third Street, corner of Fairfax ☎ (323) 933-9211 ⏰ Mon–Sat 9–8 Jun–Sep; 9–6:30, rest of year; Sun 10–5 💲 Free

8 Petersen Automotive Museum

L.A.'s ongoing love affair with the automobile gets major treatment at the Petersen, and the results can be

A Model A Ford, one of 400 vintage cars at the Petersen Automotive Museum

engrossing. Named for media mogul Robert Petersen (publisher of *Motor Trend* and *Hot Rod* magazines), the museum displays more than 400 cars, from vintage to futuristic. The first-floor **Streetscape** puts visitors into historically accurate dioramas exploring L.A.'s car-bound history.

Second-floor galleries have revolving shows: celebrity autos are everywhere; the **Bruce Meyer Gallery** features hot rods; and the **Otis Chandler Gallery** does motorcycles. The third floor offers interactive children's exhibits such as the **Vroom Room**.

The museum also holds special exhibits devoted to off-beat auto-related topics, for example, a tribute to Woodies, the wood-paneled station wagons that became icons of the California surf culture.

✚ 199 E2 ✉ 6060 Wilshire Boulevard at Fairfax Avenue ☎ (323) 930-2277; www.petersen.org ⏰ Tue–Sun 10–6 💲 Moderate–expensive

9 L.A. Craft and Folk Art Museum

Another treasure-filled gem on Museum Row, the L.A. Craft and Folk Art Museum is best known for sponsoring the hugely popular International Festival of Masks, when half the neighborhood, it seems, dons ethnic costumes and masks and goes on parade in Hancock Park. Look for it in October. The museum added "L.A." to its name a few years ago when it ran out of cash and closed; the city kicked in some funds and it reopened with a new name. Stable now, and ensconced in a handsome 1930s Georgian-style building, the museum's collections include contemporary, historic and ethnic arts and crafts, ranging from household objects to artworks in a variety of media from all over the world, plus a superb collection of masks.

🔶 199 F2 ✉ 5814 Wilshire Boulevard
☎ (323) 937-4230 🕐 Tue, Wed, Fri noon–5, Thu noon–9, Sat–Sun 11–5
💲 Adults, seniors and students inexpensive; under 12s free; free Thu 5–9

10 Hollywood Memorial Park Cemetery

This grand old Hollywood graveyard is an important stop for fans of the celebrity dead. Famous stars interred here include Rudolph Valentino, in

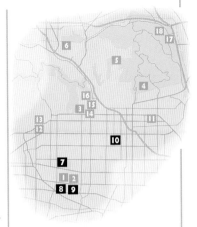

tomb number 1205 in the Cathedral Mausoleum. In 1926 10,000 people packed into the cemetery for his funeral. In a tradition dating from 1931, every year on the date of his death, Aug. 23, at least one Lady in Black arrives to mourn him. The fact that the first "Lady in Black" was a hoax (she claimed to be his former lover but was a hired actress) doesn't seem to matter – the myth lingers on.

There are plenty of other famous people buried here, including Marion

The Farmers Market is the first choice of many for fresh fruits and vegetables

Rock clubs still rule on Sunset Strip

Davies, Cecil B. DeMille, Woody Herman, Jayne Mansfield, Edward G. Robinson and Tyrone Power. One of the finest, more recent gravestones belongs to Mel Blanc, the voice of Bugs Bunny and countless other cartoon characters. His epitaph reads, "That's all, folks."

✚ 200 B3 ✉ 6000 Santa Monica Boulevard between Gower and Van Ness ⏰ Daily 8–5 🎟 Free

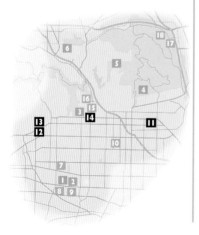

🆔 Hollyhock House

Millionaire oil heiress Aline Barnsdall envisioned an artists' colony or something vaguely Marxist when she arrived in L.A. from Chicago flush with family cash in 1915. She bought a 36-acre site called Olive Hill, on Hollywood's eastern edge, and called on Frank Lloyd Wright to plan the project. Wright responded with Hollyhock House, long-considered one of his greatest works and one of the most significant buildings of the 20th century, according to the American Institute of Architects. The concrete-and-stucco house has been decorated inside and out with an abstract pattern of a hollyhock, Barnsdall's favorite flower. The pattern works beautifully, enhanced by the pre-Columbian-influenced style of the structure. Barnsdall gave the property to the city in 1923. For decades, earthquakes, rain and neglect took their toll. It was designated a cultural monument in 1963, but bureaucrats danced around the problem until at last the place was shut down in 2000 for renovation.

The grounds, which are known as the Barnsdall Art Park, and a couple of outbuildings that now serve as municipal galleries or studios re-opened in fall 2002; the main house is scheduled to re-open in 2004.

✚ 200 C3 ✉ 4800 Hollywood Boulevard, between Vermont and Edgemont ☎ (323) 913-4157; call for hours, fees and schedule

🆔 Sunset Strip

The Strip has been legendary for decades, and rocks on still, with giant billboards, cool nightclubs, hot comedy clubs, hip hotels and chic restaurants leading the neon-lit parade. From Crescent Heights to Doheny, Sunset reigns as one of the most famous asphalt arteries on earth. In the 1930s and 1940s, movie stars gathered at Ciro's, Mocambo, the Garden of Allah and other nightclubs. After a TV-induced nightlife lull, the late 1960s arrived in full-blown, flower-powered splendor: Whisky A Go Go, the Roxy and other rock 'n' roll venues showcased such rock icons as the Doors, the Byrds, Janis Joplin and Jimi Hendrix. The Strip has been a holy ground for the rock world ever since, spiced up by new clubs like Johnny Depp's notorious Viper Room (where River Phoenix died).

Even hipper these days is the hotel scene, both old and new: Chateau Marmont, the Mondrian, the Argyle and others, with their celebrity bars and *haute* restaurants, are all the rage.

✚ 199 E4 ✉ Sunset Boulevard between Crescent Heights Boulevard and Doheny Drive

Schindler House is an icon of L.A. Modernism

🔢 Schindler House

One of the most influential L.A. architects of the 20th century, Austrian immigrant Rudolph Schindler moved to California to work for Frank Lloyd Wright on the Hollyhock House, then pursued his own successful career. Many consider the studio-residence he designed for himself and his wife in 1921 to be the best of the houses he created in L.A. The iconoclastic house was designed as a two-family home (Schindler and his wife lived there, separately, even after divorcing) with a single kitchen. But the real innovations were in the use of simple materials, and the complex relationships

between interior and exterior space. Schindler knit concrete, redwood, glass walls and removable walls into an open plan, with all the rooms flowing into patios. The "bedrooms" were sleeping baskets on the roof, embracing the sky.

The house now serves as an outpost of Vienna's esteemed MAK (School of Applied Arts), which offers tours of L.A. area buildings by Schindler and other Austrian émigré architects.

✚ 199 E4 ✉ 835 N. Kings Road between Melrose and Santa Monica boulevards ☎ (323) 651-1510 🕐 Wed–Sun 11–6, guided tours weekends ✚ Inexpensive; children free

🔢 Hollywood and Highland

This would be just another intersection, lacking the historical pizzazz of nearby Hollywood and Vine, except for the huge new $430 million shopping/ entertainment complex. The five-story Hollywood and Highland megamall has a variety of enticements: a luxury hotel and dozens of retail stores, nightclubs, restaurants and theaters. More alluring are the only-in-Hollywood features, including a grand staircase leading to an outdoor platform with a panoramic view of the Hollywood Sign; Babylon Court, a re-creation of the extravagant set from D.W. Griffith's immortal 1916 classic, "Intolerance"; a live broadcast center and the **Kodak Theatre**, the new home for the annual Oscar telecast. The theater contains a 3,300-seat auditorium, a ballroom, a press area, a media "cockpit" and an entryway designed to bestow an even higher level of self-importance on the movie stars, as they sweep in for their Oscar evening.

✚ 200 A3 ✉ Corner of Hollywood Boulevard and Highland Avenue

The Hollywood Bowl ranks among the country's top outdoor music venues

15 Freeman House

One of Frank Lloyd Wright's greatest L.A. projects is the 1924 Freeman House, created as a prototype for low-cost mass housing. It stands out in part for its wonderful location: The views of Hollywood are spectacular. The house is also admired for the elaborate patterning – a geometric synthesis of Mayan and Islamic forms designed by Wright – that decorates the concrete structural bricks both inside and out. Much of the furniture was designed by one of L.A.'s other great architects, Rudolph Schindler. The house features the world's first glass-to-glass corner windows. In its heyday, it was quite a salon: Dancer/choreographer Martha Graham, photographer Edward Weston, and architects Philip Johnson and Richard Neutra are among the many avant-gardists said to have lived there. Call ahead to make sure it's open if you want a tour – Saturday only.

➕ 199 F4 ✉ 1962 Glencoe Way, Hollywood, just below the Hollywood Bowl off Hillcrest, near Highland and Franklin avenues ☎ (323) 851-0671 🕐 Tours Sat 2 and 4 pm 💷 Moderate; students inexpensive

16 Hollywood Bowl

Listening to a well-played concert on a summer evening at the Bowl ranks among the more sublime L.A. experiences. The acoustics are excellent, the setting is exquisite and you won't find any but the best musicians performing on stage.

The L.A. Philharmonic plays their summer season here, and just about every major figure in jazz and pop has played the Bowl, from Louis Armstrong to Garth Brooks. Built in 1922 in a natural amphitheater in the Hollywood Hills, the Bowl seats 17,000, and even the budget seats are great. If you're in L.A. in summer, by all means get tickets, pack a bottle of wine and a picnic dinner – or buy the excellent take-out food available here – and settle in for a festive evening.

Off-season or during the day, you can stroll the grounds and visit the **Edmund D. Edelman Hollywood Bowl Museum** to see original drawings, early photos and footage of Leopold Stokowski, Judy Garland, the Beatles and other great concerts.

Top Tip: From Tuesday to Friday 9:30–noon you can watch rehearsals for free.

➕ 199 F4 ✉ 2301 N. Highland Avenue at Odin Street, north of Whitley Heights, west of the Hollywood Freeway ☎ (323) 850-2000 (Bowl), (323) 850-2058 (Museum); www.hollywoodbowl.org 🕐 Concert season: Jul–mid-Sep; Bowl grounds and museum: daily 10–8:30, Jun–Aug; Tue–Sat 10–4, rest of year 💷 Free

Decorated bricks enliven Frank Lloyd Wright's Freeman House

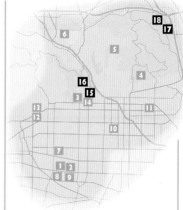

🇮🇷 Autry Museum of Western Heritage

The singing cowboy Gene Autry contributed greatly to the Hollywood version of the Old West, and so one cannot help suspect that a museum named for him might display history rewritten to match the movies. And with Autry as the museum's major donor, there is plenty of Western movie lore here. With help from Disney's special-effects Imagineers, the museum does an entertaining job of exploring America's frontier culture. Seven themed galleries evoke the Old West of myth and reality. **The Spirit of Romance**, for example, examines the real hardships of life in the West while extolling the region's enchanting natural beauty. Sponsored, fittingly, by a beer company, the **Anheuser-Busch Gallery** depicts a Wild West saloon from 1880. The artifacts are fascinating: check out Billy the Kid's gun and Wyatt Earp's badge. Lively interactive scenarios thrill the kids, and a couple of galleries display special exhibitions.

➕ 200 C5 ✉ 4700 Western Heritage Way, across from the L.A. Zoo ☎ (323) 667-2000; www.autry-museum.org
🕐 Tue–Sun 10–5, Thu till 8
🎫 Students moderate; seniors, children under 12 inexpensive (museum included in the Hollywood CityPass)

🇮🇷 Los Angeles Zoo

With 1,300 critters representing some 350 species, the L.A. Zoo houses enough interesting beasts to grab the fancies of most kids – and their parents. The Zoo has been upgrading lately, creating "natural" habitats for its residents. Two of them house primates: Orangutans cavort in the Red Ape Rain Forest, while chimps roam free in the Chimpanzees of the Mahale Mountains. Adventure Island offers an assortment of activities. In Koala House cute marsupials frolic in a simulated Australian forest with anteaters, rat kangaroos and flying possums. And check out the Komodo dragons – not long ago one of them took a bite out of the foot of actress Sharon Stone's husband, creating quite a furor.

Tip: Do the zoo and Autry Museum the same day, as they're near each other, far from everything else, and they share parking lots.

➕ 200 C5 ✉ 5333 Zoo Drive, across from the Autry Museum in Griffith Park ☎ (323) 644-4200; www.lazoo.org 🕐 Daily 10–5, closed Christmas 🎫 Adults, seniors moderate; children inexpensive

The Autry Museum of Western Heritage

Where to...
Eat and Drink

Prices

Expect to pay per person for a three-course meal, excluding tax, drinks and service

$ under $15 $$ $15–$25 $$$ over $25

RESTAURANTS

☞☞☞ Campanile $$$

Charlie Chaplin designed this building where city dwellers now flock for delectable and eclectic Mediterranean cuisine. The often-changed menu – might encompass innovative preparations of fish, lamb and prime rib. Nancy Silverton's "La Brea Bakery" breads, buns and pastries are famous, and it can be somewhat challenging to snag a table for the popular weekend brunches. You can also buy the bakery items to go.

➕ 199 F2 ⊠ 624 S. La Brea Avenue
☎ (323) 938-1447 🅐 Mon–Thu
11:30–2:30, 6–10; Fri 11:30–2:30,
5–11, Sat–Sun 9:30–1:30, 5:30–11

☞☞☞ Chaya Brasserie $$$

This consistently chic Japanese/Mediterranean restaurant serves superbly presented East/West fusion dishes. Move from sushi appetizers to the tuna tartare starters on on to a main course from a lengthy menu of seafood, steak and vegetarian entrees. Wash it down with a bottle from the equally fabulous wine list. Elegant cocktails also pour forth from the full bar.

➕ 199 E3 ⊠ 8741 Alden Drive
☎ (310) 859-9833 🅐 Mon–Fri
11:30–2:30; 6–10:30, Sat 6–11, Sun
6–10

☞☞☞ Dar Maghreb $$$

Cross the threshold into an exotic recreation of a Moroccan palace, where you'll recline on deep cushions, watch belly dancers jiggle and jangle and sup on a traditional seven-course feast. After a ceremonial washing, your hands become utensils for picking through lemon chicken, *bsteeya*, couscous and other delights.

➕ 199 F4 ⊠ 7651 Sunset Boulevard
☎ (323) 876-7651 🅐 Daily 6 pm–
11 pm (Fri 5:30 pm–11 pm, Sun
5:30 pm–10:30 pm)

☞☞☞ Diaghilev $$$

Start saving up for this Russian-with-a-French-twist splurge in the Wyndham Bel Age Hotel (➤ 43). Gear up for an amazing assortment of icy flavored vodkas, bound to whet your appetite for the smoked-fish appetizers, traditional borscht, and snazzy salmon, chicken Kiev and other entrees. And, of course, there's caviar.

➕ 199 D3 ⊠ 1020 N. San Vicente
Boulevard ☎ (310) 854-1111
🅐 Tue–Sat 6:30–10 pm

☞☞☞ Le Carafe $$$

Save yourself the trip to Paris and come dine in this French restaurant with authentic decor, ambience and cuisine. Try such Francophile favorites as frogs' legs, duck *foie gras* and crispy sweetbreads. Even regular visitors are in for surprises, with a changing menu that captures current trends and incorporates fresh offerings.

➕ 199 E3 ⊠ 8284 Melrose Avenue
☎ (323) 655-8880 🅐 Tue–Thu
6–10 pm, Fri 11:30–2:30, 5:30–10,
Sat 5:30–10, Sun 5:30–9:30

☞☞☞ Le Dome $$$

Opened in 1978, Le Dome's French cuisine, Sunset Strip location and flattering lighting continue to draw a steady stream of celebrities, agents and other in-the-biz clientele. The bistro menu appeals to all appetites with tasty renderings of leg of lamb, hearty cassoulet, warm duck salad and other feels-like-France delights, all presented by attentive servers.

➕ 199 E3 ✉ 8720 Sunset Boulevard 🕐 Mon–Fri noon–11:45, Sat 6:30–11:45

☞☞☞ L'Orangerie $$$

Men need a jacket to enter this marvelous restaurant that turns out classic French dishes with a hint of originality, including sublime presentations of seafood, rack of lamb and other grilled meats. Everything here is perfect and diners certainly pay the price, but the setting is opulent and the food somehow never disappoints. Keep an eye out for the ambrosiac chocolate cake – a recipe tenderly supplied by the chef's mother.

➕ 199 E3 ✉ 903 N. La Cienega Boulevard ☎ (310) 652-9770 🕐 Tue–Sun 6–11

☞ Musso & Frank Grill $$

For the ultimate Hollywood-noir experience, ask for a seat in the original side of this expanded restaurant, and order from a menu that features traditional American dishes such as liver and onions, juicy steaks, mashed potatoes and creamed spinach. Cocktails are perfectly mixed and the waiters (who seem like a holdover from the golden era) display a befitting crusty attitude while tending to your every need.

➕ 200 A3 ✉ 6667 Hollywood Boulevard ☎ (323) 467-5123 🕐 Tue–Sat 11–11

☞☞ Palm Restaurant $$$

The menu at this traditional steakhouse with wood booths and brass rails features thick cuts of melt-in-your-mouth steak, succulent lobsters, chunky cottage fries and wedges of rich New York cheesecake. Be prepared for plenty of noise, no-nonsense service and drop-dead prices.

➕ 199 D3 ✉ 9001 Santa Monica Boulevard ☎ (310) 550-8811 🕐 Mon–Fri noon–2:30, 5–10:30, Sat 5–10:30, Sun 5–9

☞☞☞ Patina $$$

Chef Joachim Splichal's flagship restaurant offers an expanded menu along with its roomier space. Here they serve wondrous French/Californian selections that are always ahead of the game in this taste-trendy town. The modernist environment features two main dining rooms, a patio and tables laden with the finest European linens and tableware.

➕ 200 A3 ✉ 5955 Melrose Avenue ☎ (323) 467-1108 🕐 Fri 11:30–2, 6–10, Sat–Thu 6–10

☞ Sonora Café $

If you fancy Southwestern cuisine, head to this eatery that dishes up incredibly nouvelle pleasures in an industrial-chic setting. Feast on innovative recipes incorporating smoked salmon, corn pudding,

cowboy steak or south Texas antelope. The signature dish is Texas-style barbeque pork chops. As an alternative to red meat, try the *ahi* or one of the other seafood dishes.

➕ 199 F3 ✉ 180 S. La Brea Avenue ☎ (323) 857-1800 🕐 Mon 11:30–9, Tue–Thu 11:30–10, Fri 11:30–11, Sat 5–11 pm, Sun 5–9 pm

CAFÉS

Hollywood Hills Coffee Shop $

The age of the "swingers" was immortalized in this "authentic" Hollywood coffee shop, where the anti-cappuccino era crowd drops by for real diner fare, albeit with celebrities and film industry types seated at the table next to you.

➕ 200 C3 ✉ 1745 N. Vermont ☎ (323) 661-3319 🕐 Daily 8 am–midnight

Insomnia Café $

Entertainment industry moguls and those who want to be their best friends inhabit this café where the coffee's strong and the patrons are enthusiastic.

➕ 199 F3 ⊠ 7286 Beverly Boulevard ☎ (323) 931-4943 ⏰ Sun–Thu noon–2 am, Fri–Sat noon–4 am

Pink's Famous Chili Dogs $

It may look like just a funky hot dog stand, but Pink's is famous with everyone from movie stars to the hapless homeless for it's wondrous, luscious, messy-as-can-be chili dogs. The person in line ahead of you might well be the hottest star in Hollywood – or not.

➕ 199 F3 ⊠ 709 N. La Brea Avenue ☎ (323) 931-4223 ⏰ Mon–Fri 9:30 am–2 am, Sat–Sun 9:30 am–3 am

B.B. King's Blues Club

Universal CityWalk sets the stage for the legendary guitarist's local franchise, where blues fans and curious visitors clamor in for hot tunes to go with cool drinks. The cover charge is quite expensive,

but those in the neighborhood prefer this kind of jam over that in traffic!

➕ 199 F5 ⊠ 100 Universal City Drive ☎ (818) 622-5464 ⏰ Daily 4 pm–1 am

The Bar at the Standard

You'll dig the bubble chairs and white shag rugs, while sipping martinis in a spaced-out atmosphere. When the bar shuts down at 2 am, the action moves next door to the 24-hour diner.

➕ 199 E4 ⊠ 8300 Sunset Boulevard ☎ (323) 650-9090 ⏰ Daily till 2 am

Bar Marmont

Attached to the celebrity-hideaway Chateau Marmont Hotel, Bar Marmont offers a deliciously dark, elegant and intimate environment to sip on a cocktail amid some of the coolest cats in Hollywood. This bar is far less pretentious than most others along the Sunset Strip.

➕ 199 E4 ⊠ 8171 Sunset Boulevard ☎ (323) 650-0575 ⏰ Daily 6 pm–2 am

Barney's Beanery

Legend has it that Jim Morrison and Janis Joplin got into a brawl at this unassuming local icon where bikers, 1960s holdovers and authentic rednecks gather for brews, beans and roadhouse fare, while a jukebox belts out rock 'n' roll tunes.

➕ 199 E3 ⊠ 8447 Santa Monica Boulevard ☎ (323) 654-2287 ⏰ Daily 11 am–2 am

Cat & Fiddle

The outside patio of this atmospheric pub is filled with comedians and sitcom stars who mingle with other customers over a pint, a game of darts or some authentic English pub grub.

➕ 200 A3 ⊠ 6530 Sunset Boulevard ☎ (323) 468-3800 ⏰ Daily 11:30 am–2 am

The Derby

This superbly glamorous club, featured in the movie "Swingers" (1996), reeks with swankiness,

retro glamour and swing dancers. After the movie, The Derby became a pinpointed sight on the tourist trail; it has since been reclaimed by locals who dress up to drink, then sashay on the dance floor.

➕ 200 C4 ⊠ 4500 Los Feliz Boulevard ☎ (323) 663-8979 ⏰ Daily 4 pm–2 am

Formosa Café

Step back into Hollywood's film-noir days in this wonderful 1930s café/bar across the street from Warner Bros. Hollywood Studios. It was once a favorite spot for such world-famous stars as Marilyn Monroe and Humphrey Bogart. More recently the Formosa was the set for a scene in the movie "L.A. Confidential" (1997). Sip on a mai tai or other exotic concoctions in a dark booth or on the rooftop patio.

➕ 199 F3 ⊠ 7156 Santa Monica Boulevard ☎ (323) 850-9050 ⏰ Mon–Fri 11 am–2 am, Sat–Sun 5 pm–2 am

Where to... Shop

Shopping in Hollywood and its environs must rank as one of the truly unique experiences in the world. Although the new Hollywood and Highland complex has taken center stage, there are still plenty of other interesting choices.

You'll find hundreds of stores and plenty of bright lights/big city

HOLLYWOOD

The new **Hollywood and Highland** retail and entertainment complex (corner of Hollywood Boulevard and Highland Avenue) is already bringing shoppers back to an area that in past years had become little more than a strip of tawdry souvenir shops.

within this uniquely designed complex centered around the showpiece Babylon Court. There are no large department stores, but major retailers include Gap (and Gap Kids and Baby Gap), Victoria's Secret, Banana Republic, Ann Taylor Loft, bebe and United Colors of Benetton.

The huge two-level **DFS Galleria** showcases both "duty free" and taxable merchandise and includes such upscale lines as Celine, Fendi, Polo Ralph Lauren, Louis Vuitton, Coach, Bulgari, Ferragamo and Burberry. M-A-C Cosmetics features private makeup areas and moveable stations where customers can try out a new face. For fine jewelry, scout out Red Diamond or Dejaun Jewelers, both with classy collections of baubles and watches.

The rest of **Hollywood Boulevard** pales for local shoppers, but souvenir hunters will find gaudy bargain stores selling imprinted T-shirts, baseball caps, shot glasses and other "been there" merchandise.

You can't miss the purple-and-pink **Frederick's of Hollywood** (No. 6608), famous for its kinky lingerie, feather boas, frou-frou stilettos and other accessories – many in hard-to-find sizes.

Hollywood Toys & Costume (No. 6600) offers a boggling assortment of costumes, masks and makeup for both adults and children, as well as a trove of stuffed animals, toys and model sets.

Larry Edmund's Cinema and Theater Bookshop (No. 6644) is another Hollywood mainstay, with one of the world's largest collections of books on the entertainment industry.

You'll also find numerous tomes of new and used Hollywood-related and other titles at **Hollywood Book City** (No. 6627).

The racks at the **Universal News Agency** (corner of Hollywood Boulevard and Las Palmas Avenue) are stacked with foreign and domestic newspapers, magazines and journals.

MELROSE AVENUE

Melrose Avenue continues to be a favorite shopping street. Trinkets and vintage apparel now dominate the area between Citrus and La Brea avenues, while upscale home decor and design houses are grouped around La Cienega and Robertson avenues, close to Beverly Center and the Pacific Design Center.

Cutting-edge furnishings, housewares and boutiques can be found along La Brea Avenue and on Beverly Boulevard (the major intersection south of Melrose Avenue).

Aardvark's Odd Ark (No. 7579) is a vintage clothing collector's dream filled with racks of reasonably priced pre-worn Hawaiian shirts, beaded sweaters, men's suits, women's gowns, hippie wear and tons of accessories and other items.

Try on some of the designer and collectible eyewear at **l.a. Eyeworks** (No. 7407) or the less-costly inventory of costume jewelry at **Maya** (No. 7452).

Vintage Americana is the specialty at kitsch-filled **Off the Wall** (No. 7325).

The astounding conglomeration of vintage, imported and reproduction wind-up toys at **Wound & Wound** (No. 7374) seldom fails to beckon people in from the street – that's kids and adults.

Find a different variety of wind-ups at **Wanna Buy a Watch** (No. 7366) with everything from antique pocket watches and cuckoo clocks to costly Rolexes.

You'll find the newest L.A. sounds and other difficult-to-locate music at **Vinyl Fetish** (No. 7305).

Hard-to-find 1930s–1960s designer furniture, lighting and artwork are highlighted at **Fat Chance** (162 N. La Brea Avenue).

American Rag (150 S. La Brea Avenue) is noted for fine vintage clothing as well as new edgy styles, and it's all pretty expensive.

Actors and movie studios are the main donors of jewelry, used clothing and decorative items at **Cinema Glamour Shop** (343 N. La Brea Avenue), where proceeds benefit actors' charities.

Excellent Modernist furnishings, including one of the largest collections of Eames bucket chairs, are showcased at **Modernica** (7366 Beverly Boulevard).

NEAR BEVERLY CENTER

The windowless Beverly Center (Beverly and La Cienega boulevards) houses three levels of high-caliber brand-name retailers, along with branches of department stores **Macy's** and **Bloomingdale's**.

You can visit more than 200 showrooms in the vast **Pacific Design Center** (8687 Melrose Avenue) – the West Coast's largest interior-design marketplace – but you'll need to employ the services of a designer (many are nearby) to make purchases.

Check out the incredible furnishings at **Pieces** (8380 Melrose Avenue), where most items metamorphose into another piece with the flip of a latch or some other type of gizmo.

The Bodhi Tree (8585 Melrose Avenue), Los Angeles's favorite New Age bookstore, offers good vibes to go with a really vast selection of books on meditation, healing and all things spiritual, as well as music.

Every trendy in town, and many a celebrity, eventually waltzes into the original **Fred Segal** (8118 Melrose Avenue), a block-large complex with designer wear, kid's clothes, gadgets, luggage, shoes and other necessities of life in Los Angeles.

SUNSET STRIP

Along Sunset Strip, you'll find designer boutiques in and around **Sunset Plaza**, near the corner of Doheny Drive.

Book Soup (8818 Sunset Boulevard) is a top shop for entertainment-related titles, classics, literature and international newspapers and magazines.

Just about every type of music can be found at the **Tower Records** flagship store (8801 W. Sunset Boulevard), or at **Tower Classical** (8840 W. Sunset Boulevard).

OTHER AREAS

L.A.'s landmark **Farmers Market** (Third Street and Fairfax Avenue), carved up to make way for **The Grove at Farmers Market** complex, still provides plenty of nostalgia where you can buy fresh produce, meat, poultry, handmade candies and other tasty treats.

Don't overlook the museum stores on **Museum Row** (Fairfax Avenue and Wilshire Boulevard) for high-quality art prints, books, cards and unique gift items.

Universal CityWalk (► 122–123) offers an architecturally striking stretch filled with eateries, clubs and dozens of retailers and novelty shops.

Where to...
Be Entertained

THEATER

Actors' Gang Theater
Classics, musicals and alternative works are performed in this theater co-founded by actor Tim Robbins.
🏛 200 A3 ⬛ 6209 Santa Monica Boulevard ☎ (323) 465-0566

Henry Fonda Theater
Touring shows and musicals are the main offerings in this fine theater, named for the great actor.
🏛 200 B3 ⬛ 6126 Hollywood Boulevard ☎ (323) 468-1700

James A. Doolittle Theater
This 1,038-seat theater presents a year-round schedule of musicals, comedies, dramas and new works.
🏛 200 A3 ⬛ 1615 N. Vine Street ☎ (213) 628-2172

Matrix Theater Company
View off-Broadway-caliber productions of works by the likes of Samuel Beckett and Harold Pinter.
🏛 199 E3 ⬛ 7657 Melrose Avenue ☎ (323) 852-1445

Pantages Theater
See lavish Broadway spectacles and concerts in this grandiose 2,600-seat art-deco performance hall.
🏛 200 A3 ⬛ 6233 Hollywood Boulevard ☎ (323) 468-1700

COMEDY AND CABARET

Cinegrill
This celebrated club in the Clarion Hollywood Roosevelt Hotel might be a bit dated, but nostalgia buffs and locals still consider it the finest cabaret spot in town.
🏛 199 F4 ⬛ 7000 Hollywood Boulevard ☎ (323) 466-7000 🕐 Re-opened May 2002, hours vary according to shows

Comedy Store
Top comedy club presenting well-received comics; legends such as Jerry Seinfeld make appearances.
🏛 199 E4 ⬛ 8433 Sunset Boulevard ☎ (323) 656-6225 🕐 Daily, hours according to shows

Groundlings Theatre
Few can keep a straight face during the groundbreaking stand-up acts that launched the career of stars such as Pee Wee Herman.
🏛 199 F3 ⬛ 7307 Melrose Avenue ☎ (323) 934-9700 🕐 Daily 10–5

The Improvisation
This branch of New York's famous Improv brings big names and hot newbies to the stage.
🏛 199 E3 ⬛ 8162 Melrose Avenue ☎ (323) 651-2583 🕐 Daily, hours according to shows

MUSIC AND DANCE

The Baked Potato
This place offers a trove of jazz greats and jam sessions.
🏛 199 F5 ⬛ 3787 W. Cahuenga Boulevard ☎ (818) 980-1615 🕐 Daily 8 pm–2 am

Catalina Bar and Grill
Top jazz legends perform at this intimate club with superior acoustics.
🏛 200 A3 ⬛ 1640 N. Cahuenga Boulevard ☎ (323) 466-2210 🕐 Daily 7 pm–midnight

El Rey Theatre
Snazzy art-deco former movie theater with sunken dance floor where hipsters move to the live tunes of cutting-edge bands.
🏛 199 F2 ⬛ 5515 Wilshire Boulevard ☎ (323) 936-4790

Greek Theatre
Located in Griffith Park, this outdoor Greek-style amphitheater

offers a summer schedule of big-name artists.

🏠 200 C4 🗺 2700 N. Vermont Avenue 🕾 (323) 665-1927 🕘 Hours vary according to shows

The Hollywood Bowl

This landmark outdoor venue (▶ 128) has hosted everyone from the Beatles to Frank Sinatra.

🏠 199 F4 🗺 2301 N. Highland Avenue 🕾 (323) 850-2000 🕘 Hours vary according to shows

House of Blues

Blues performances as well as reggae, rock and hip hop.

🏠 199 E4 🗺 8430 Sunset Boulevard 🕾 (323) 848-5100 🕘 Daily 6 pm–2 am

Key Club

This large multi-level club entertains with top rock and other bands, plus DJs.

🏠 199 D3 🗺 9039 Sunset Boulevard 🕾 (310) 274-5800 🕘 Daily 7 pm–2 am

Kibbutz Room

There's live music almost every night at this hip and kitschy club.

🏠 199 E3 🗺 419 N. Fairfax Avenue 🕾 (323) 651-2030 🕘 Daily 10 am–2 am

Kodak Theatre

The Kodak Theatre became the permanent home of the Academy Awards in 2002. The theater also puts on a variety of other presentations such as concerts and ballet.

🏠 199 F4 🗺 6801 Hollywood Boulevard 🕾 (323) 308-6363 🕘 Hours vary according to shows

Roxy

One of the hottest clubs on the Strip, hosting national touring acts as well as lesser-known wannabes.

🏠 199 D3 🗺 9009 W. Sunset Boulevard 🕾 (310) 278-9457 🕘 Daily 7 pm–2 am

The Troubadour

This famous venue has changed with the times, but rock 'n' roll still

shares the line-up with an assemblage of raunchier bands.

🏠 199 D3 🗺 9081 Santa Monica Boulevard 🕾 (310) 276-6168 🕘 Daily 6 pm–2 am

Viper Room

Hosts big-name musicians, local bands and impromptu acts (such as Keanu Reeves and Neil Young).

🏠 199 D3 🗺 8852 Sunset Boulevard 🕾 (310) 358-1880 🕘 Daily 9 pm–2 am

Whisky A Go Go

This legendary 1960s club still thrills music fans who come to see the current era's prime rock and alternative bands.

🏠 199 D3 🗺 8901 Sunset Boulevard 🕾 (310) 652-4202 🕘 Daily 8 pm–2 am

MOVIES

El Capitan Theater

This spectacular art-deco movie theater showcases Disney features.

shares the line-up with an assemblage of raunchier bands.

Egyptian Theater

The American Cinemateque presents art films, foreign entries and experimental works.

🏠 200 A3 🗺 6712 Hollywood Boulevard 🕾 (323) 466-3456

Mann's Chinese Theatre

(▶ 115–117)

🏠 200 A3 🗺 6925 Hollywood Boulevard 🕾 (323) 464-8111

New Beverly Cinema

Presents the rare double bill. See such nostalgic combinations as "Rebel Without a Cause" and "The Blackboard Jungle."

🏠 199 F3 🗺 7165 Beverly Boulevard 🕾 (323) 938-4038

Silent Movie Theatre

The silent-film era is alive and well in this unpretentious movie house.

🏠 199 E3 🗺 611 N. Fairfax Avenue 🕾 (323) 655-2520

🏠 199 F4 🗺 6838 Hollywood Boulevard 🕾 (323) 467-7674

Downtown and Pasadena

Getting Your Bearings

While Hollywood's image may have suffered from tawdriness at times, Downtown L.A.'s image problem has been simpler: It's never had an image until now, perhaps. In addition to a proud new skyline and new metro, L.A. has added world-class museums, new concert halls and other amenities. In truth, Downtown has always had plenty to offer open-minded visitors, whose sense of adventure was rewarded when they wandered into the Bradbury Building or took in the fragrant pleasures of the Markets. Note: Downtown is still a gritty urban environment, with all the good and bad that entails.

A few miles north by freeway, once-sleepy Pasadena and its San Gabriel Valley neighbors have gone along quietly for decades, it seems, without getting much attention from travelers (other than football and Rose Parade fans). That has all changed. The heart of Old Pasadena has emerged as a shopping, dining and cultural mecca without losing its historic soul, while the region's museums, gardens and period houses enchant visitors.

★ Don't Miss

1. MOCA and MOCA at the Geffen Contemporary ➤ 142
2. Olvera Street and Union Station ➤ 147
3. Norton Simon Museum ➤ 149
4. Gamble House ➤ 152
5. The Huntington ➤ 154

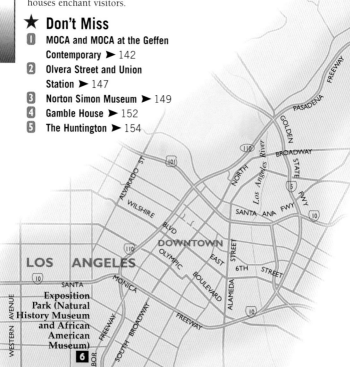

At Your Leisure

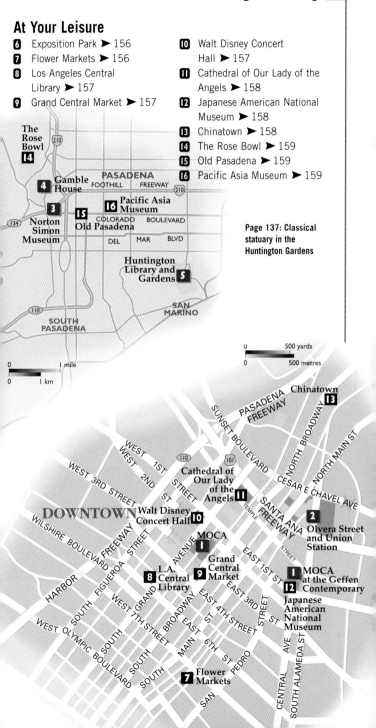

The Rose Bowl **14**

4 Gamble House

3 Norton Simon Museum

15 Old Pasadena

16 Pacific Asia Museum

PASADENA

FOOTHILL FREEWAY

COLORADO BOULEVARD

DEL MAR BLVD

Huntington Library and Gardens **5**

SOUTH PASADENA

SAN MARINO

Page 137: Classical statuary in the Huntington Gardens

0 | 1 mile
0 | 1 km

0 | 500 yards
0 | 500 metres

Chinatown **13**

SUNSET BOULEVARD

PASADENA FREEWAY

NORTH BROADWAY

NORTH MAIN ST

WEST 1ST STREET
WEST 2ND ST
WEST 3RD STREET

Cathedral of Our Lady of the Angels **11**

CESAR E CHAVEL AVE

SANTA ANA FREEWAY

DOWNTOWN

Walt Disney Concert Hall **10**

MOCA **1**

2 Olvera Street and Union Station

WILSHIRE BOULEVARD

HARBOR FREEWAY

SOUTH FIGUEROA STREET

WEST GRAND AVENUE

8 L.A. Central Library

9 Grand Central Market

EAST 1ST ST

EAST 2ND ST

EAST 3RD ST

1 MOCA **12** at the Geffen Contemporary

Japanese American National Museum

WEST 7TH STREET

SOUTH BROADWAY

EAST 4TH STREET

WEST OLYMPIC BOULEVARD

SOUTH MAIN ST

EAST 6TH ST

SOUTH SAN PEDRO ST

CENTRAL AVE

SOUTH ALAMEDA ST

Flower Markets **7**

L.A.'s increasingly urbane Downtown offers many attractions, while nearby Pasadena charms with chic shopping, great museums and lavish gardens.

Downtown and Pasadena in Two Days

Day One

Morning
Take a pre-breakfast walk through the fragrant stalls of the **7 Flower Markets** (➤ 156). Breakfast at one of Downtown's classic eateries. Take the Metro Blue Line to the 103rd Street Station (or drive) for a visit to the **Watts Towers** (➤ 157, right). Return to Downtown by car or Metro. Take in the Downtown sights on foot and on the Bunker Hill Trolley. There's a wide choice: **9 Grand Central Market** (➤ 157), **8 Central Library** (➤ 157), **10 Walt Disney Concert Hall** (➤ 157), **11 Cathedral of Our Lady of the Angels** (➤ 158) and whatever else strikes your fancy. Then go to **2 Olvera Street and Union Station** (➤ 147–148). Lunch at Olvera Street or in nearby **13 Chinatown** (➤ 158). Tour Chinatown on foot.

Afternoon
Spend the afternoon at **1 MOCA and MOCA at the Geffen Contemporary** (you can shuttle from one to the other; ➤ 142–146, below). If time permits, also visit the **12 Japanese American National Museum** (➤ 158).

Evening
Cocktails at the elegant Millennium Biltmore (➤ 43) or at the lively Engine Company No. 28 (➤ 161). Dine Downtown. Highly recommended for food, ambience or both: Bernard's at the Biltmore (➤ 43), Traxx at

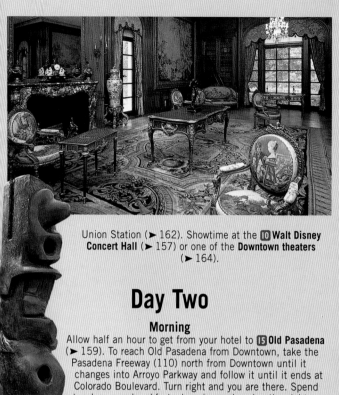

Union Station (► 162). Showtime at the **10 Walt Disney Concert Hall** (► 157) or one of the **Downtown theaters** (► 164).

Day Two

Morning

Allow half an hour to get from your hotel to **15 Old Pasadena** (► 159). To reach Old Pasadena from Downtown, take the Pasadena Freeway (110) north from Downtown until it changes into Arroyo Parkway and follow it until it ends at Colorado Boulevard. Turn right and you are there. Spend two hours on breakfast, shopping and seeing the sights along Colorado Boulevard and the other streets of Old Pasadena. Take time to drive down to Arroyo Seco and have a look at the **14 Rose Bowl** (► 159), then head up and park at the **4 Gamble House** (► 152–153). While waiting for it to open (sign up for the first tour), take a walk to see the several splendid Greene & Greene houses on Arroyo Terrace near by. Take the one-hour Gamble House tour. Explore the nearby **3 Norton Simon Museum** (► 149–151, left, see below), taking time to have lunch in the gardens.

Afternoon

Drive to **5 The Huntington** (► 154–155, top). Tour the gardens and library. Have tea in the Rose Garden Room (► 162). If you're not dining or staying at the **Ritz-Carlton** (► 43), at least drive by to have a look and a quick tour. And take a spin through the gorgeous streets of San Marino.

Evening

Cocktails in one of the lively bistros in Old Pasadena, followed by dinner in the Playhouse District (► 163). Or treat yourself to a cocktail and/or dinner at the Ritz-Carlton. Showtime at the **Pasadena Playhouse** (► 164), one of L.A.'s finest traditional theaters. If nothing's on, take another Old Pasadena walk; better yet, on Friday, the Norton Simon Museum is open until 9 pm so you could return to finish your visit there if you need to.

❶ MOCA and MOCA at the Geffen Contemporary

When seen from outside, this low-rise 1980s building, designed by Japanese architect Arata Isozaki, offers an understated yet powerful geometric assemblage of pyramids, cylinders and cubes clad in rough red sandstone, flanking a copper-sheathed barrel vault. The structure, located on Bunker Hill in a development called California Plaza, grace-fully holds its own against the Downtown skyline. Bathed in rich washes of natural light from rooftop skylights, the galleries have a serene, sanctuary-like quality – an ambience attained, in part, by placing them "underground," away from the business of the street.

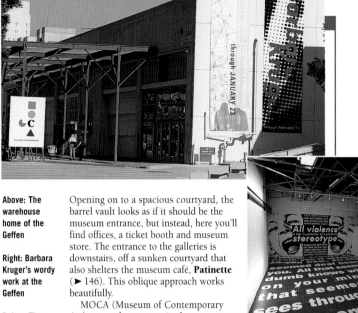

Above: The warehouse home of the Geffen

Right: Barbara Kruger's wordy work at the Geffen

Below: The MOCA plaza, encircled by graceful structures

Opening on to a spacious courtyard, the barrel vault looks as if it should be the museum entrance, but instead, here you'll find offices, a ticket booth and museum store. The entrance to the galleries is downstairs, off a sunken courtyard that also shelters the museum café, **Patinette** (▶ 146). This oblique approach works beautifully.

MOCA (Museum of Contemporary Art) presently operates in three separate locations: **MOCA at California Plaza** is the museum's primary location; a second location is known as **MOCA at the Geffen Contemporary**; and a third **MOCA** holds forth at the **Pacific Design Center** on Melrose Avenue in West Hollywood.

The Geffen Contemporary was an old warehouse structure converted by architect Frank Gehry into a temporary museum space to house the growing MOCA collections during its construction phase in the 1980s. Gehry did a masterful job of utilizing the structure's inherent strengths – massive doors, redwood ceilings, steel columns, trusses and beams and a vast, open floor space – and the Temporary Contemporary, as it was dubbed, proved enormously popular, staking a claim for itself as a permanent part of the L.A. art scene. After closing for a couple of years in the early 1990s when MOCA at California Plaza opened, the Temporary Contemporary reopened with an endowment from entertainment mogul David Geffen, whose name now graces the building.

Finally, in what appears to be an effort to have a presence farther west, where most of L.A.'s new money is and where LACMA and the Getty rule, in 2001 MOCA opened a third outpost, devoted to temporary exhibitions, on the grounds of the Pacific Design Center in West Hollywood.

According to MOCA's rules of engagement, contemporary art means anything made after 1940 and within those parameters MOCA's collection is probably the best in the western United States. The museum's emphasis is slanted toward temporary exhibitions: for example, a magnificent show devoted to David Hockney's photography enthralled much of L.A. through the summer of 2001. Given the unpredictable nature of the contemporary art scene, the commitment to temporary exhibitions makes sense. MOCA's curators host about 20 such shows every year, highlighting the work of artists ranging from the internationally famous to relative unknowns in the formative stages of their careers.

There is plenty of outstanding work on permanent display – enough to engage even the most demanding connoisseur of post-1940 art. The permanent collections include over 5,000 pieces, beginning with the Abstract Expressionists and ending with the latest art stars of the new millennium. Some of the famous names whose works have been collected at MOCA include Diane Arbus, Willem de Kooning, Sam Francis, Arshile Gorky, Robert Irwin, Jasper Johns, Roy Lichtenstein, Joan Miró, Louise Nevelson, Claes Oldenburg, Jackson Pollock, Robert Rauschenberg, Mark Rothko, Cy Twombly and Andy Warhol.

Not surprisingly, the collections are particularly strong on L.A. artists and collectors. The original MOCA board of trustees, formed in the late 1970s, included artist Sam Francis, who gave 10 major pieces to the collections. (Francis was also instrumental in commissioning Arata Isozaki to design the California Plaza building.) Artist Ed Moses contributed 11 paintings and drawings, while trustee Marcia Simon Weisman honored the museum with a collection of 83 drawings and prints, including major pieces by de Kooning, Gorky and Johns. The

museum purchased a major collection of 80 abstract expressionist and pop art pieces from the Italian count Giuseppe Panza; later, Panza gave the museum another 70 pieces, and bequests from assorted L.A. media millionaires have deepened the collections of contemporary work over the past two decades.

Since early 2001 and continuing indefinitely, in addition to various temporary exhibitions the two Downtown MOCAs have hosted a single exhibition divided into two parts. At California Plaza, it's **A Room of their Own: From Rothko to Rauschenberg**; at the Geffen Contemporary,

Alternative Shows

MOCA has also achieved quite a reputation for its architecture shows, offering one-man exhibitions that explore the work of stellar designers like Louis Kahn and Frank Gehry and focusing attention on lesser-known architects like Rudolph Schindler and other early L.A. Modernists.

A Room of Their Own: From Arbus to Gober. Each attempts an in-depth survey of the work of a number of leading artists. You'll see the "classics" of post-World War II art, such as the Abstract Expressionists, at California Plaza; the Geffen exhibition focuses on the most contemporary works.

Amid all the riches to be found in both Downtown MOCAs, a number of works should not be missed: Pollock's powerful **Number One** and **Number Three** show the master of over-scale splatter painting at his best. Rauschenberg's **Coca-Cola Plan** is an amusing item, a battered cabinet with old bottles and wings. Jasper Johns' **Map** from 1962 is a richly layered and textured map of the U.S. that has become an icon of the Abstract Expressionist movement; Warhol's **Telephone** is a pop art stand out.

Several of the New York art stars of the postmodern, post-pop 1980s – Julian Schnabel, David Salle, Eric Fischl and Barbara Kruger among them – also have artwork in the collections, so you can see for yourself what all that 1980s art hype was

Jasper Johns' *Map* is one of the great modern works in the MOCA collection

about. Schnabel's monumental *Owl*, from 1980, illustrates his powerful way with paint and other materials and the Salle piece, cleverly named ***View the Author Through Long Telescopes***, is representative of his mocking, ironically charged work.

Also in that 1980s vein, don't miss Cindy Sherman's bizarre photographic self-portraits, or the two pieces by the tragically short-lived Jean Michel Basquiat.

TAKING A BREAK

Allow time for a snack or a meal at the chic **Patinette** at the California Plaza MOCA. This little café is a small version of Patina (➤ 131), the celebrated restaurant of Joachim Splichal.

This is the place for great art books and gifts

MOCA at California Plaza (on Bunker Hill)
🛉 197 E4 ⊠ 250 S. Grand Avenue ☎ (213) 626-6222; www.moca-la.org (for all three sites) 🕐 Tue–Sun 11–5, Thu till 8 💰 Adults moderate; students and seniors inexpensive; children free; Thu 5–8 free

MOCA at the Geffen Contemporary (in Little Tokyo)
🛉 197 F4 ⊠ 152 N. Central Avenue ☎ (213) 626-6222 🕐 Tue–Sun 11–5, Thu till 8 💰 Adults moderate; students and seniors inexpensive; children free; Thu 5–8 free

MOCA at the Pacific Design Center (in West Hollywood)
🛉 199 E3 ⊠ 8687 Melrose Avenue ☎ (310) 289-5223 🕐 Tue–Sun 11–5, Thu till 8 💰 Adults moderate; students and seniors inexpensive; children free; Thu 5–8 free

MOCA/MOCA AT THE GEFFEN CONTEMPORARY: INSIDE INFO

Top tips When you pay to enter either of the two main museums, **you're also covered at the other**; a free, continuously running shuttle bus makes it easy to do them both in a single session.
• You could see each of the Downtown MOCAs in an hour if you had to, but **two to three hours** should allow plenty of time to see the best of what's on hand. If you must choose, remember that MOCA at the Geffen is the more contemporary of the two contemporaries.

Don't miss Visit the museum's **book and gift shop** on the upper level – it's a great one.

2 Olvera Street and Union Station

Those curious about the early history of Los Angeles need go no farther than El Pueblo de Los Angeles State Historic Park. This collection of 27 historic buildings on a 44-acre site (everyone calls it Olvera Street) just north of Downtown encapsulates L.A.'s Hispanic roots and its transformation from dusty Spanish pueblo to thriving Anglo-Mexican town.

It's best to see El Pueblo on foot. Whichever route you take (buy a self-guided walking tour brochure at Sepulveda House), there are several must-sees. Start with the **Pobladores (Founders) Plaque** in the old plaza. It lists the names of the 44 settlers who came from Mexico in 1781 to bolster the Spanish claim to California by settling El Pueblo. The original village is long gone; the oldest building on Olvera is the 1818 **Avila Adobe**, now a museum on the Hispanic lifestyle of 1840s California. Other pre-Anglo sites include the **Plaza Catholic Church** (1818–22), across North Main Street from the plaza and the adjacent **Campo Santo**, site of the pueblo's first cemetery.

During the 1840s California changed from Mexican to American rule – a change reflected in the buildings in the historic district, as brick and wood replaced adobe. Several fine examples of late 19th-century architecture have been restored and transformed into museums. L.A.'s first firehouse, from 1884, across the plaza from Olvera Street, is now a **museum** about 19th-century firefighting. The Italianate 1870 **Pico House** was originally a hotel belonging to Pio Pico, the last governor of Alta (upper) California. Today it houses a museum devoted to the history of his family.

A Mexican-style homestead on Olvera Street

Olvera Street was a run-down, muddy little alley surrounded by decrepit buildings in the 1920s, scheduled for razing until Christine Sterling, a local preservationist, convinced the powers-that-be to save the street. Lined with a mix of nicely restored old buildings (dating from 1818 to 1926) that now house restaurants, curio shops, museums and historic sites, Olvera Street is a lively pedestrian arcade. Don't miss the **Avila Adobe**, **Sepulveda House**, the **Biscailuz Building** and the **Pelanconi Building**, which now contains La Golondrina Café, one of the city's oldest eateries. Have a margarita, let the mariachis play and enjoy L.A.'s Mexican heritage.

Union Station

Slip across Alameda Street for a quick tour of Union Station, a grand 1930s terminal worth a walk-through even if you're not headed for the Metro (via a tunnel to the Gateway Transit Center east of the station) or dining at **Traxx**, the chic in-station restaurant (► 162). Anchored by a Mediterranean-style clock tower, the red-tile-roofed station gracefully mixes Mission, Streamline Moderne and Moorish design elements. Its 52-foot-high lobby ceilings soar overhead, supported on massive wooden beams, and great swatches of original tilework display patterns inspired by everything from art deco to Navajo.

TAKING A BREAK

Have a French dip sandwich at nearby **Philippe the Original** (1001 Alameda Street at Ord Street, tel: 213/628-3781, daily 6 am–10 pm), one of the city's first fast-food stands. Or there's always **Traxx** (► 162).

El Pueblo de Los Angeles
➕ 197 F5 ✉ 125 Paseo de la Plaza (bordered by Alameda Street, Spring Street, Sunset Boulevard ☎ (213) 628-1274

Sepulveda House Visitor Center
➕ 197 F5 ✉ 662 N. Main Street ☎ (213) 628-1274 🕐 Daily 11–11 (restaurants), 11–7 (retail)

Union Station
➕ 197 F5 ✉ 800 N. Alameda Street ☎ (909) 789-7867 🕐 Daily 24 hours

---

OLVERA STREET AND UNION STATION: INSIDE INFO

Top tip Union Station has "starred" in several movies, among them "The Way We Were" (1973), "Blade Runner" (1982) and "To Live and Die in L.A." (1985).

Hidden gem As you're strolling Olvera Street, you may see a series of **marked bricks** that trace the course of the centuries-old *zanja madre*, or mother ditch, which ran from the original Los Angeles River along what is now Olvera Street. The original settlement of Los Angeles grew up around this manmade canal.

3 Norton Simon Museum

One cannot help but think, visiting this museum, that Norton Simon made his food-packing and magazine-publishing fortune with one thing in mind – so that he could afford to gather as much of the world's most beautiful art as possible. The range of this collection is astonishing. Simon may have been the last of the great private collectors.

Left: Union Station's soaring interior: Dig those comfy chairs

Simon began acquiring European art in the 1950s, starting with the masters of the 19th and early 20th centuries including Degas, Cézanne, Renoir and Gauguin. In the 1960s he added a large number of Old Master paintings from the 16th to the 18th centuries. The collection grew to include hundreds of artworks from the last 700 years of European painting and sculpture.

Simon educated himself in south Asian art and began acquiring works from that part of the world as well. He put his collection on tour, lending it to a number of museums prior to settling in Pasadena in 1974, where he took over the

Works are displayed with style in the galleries of the Norton Simon

financially troubled Pasadena Museum of Modern Art (built in 1969) and transformed it into a home for his 12,000 pieces.

Simon's passionate commitment to his museum left everyone uncertain as to what would happen when he died in 1993. Fortunately, his widow, actress Jennifer Jones Simon,

did the right thing: In the mid-1990s she announced a $3 million plan to renovate the building and gardens. Architect Frank Gehry masterminded the work, completed in 1999, which turned out surprisingly subdued and elegant, given his radical reputation. In fact, Gehry has always been an artists' architect and here, with one of the world's great collections of Old Masters to inspire him, he worked quiet wonders. The galleries have been made more intimate, the lighting vastly improved and the flow of spaces matches the stylistic and chronological flow of the artworks. Outside the building, landscape architect Nancy Goslee Powers redesigned the museum's 80,000-square-foot formal sculpture gardens to evoke the spirit of Monet's gardens at Giverny.

Rodin's magnificent *The Burghers of Calais* greets visitors outside the entry; Henry Moore's *King and Queen*, from 1952–53, offers up a second greeting by the doors.

The greatness of Norton Simon's collection lies in its extensive European art holdings. From the entrance lobby, the 19th- and 20th-century galleries lie to the left. Here, you'll find more than 100 pieces by Edgar Degas, including a complete set of bronze sculptures cast from the artist's waxes found in his studio after his death, and dozens of paintings and drawings of his elegant dancers, such as *Dancers in the*

Wings (1880). Don't miss Manet's *The Ragpicker*; Cézanne's *Portrait of Uncle Dominique, Vase of Flowers* and *Tulips in a Vase*; Monet's *The Artist's Garden at Vetheuil*; and Renoir's fascinating group portrait, *The Artist's Studio*.

Van Gogh is represented by several works, including *Portrait of the Artist's Mother* (1888) and the striking *Mulberry Tree* (1889). A letter from the artist dated May 21, 1890, is also on display; it was one of the last he wrote before he took his own life. Gauguin's *Tahitian Woman and Boy* (1899), Rousseau's *Exotic Landscape* (1910) and dozens of other great artists' works are here, including some by Picasso and Matisse, with a generous selection of outstanding pieces.

The list of masterpieces seems endless, but the museum is really not all that large and you can do a focused tour in an hour or two.

After the Impressionists, head across the hall and immerse yourself in an earlier Europe, when the artists concentrated on painting religious figures – along with portraits of the wealthy and scenes from Testaments Old and New. Don't miss Botticelli's *Madonna and Child with Adoring Angel*, Raphael's *Madonna and Child with a Book* and Lucas Cranach's *Adam and Eve*.

Left: *Waiting* by Edgar Degas

Below: One of Rodin's masterful statues

There are masterpieces everywhere; one of the most captivating paintings in the collection is the *Self-Portrait* by Rembrandt (1636–38). Canaletto's several views of Venice in the 18th century are exquisite.

TAKING A BREAK

The Norton Simon's 80,000 square feet of sculpture gardens, ponds and plantings gracefully evoke Monet's gardens at Giverny; the small outdoor **café** ($–$$) makes a wonderful place to stop for a snack or lunch while touring the museum. Open during museum hours; very casual.

🚼 201 D5 ✉ 411 W. Colorado Boulevard, corner of Colorado and Orange Grove boulevards, intersection of Foothill (210) and Ventura (134) freeways, a few blocks west of Old Pasadena ☎ (626) 449-6840; www.nortonsimon.org 🕐 Wed–Sun noon–6, Fri till 9 💰 Adults moderate; seniors inexpensive; students and children under 12 free

NORTON SIMON MUSEUM: INSIDE INFO

Top tips There are numerous famous **sculptures** to the rear, artfully placed around the ponds and plantings.
• Downstairs, be sure to see the museum's enthralling collection of **South Asian sculptures**.

4 Gamble House

The architectural side of the Arts and Crafts movement doesn't get any better than this. Brothers Charles and Henry Greene put all their considerable skills to work in creating the gorgeously detailed Gamble House, built in 1908 as a winter getaway for midwestern millionaires David and Mary Gamble, of Procter and Gamble money and fame.

Rather than imitate the other wealthy Pasadena snowbirds, who built their beaux arts winter palaces along Orange Grove Boulevard (nicknamed Millionaires' Row), the Gambles set up shop nearby on Westmoreland Terrace and hired the Greenes to make their vacation home. The Greenes already had a reputation for their brilliant interpretations of the English-originated Arts and Crafts style, translated into Southern California. Swiss and Japanese influences are lovingly integrated into this bungalow.

The building unquestionably ranks among the finest house museums in America. The obvious exterior elements that define the Arts and Crafts style include broad, deep overhanging eaves and generously proportioned porches. However, the real allure lies inside, behind the stained-glass front door, featuring an image of a California oak tree designed by Henry Greene and executed in leaded glass by Emil Lange. The built-in cabinetry, walls, floors, doors, indeed every last bit of wood and hardware, was handcrafted for the house in the Greenes' Pasadena studio. Woods include everything from teak and redwood to maple, mahogany and oak, all meticulously finished and impeccably preserved. The interior is rich, dark, flooded with warm light streaming through leaded glass windows and marvelously detailed.

Above: The California bungalow at its Arts and Crafts best

Right: The dining room has original furnishings and fixtures

Detail right: A stained-glass oak tree sets the front door glowing

GAMBLE HOUSE: INSIDE INFO

Top tips A collection of 80 pieces of Greene & Greene-designed furniture and decorative artworks has been moved from the Gamble House for display and safekeeping in the **Virginia Steele Scott Galleries** at the Huntington Gardens and Library. Don't miss it when you visit the Huntington (▶ 154–155).
• For **guided tours** of the area's architectural riches, including the Arts and Crafts bungalows, contact Pasadena Heritage (tel: 626/441-6333).

The Greenes created a number of smaller but equally well-crafted houses in the neighborhood. Visitors can arrive at the Gamble House around 11 am and begin the architectural activity by exploring the landscaped grounds. Then take a few moments to browse the well-stocked gift shop and sign up for one of the one-hour docent-guided tours of the house (no unguided tours are permitted) that start at noon.

Take a walking tour on your own of the other Greene & Greene houses on Arroyo Terrace, near Westmoreland Place. Along with the **Cole House** next door on Westmoreland (now a Unitarian Community House), the following privately owned houses on Arroyo Terrace are all Greene & Greene designs: Nos. 440, 424, 408, 400, 370 and 368; also, Nos. 210, 240 and 235 Grand Avenue, around the corner.

To the north lies **Prospect Park**, another residential enclave and in the distance, the **Rose Bowl** (▶ 159). At Prospect Park, Frank Lloyd Wright designed one interesting little number, the **Millard House**, 645 Prospect Crescent. Known as La Miniatura, it was the first of his concrete block houses and looks something like a Mayan ruin buried in the jungle.

TAKING A BREAK
Drive to **Goldstein's Bagel Bakery** (86 Colorado Boulevard, Old Pasadena, $) for fresh-baked, New York-style bagels.

➕ 201 D5   ✉ 4 Westmoreland Place, Pasadena   ☎ (626) 793-3334
🕐 Wed–Sun noon–3   💲 Inexpensive. One-hour docent-led tours only

5 The Huntington

Reigning over a 207-acre hilltop site in the upscale town of San Marino, the Huntington Library, Art Collections and Botanical Gardens bring together in one place three distinct attractions, each of which is unmissable. The Huntington is a magnificent gift from a magnanimous millionaire, Henry Edwards Huntington. He came west with inherited money, established L.A.'s once-great transit system, made a large fortune larger and retired in 1908 to his San Marino ranch to pursue his real passion: collecting English and American books and paintings.

Huntington collected art for the rest of his life (he died in 1927) and his widow and then his foundation continued collecting after his death, often buying entire libraries from individuals or institutions. Today the Library possesses more than 4 million pieces. While most of the books, manuscripts, maps, photographs and other items are in storage, available primarily to scholars, the **Exhibition Hall** on the ground level houses a fascinating selection. Here you'll find the *Ellesmere Chaucer*, an illuminated draft of the *Canterbury Tales* from 1405; a Gutenberg Bible from 1455 is displayed in a permanent exhibition devoted to the transition from handwritten to printed books.

Chaucer himself, from the *Ellesmere Chaucer*

The **Shakespeare collection** is one of the best in the world. You might also see the original handwritten draft of Benjamin Franklin's *Autobiography*, or works by Copernicus, Charles Dickens, James Joyce and hundreds of other writers, artists and printmakers. One of the most famous books on display is William Blake's *Songs of Innocence and Experience*, with its illustrated version of his great poem *The Tyger*. The library also has an original 1778 copy of *The Federalist Papers* and 400 documents written by George Washington.

Displayed in a palatial beaux arts building, the art collection focuses primarily on English paintings of the 18th and early 19th centuries. Some of the galleries are resplendent with Louis XIV-style carpets, chairs, tables and statuary. Others may want to focus on the greatest hits; one of Gilbert Stuart's famed George Washington portraits hangs in the dining room.

In the **Main Gallery**, highlights include the *Blue Boy* by Thomas Gainsborough, *Pinkie* by Thomas Lawrence, *Grand Canal, Venice* by J.M.W. Turner and Sir Joshua Reynolds' *Mrs. Siddons as the Tragic Muse*.

The **Virginia Steele Scott Gallery for American Art** features works from every period of American history. Look for Mary Cassatt's *Breakfast in Bed* (1897) and Edward Hopper's evocative *The Long Leg* (1935). Surrounded by the **Dorothy Collins Brown Gardens**, the **Boone Gallery** hosts traveling exhibitions. It stands near the Scott Gallery in the northwestern part of the grounds, as does Huntington's Greek-style mausoleum.

Botanical Gardens

Many visitors come just for the Botanical Gardens. You'll need a brochure with a map, available at the entrance, to best explore them. The **North Vista**, a grand allée flanked by rows of 17th-century statuary, features a formal sweep of lawn that shapes a view of the San Gabriel Mountains. The **Shakespeare Garden** displays plants mentioned in his works. In the **Rose Garden**, take in 1,000 years of rose history told through some 2,000 cultivars. Stroll through the Australian Garden, the Subtropical Garden, the Tropical Garden and the Palm Garden and visit the Lily Pond en route to the most compelling site of all: the **Desert Garden**, home to the world's largest collection of desert plants.

TAKING A BREAK

Tea in the **Rose Garden Room** is a lovely event (tel: 626/683-8131).

➕ 201 F4 ✉ 1151 Oxford Road, San Marino (second entrance on Orlando Road at Allen Avenue) ☎ (626) 405-2100; www.huntington.org 🕐 Tue–Fri noon–4:30, Sat–Sun (and every day in summer) 10:30–4:30 💲 Moderate; free for children under 12; free first Thu every month

THE HUNTINGTON: INSIDE INFO

Top tips Pasadena can be very **hot in summer and fall**. Plan your time at the Huntington so you're ouside in the gardens in the earlier, cooler part of the day, then move to the indoor attractions as the temperature rises.
• One of the Huntington's most sublime elements, the **Japanese garden complex**, located in a once-wild canyon west of the mansion, includes an authentic, reconstructed Japanese house, a traditional landscape with a moon bridge, an extensive bonsai garden and a raked gravel and rock garden in the style of Zen Buddhist gardens of the Muromachi period.

At Your Leisure

🔟 Exposition Park

Located southwest of Downtown next to the University of Southern California, Exposition Park served as an open-air farmer's market from 1872 until 1910. Its first great moment arrived back in 1932, when the Memorial Coliseum, now a national historic landmark, hosted the Olympic Games. With the Coliseum, the Rose Garden and several fine museums, the park remains a major draw. Note: This part of L.A. can be dangerous, especially after dark.

The **African-American Museum** (600 State Drive, off Figueroa Street, tel: 213/744-7432, Tue–Sun 10–5, free) moved into its sleek new Exposition Park home in 1984. The building has an impressive sculpture court under a tinted-glass roof. The permanent collection offers paintings, sculptures, photographs and works in other media by African-American artists from the 19th century to the present. An excellent long-term exhibit on the life of singer Ella Fitzgerald has been mounted in the form of a backstage dressing room.

The **Natural History Museum** (900 Exposition Boulevard, tel: 213/744-3466, Tue–Sun 10–5, moderate–expensive) serves as one of the nation's most comprehensive collections of artifacts relating to the history of the earth. There is so much to choose from, you might want to focus on

just one of the four main departments. **Life Sciences** features birds, mammals, reptiles, fish and the like. The highlight here is the Insect Zoo. **Earth Sciences** covers dinosaur bones, fossils, gems and minerals. Don't miss the dueling dinosaurs in the lobby of the Dinosaur Hall. Native American, pre-Columbian and Pacific civilizations are in **Anthropology**, and **History** covers American and Southwest civilizations.

🞢 196 A1 ⊠ Bordered by Figueroa Street, Vermont Avenue, Exposition Boulevard and Martin Luther King Jr. Boulevard

🔟 Flower Markets

A pre-breakfast trip to the Flower Markets adds an aromatic beginning to your day. With all the bustle going on, it's very atmospheric and a stunningly colorful scene. Since these markets supply most of the flower shops in L.A., the stalls sell out fast: Arrive early if you want to see it in full bloom and have your pick. They've got every flower imaginable, from gerbera daisies to long-stem roses. The two markets (across the street from each other) are near

Dinos duke it out in the Dinosaur Hall, Natural History Museum

L.A.'s Skid Row sleaze, so park as close as possible.

🔢 197 E3 ✉ **American Florist Exchange**, 754 Wall Street ☎ (213) 622-1966 ✉ **Southern California Flower Markets**, 742 Maple Avenue ☎ (213) 627-2482 🕐 Mon, Wed, Fri 2 am–noon, Tue, Thu, Sat 6 am–noon, closed Sun 💰 Inexpensive, secure parking inside or on roof inexpensive

8 Los Angeles Central Library

The Central Library has a wealth of engrossing architectural details, highlighted by a series of interior wall murals on California's history. The original building is a vision of L.A. eclecticism. The exterior has a Moderne look, with Egyptian detailing. Inside are more classical forms: a dome, arches and vaults. Don't miss the limestone figures of literary greats on the exterior, or the awesome sweep of the central rotunda ceiling with its 1933 murals. In the west garden you'll find Jud Fine's intriguing sculpted entryway, "Spine." Since a disastrous fire in 1986, the original spaces have been beautifully restored; the new atrium features three artist-designed chandeliers.

🔢 197 D4 ✉ 630 W. Fifth Street ☎ (213) 228-7000; www.lapl.org 🕐 Mon, Thu–Sat 10–5, Tue–Wed noon–8, Sun 1–5 💰 Free; tours daily

9 Grand Central Market

Since 1917 the Grand Central Market has served L.A. as an indoor market for fresh meat, veggies, fruit – whatever. Given the Market's overwhelmingly immigrant clientele, you can find good prices on everything, hear exotic languages and see several stands selling the stranger parts of cows, pigs and sheep. Look for handmade tortillas, mango ice-cream cones and more than 20 varieties of fresh juice. Mariachi bands often play by the Hill Street entrance on weekends.

🔢 197 E4 ✉ 317 S. Broadway, second entrance on Hill Street ☎ (213) 624-2378 🕐 Daily 9–6 💰 Free

10 Walt Disney Concert Hall

Until the Walt Disney Concert Hall began rising on the Downtown skyline, Frank Gehry had never had a truly major L.A. commission. With the sculpted elegance of the

Watts Towers

Watts Towers (1765 E. 107th Street, 6 miles south of Downtown) is one of the great folk-art monuments in the country. Allow an hour's travel time, roundtrip (take the Metro Blue Line, or drive) and half an hour to view. Italian immigrant Simon Rodia spent 33 years, from 1921 to 1954, on the eight 100-foot towers. He worked alone, building the openwork iron frames with salvaged steel rods, pipes and assorted debris, and then embellishing them with 70,000 crushed sea-shells and bits of broken glass and ceramics. The Northridge earthquake in 1994 did significant damage, but they are now back in shape, with limited accessibility: call Watts Towers Art Center (213/847-4646). Note: They are in a high crime area, so visit in the daytime.

surrealistically swooping steel frame, rising on its Bunker Hill site, the new Concert Hall is spectacular. Voluptuous sails of stainless steel encircle the auditorium, reception areas, lobby and rehearsal halls. A separate theater downstairs is part of CalArts, an L.A.-based art school. There are also gardens and an outdoor amphitheater.

➕ 197 E5 ✉ S. Grand Avenue between First and Second streets

🔟 Cathedral of Our Lady of the Angels

L.A.'s brand-new cathedral merits a visit from even the most jaded traveler. Designed by José Rafael Moneo, it should prove to be one of the world's great modern places of worship: an exposed concrete structure infused with light and spirituality. With its traditional sacramental forms and elements seamlessly integrated into a dynamic contemporary space, the church seats around 3,000, while the adjacent plaza provides a gathering space for 6,000.

➕ 197 E5 ✉ 555 W. Temple Street
🕐 Open 24 hours for worship

🔢 Japanese-American National Museum

Located in the Little Tokyo district, this museum offers a changing series of exhibitions devoted to Japanese-American history and culture. It housed a Buddhist temple from 1925 until 1992, when a massive renovation transformed it into a striking, contemporary museum space.

Chinatown is recognizable by pagoda-style rooflines and Chinese writing

Exhibitions change frequently and focus on the lives and contributions of Japanese-Americans and on the tragedy of forced internment of some 100,000 Japanese-American citizens during World War II. Permanent displays integrate photographs, artifacts, family mementos and old home movies into moving tributes to Japanese immigrants and their contributions to American culture.

➕ 197 F4 ✉ 369 E. First Street at Central Avenue ☎ (213) 625-0414; www.janm.org 🕐 Tue–Sun 10–5, Thu till 7:30 💲 Adults moderate; seniors and students inexpensive; free third Thu of every month and Thu after 5

🔢 Chinatown

The original Old Chinatown evolved in the 1870s when L.A.'s Chinese were forced out of a downtown area by discriminatory housing laws. They formed their own community, which was razed in the late 1930s to make way for Union Station. Thus was born "New Chinatown," the first such enclave in the country to be owned and financed by Chinese. The main street is North Broadway, where the buildings are embellished with the ornamental facades and rooflines that lend the district its Chinese identity. Between Broadway and Hill Street, Gin Ling Way offers a pedestrians-only strip of stores and restaurants. Try *dim sum* at **Ocean Seafood** (747 N. Broadway, tel: 213/687-3088)

or spicy Szechuan at **Yang Chow**
(819 N. Broadway, tel: 213/625-
0811). There are several trendy new
art galleries on Chung King Road.

➕ 197 F5 ✉ Bordered by N.
Broadway, N. Hill Street, Bernard Street
and Cesar Chavez (Sunset) Boulevard

⓮ The Rose Bowl

One of the United States' great sports
events takes place here every New
Year's Day, following the Tournament
of Roses Parade: the Rose Bowl football game, pitting the championship
team of the Pac Ten (west coast
universities) versus the Big Ten
champions from the midwest. Every
four years or so, according to a
revolving schedule, the Rose Bowl
hosts the national college football
championship. Both meetings are
quite a show. The Rose Bowl also
hosts UCLA's home football games,
the occasional Super Bowl and other
sports events. It also hosts one of the
largest **flea markets**.

➕ 201 D5 ✉ 1001 Rose Bowl Drive,
Pasadena ☎ (626) 577-3100 ⏰ Flea
market 9–3, second Sun every month
💲 Moderate–expensive

⓯ Old Pasadena

Old Pasadena is a historic district
brimming with trendy boutiques,
coffee shops, hip bistros, nightclubs,
music and bookstores, antiques
dealers and funky gift shops.
Lined with vintage buildings,
Colorado Boulevard may be
the district's liveliest retail axis,
but try to see the Venetian
Revival Building (17 S.
Raymond), the impressive
Castle Green (99
S. Raymond), the
Santa Fe Railroad
Station
(222 S.

Raymond) and the White Block (Fair
Oaks Avenue). Farther down
Colorado, stroll over to see the
Pasadena Civic Auditorium (300 E.
Green Street), the 1925 Pasadena
City Hall (100 N. Garfield) and the
Central Library (285 E. Walnut).

➕ 201 D4 Pasadena Heritage ✉ 651
St. John Avenue ☎ (626) 441-6333

⓰ Pacific Asia Museum

Grace Nicholson built her Chinese
Treasure House in 1924 and willed
the building to Pasadena on her
death in 1948. It served as the
Pasadena Art Museum, then in 1971
it became home to the Pacific Asia
Museum's 17,000 pieces. Collections
of Chinese textiles, Ming and Ching
Dynasty porcelain, carved jade and
Japanese Edo paintings are shown
in revolving displays in lower-level
galleries. The museum's temporary
exhibitions and programs range from
workshops in *mah-jongg* (an ancient
Chinese tile game) and *ikebana*
(flower-arranging) to displays of
works by contemporary Asian and
Asian-American artists. Even if you
don't visit the exhibitions, you
should see the building.

➕ 201 E5 ✉ 46 N. Los Robles Avenue,
Pasadena ☎ (626) 449-2742;
www.pacasiamuseum.org ⏰ Wed–Fri
noon–5, Thu till 8, Sat–Sun 11–5
✋ Inexpensive;
free third Sat
each month
and for
children
under 12

Where to...
Eat and Drink

Prices
Expect to pay per person for a three-course meal, excluding tax, drinks and service

$ under $15 $$ $15–$25 $$$ over $25

RESTAURANTS

☞☞☞ A Thousand Cranes Restaurant $$$

Set inside the New Otani Hotel in Little Tokyo (➤ 43), this Japanese dining spot offers an oasis of calm in the middle of Downtown. Diners relax over traditional Japanese dishes such as sukiyaki, or make delectable selections at the sushi and tempura bars. The festive Sunday brunch is a crowd pleaser, with both Japanese and Western selections.

✚ 197 E4 ⊠ 120 S. Los Angeles Street ☎ (213) 253-9255

🕐 Mon–Sat 7–10, 11:30–2, 6–9.30, Sun 11–2, 6–9.30

☞☞☞ Arroyo Chop House $$$

This serious steakhouse is a bastion of dark woods and clubby atmosphere, Craftsman-style decor and live piano music. The tab is easily racked up by an a la carte menu consisting of stylish shoot-from-the-hip steaks and chops with cream sauces, substantial starters, hearty side dishes and straightforward desserts.

✚ 201 D4 ⊠ 536 S. Arroyo Parkway, Pasadena ☎ (626) 577-7463 🕐 Daily 5–10 pm

☞☞☞ Bistro 45 $$

California-French cuisine, with a hint of Pacific Rim, is showcased in this restored art-deco building – a favorite haunt for romantic-minded locals who duck into the several intimate rooms. Dishes are prepared with the highest quality seasonal seafood, game and veal, with scintillating reduction sauces and expertly woven flavors. Cassoulet and lighter fare are also offered and all are complemented by a fine wine list.

✚ 201 E4 ⊠ 45 S. Mentor Avenue, Pasadena ☎ (626) 795-2478 🕐 Tue–Fri 11:30–2:30, 6–10, Sat 5:30–10, Sun 5–9

Café Pinot $

Famed chef Joachim Splichal has installed his California-French bistro fare in this wonderful bucolic setting adjacent to the Los Angeles Central Library. Bookworms are not the only ones who stop in for first-class risottos, rotisserie chicken and snappy salads; this pleasurable eatery is also a wow with locals and pre-theater diners (with shuttle service available to the Performing Arts Center).

✚ 197 D4 ⊠ 700 W. Fifth Street ☎ (213) 239-6500 🕐 Mon–Thu 11:30–9, Fri 11:30–10, Sat 5–10, Sun 5–9

☞☞☞ Checkers $$

Housed in the Wyndham Checkers Hotel (➤ 43), Checkers offers delicacies such as pâté de foie gras terrine, veal- and duck-filled ravioli and some truly succulent salads. The dessert menu measures up to high standards and the wine list offers fine California chardonnays and cabernets.

✚ 197 D4 ⊠ 535 S. Grand Avenue ☎ (213) 624-0000 🕐 Mon–Sat 7 am–10.30 pm, Sun 11–2:30, 5–10.30

Empress Pavilion $

You'll be hard-pressed to find better Hong Kong-style dim sum or a more impressive just-like-China environment than this landmark restaurant in Chinatown's Bamboo Plaza. There seems to be a perpetual throng of diners at this 500-seat restaurant waiting to get some of the hundreds of steaming, sizzling morsels down their throats. You'll be dazzled by the staff's well-tuned choreography and efficient service.

✚ 201 E2 ⊠ 988 N. Hill Street ☎ (213) 617-9898 ⓖ Mon–Fri 9 am–10 pm, Sat–Sun 8 am–10 pm

🍷🍷 Engine Company No. 28 $$

Savor an a la carte menu of beef, chicken, seafood and Cobb salad inside this historic converted firehouse. The all-American menu leans heavily toward rib-sticking and easily recognizable meat, potatoes and satisfying side dishes. Evenings and weekends bring in the pre-theater crowd, tempted by both the food and the free shuttle over to the Performing Arts Center.

✚ 197 D4 ⊠ 644 S. Figueroa Street ☎ (213) 624-6996 ⓖ Mon–Sat 11:15–9, Sat–Sun 5–9 pm

🍷🍷 Mi Piace $

This always-busy Italian place on always-busy Colorado Boulevard will have you tucking into traditional Italian pastas and entrees, as well as crispy-crusty New York-style pizzas with such no-nonsense, nonouvelle toppings as pepperoni, sausage and anchovies. One unpredictable treat is the dessert case, filled with fine French cakes and pastries.

✚ 201 D5 ⊠ 25 E. Colorado Boulevard, Pasadena ☎ (626) 795-3131 ⓖ Mon–Thu 7:30 am–11:30 pm, Fri–Sat 7:30 am–12:30 am

🍷🍷 Parkway Grill $$

Often referred to as Pasadena's "Spago," the 1980s Parkway Grill was indeed at the forefront of the local food scene. This popular restaurant is perpetually crowded with die-hard diners who feast on creative California cuisine prepared on an open mesquite-fired grill. The black bean soup and brick-oven pizzas are favorite starters.

✚ 201 D4 ⊠ 510 S. Arroyo Parkway, Pasadena ☎ (626) 795-1001 ⓖ Mon–Thu 11:30–2:30, 5:30–10, Fri–Sat 5–11, Sun 5–10

🍷🍷 Raymond Restaurant $$$

While the ambience is decidedly early-Pasadena in this beautifully restored Craftsman bungalow, the cuisine at Raymond's is a blend of California and Continental flavors. The limited menu is nonetheless compiled of carefully prepared dishes such as fig-wrapped pancetta and rack of lamb. An extravagant afternoon tea is also served and a full bar is on hand.

✚ 201 D4 ⊠ 1250 S. Fairoaks Avenue, Pasadena ☎ (616) 441-3136 ⓖ Tue–Thu 11:30–2:30, 6–10, Fri–Sat 11:30–2:30, 5:45–10, Sun 10–2:30, 4:30–8

🍷🍷 Saladang $

Some insist that this high-tech spot ranks as the best Thai restaurant in Greater L.A. Classic Thai favorites, incorporating super-fresh ingredients, are presented like fine works of art. Ginger-and-chicken pearly rice soup might be on the breakfast menu, while a large assortment of noodle soups and heavier meat, fish, seafood and vegetarian dishes progress into lunch and dinner.

✚ 201 D4 ⊠ 363 S. Fairoaks Avenue, Pasadena ☎ (626) 793-8123 ⓖ Daily 10–10

🍷🍷 Water Grill $$

It may not be close to the ocean but the Water Grill is known around town as one of the finest seafood restaurants in the city. The atmosphere is sophisticated and clubby. Raves go to the heavenly clam chowder, the incredibly fresh seafood selections, seasonal oysters and plucked-from-the-tank Maine lobsters and Dungeness crabs. But leave room for the equally mouthwatering desserts.

✚ 197 D4 ⊠ 544 S. Grand Avenue ☎ (213) 891-0900 ⓖ Mon–Fri 11–2:30, 5–10, Sat–Sun 5–10

🍜🍜 Yujean Kang's $

Prepare yourself for Chinese dishes with a modern twist, infused with wunderkind chef Yujean Kang's uncanny and now revered flavor combinations and exquisite presentation. Beijing duck, a masterwork, must be ordered two days ahead.

➕ 201 D5 ⊠ 67 N. Raymond Avenue, Pasadena ☎ (626) 585-0855 ⏰ Mon–Thu, Sun 11:30–2:30, 5–9:30, Fri–Sat 11:30–2:30, 5–10

CAFÉS AND TEAROOMS

Downtown cafés are sprinkled about the business district and located inside most hotels and some cultural attractions. There are numerous cafés and bakeries throughout Pasadena.

Rose Garden Room $

As though there wasn't enough to ooh and aah over at the Huntington (▶ 154–155), visitors can also absorb all the sensory delights of traditional high tea and luxuriate in turn-of-the-20th-century ambience. Served in the blissful Rose Garden Room, the buffet-style treats include flaky scones, finger sandwiches, dainty pastries and – of course – the Huntington's well-known elegant blends of tea, perhaps one that's laced with delicate pink rose petals.

➕ 201 F4 ⊠ 1151 Oxford Road, San Marino ☎ (616) 683-8131 ⏰ Tue–Sun 11:30–4:30

BARS

Atlas Supper Club

Located around the corner from the Wiltern Theatre, the Atlas is a swanky throwback to the see-and-be-seen supper clubs of the past. Live contemporary jazz, lounge acts and other performers regale, as you sip a cocktail enhanced by lighting that makes everyone look good.

➕ 200 A2 ⊠ 3760 Wilshire Boulevard ☎ (213) 380-8400 ⏰ Mon–Fri 11:30–3, Tue–Sat 6–11 pm

Fox Sports Sky Box

Sports fanatics can cheer the action from right inside the Staples Center (▶ 164), home to the L.A. Lakers and many of the city's other major sports teams. Huge screens and crowd-pleaser appetizers are right on the mark, but the drinks are on the costly side. Located adjacent to the VIP entrance, this is as close to the glitz as you can get without a ticket.

➕ 197 D5 ⊠ 111 S. Figueroa Street ☎ (213) 742-7345 ⏰ Daily 11–11

Grand Avenue Sports Bar

Housed inside the Millennium Biltmore Hotel (▶ 43), this is the perfect sports bar for an upscale and more refined clientele wanting a cut above the usual screaming mayhem as they watch whatever game is showing. Fifteen screens show the action for fans still dressed for business.

➕ 197 D4 ⊠ 506 S. Grand Avenue ☎ (213) 612-1532 ⏰ Mon–Fri 4:30–1 am, weekend hours vary

McMurphy's Tavern

There's something for everyone at this energetic Old Pasadena hangout with live music, dancing, sports screens and a singles scene.

➕ 201 D5 ⊠ 72 N. Fairoaks Avenue, Pasadena ☎ (626) 666-1445 ⏰ Daily 11 am–1:30 am

Traxx

Union Station's old telephone room has been transformed into a chic, art-deco bar, where it feels like the 1920s, especially for rail buffs and those waiting for a train to pull in.

➕ 197 F5 ⊠ 800 N. Alameda Street ☎ (213) 625-1999 ⏰ Mon–Fri 11–10, Sat 6–10

Twin Palms

On weekend nights, Pasadena locals swarm to this calm-by-day eatery that rolls out the dance floor, brings in big bands and lets couples frolic under the tent-covered starry night.

➕ 201 D4 ⊠ 101 W. Green Street, Pasadena ☎ (626) 577-2567 ⏰ Daily 11:30–3, 5:30–10

Where to...
Shop

Branches of Robinsons-May and more-upscale Bullocks department stores anchor **Seventh Market Place** (735 S. Figueroa Street), with another few dozen stores and eating places surrounding the courtyard space. Locals go to the six-story **L.A. City Mall** (201 N. Los Angeles Street) near City Hall for break-from-work shopping and dining. Both **ARCO Plaza** (505 S. Flower Street) and **Broadway Plaza** (Seventh and Wall streets) have trendy stores and restaurants.

Bound by Broadway, Pico Boulevard and Seventh and Wall streets, the vast 30-square-block **Garment District** draws bargain hunters who sort through the heavily discounted designer- and brand-name clothing and accessories. Most of the action is centered around the **California Mart** (910 S. Los Angeles Street), **Cooper Building** (860 S. Los Angeles Street) and **Santee Alley**.

The bustling and atmospheric **Grand Central Market** (➤ 157, open daily) offers a trove of stands selling fresh produce, meat and poultry, fresh fish, baked goods, Latin American staples, fresh tortillas and fruit milkshakes.

Casa de Sousa (19 Olvera Street) is famed for its fine selection of imported Mexican and Central American folk arts, particularly the lustrous Oaxacan vases.

Those more inclined toward pen and ink will delight in the gorgeous handmade papers at **McManus and Morgan** (2506 W. Seventh Street).

Cirrus Gallery (542 Alameda Street), one of the first (and last) art dealers in the Downtown area, offers fine art prints by many big-name California artists.

Pasadena is full of stores, compartmentalized in three areas.

South Lake Avenue is the major district, where hundreds of stores and department stores stretch 10 tree-lined blocks between California and Colorado boulevards.

The 20-block Old Pasadena historic enclave (bound by Colorado Boulevard, Fair Oaks Avenue, De Lacey Avenue and Union Street) is anchored by the One Colorado building and offers many national retailers as well as specialty stores and boutiques.

Antiques dealers, bookstores and eclectic merchants surround the **Pasadena Playhouse District** (Colorado Boulevard and El Molino Avenue). The three-block, open-air **Paseo Colorado** complex (Colorado Boulevard, between Los Robles and Marengo) re-creates an urban village with dozens of shops, outdoor cafés, a gourmet market and 14-screen Cineplex movie theater.

Bookworms need go no farther than **Vroman's** (695 E. Colorado Boulevard), a century-old icon with a huge selection.

The **House of Fiction** (663 E. Colorado Boulevard) stocks used books including some rare titles and first editions.

Distant Lands (56 S. Raymond Avenue) is well-known for travel guides and literature.

Canterbury Records (805 E. Colorado Boulevard) specializes in big band, jazz, classical and world music CDs and albums, while **Pooh-Bah Records** (1101 E. Walnut Street) offers an eclectic range of new, used and hard-to-find CDs.

When hunger hits, purchase the authentic fruit cobblers at **The Cobbler Factory** (33 N. Catalina Avenue), or the luscious baked goods at **EuroPane** (950 E. Colorado Boulevard). **Mission Wines** (1114 Mission Street) may not possess the largest inventory, but makes up for it with friendly and knowledgeable service.

Where to...
Be Entertained

THEATER

Ahmanson Theater

L.A.'s top theater, with 2,000 seats, is the setting for huge Broadway musicals and other spectacles.

✚ 197 E5 ⊠ 135 N. Grand Avenue
☎ (213) 972-7401

Mark Taper Forum

The glamorous Performing Arts Center offers classics and contemporary works.

✚ 197 E5 ⊠ 135 N. Grand Avenue
☎ (213) 972-7211

Pasadena Playhouse

Pasadena's landmark theater has been the jumping-off point for many celebrated actors.

✚ 201 E4 ⊠ 39 S. El Molino Avenue
☎ (626) 356-7529

MUSIC AND DANCE

Dorothy Chandler Pavilion

This 3,200-seat, acoustically divine auditorium is home to the Los Angeles Opera, Los Angeles Philharmonic Orchestra (scheduled to move to the Walt Disney Concert Hall, also part of the Performing Arts Complex) and the Los Angeles Master Chorale. Touring ballet companies also perform here.

✚ 197 E5 ⊠ 135 N. Grand Avenue
☎ (213) 972-8001

Mayan Theatre

Prepare for a high-energy dance club, inside one of L.A.'s historic theaters, where dancers move to salsa and merengue (downstairs), or DJ-spun house, hip-hop and oldies (upstairs).

Pasadena Civic Auditorium

This large complex hosts the Pasadena Symphony Orchestra and other performing groups such as The Women of the Pacific Chorale, the "Riverdance" touring show and the Moscow Classic Ballet.

✚ 201 D4 ⊠ 300 E. Green Street, Pasadena ☎ (626) 584-8833

Shrine Auditorium

Choral gospel groups, as well as such prominent dance companies as the Bolshoi and Kirov, are the highlights here.

✚ 196 B2 ⊠ 665 W. Jefferson Boulevard ☎ (213) 749-5123

Staples Center

Downtown's fabulous new sports venue also hosts high-profile rock concerts that reel in crowds of preteens to baby boomers.

✚ 196 C3 ⊠ 1111 S. Figueroa Street ☎ (213) 742-7340

✚ 197 D3 ⊠ 1038 S. Hill Street
☎ (213) 746-4287

Wiltern Theatre

Staging area for top-name performers and eclectic musical events.

✚ 200 B1 ⊠ 3790 Wilshire Boulevard ☎ (213) 480-3232

COMEDY AND CABARET

The Ice House and Annex

This famous club, located in a former 1920s ice factory, features established comedians, newcomers and improv acts. Theme-oriented sketch comedy is also staged here.

✚ 201 E5 ⊠ 24 N. Mentor Avenue, Pasadena ☎ (626) 577-1894

MOVIES

The new **Paseo Colorado** retail complex houses a 14-screen movie theater with first-run movies.

USC, **CalTech** and **California State University** at Los Angeles often screen student works and interesting film fests. Check the Sunday *Los Angeles Times* "Calendar" section for listings.

Excursions

Beyond Greater L.A. are charming coastal towns, chic desert outposts, snow-capped mountains and rugged islands, and, of course, amusement parks, most notably the Disney marvels in nearby Anaheim.

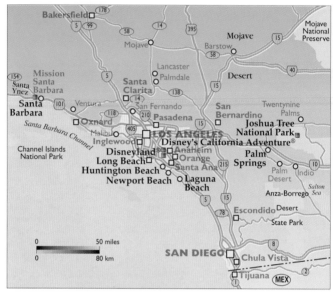

Disneyland

Thirty miles by freeway from Downtown L.A., Disneyland reigns as the most famous theme park in the world, a monumental construct of pop cultural fantasy that remains unmatched – except by its bigger sister park in Florida. With the 2001 opening of Disney's California Adventure right next door to the Disneyland Park, visitors can now find a compressed, sanitized and ultra-safe version of California all in one place.

Disneyland

Disneyland opened in 1955, brainchild of the late, great animator, movie-maker and dream-weaver Walt Disney. Carved out of orange groves in the sleepy Orange County town of Anaheim, it quickly became a world-famous destination, much-admired, much-copied and packed with entertaining attractions and characters drawn from comic books and fairy tales, outer space, culture and history.

Over the decades, with the competition getting bigger, louder and more exciting, Disneyland's once fail-safe allure began to fade. In response, Disney

Above: Big Thunder Mountain

Page 165: The Joshua Tree, emblem of the California desert

A Mad Tea Party thrills the kids in Fantasyland

management has updated the park, added Disney's California Adventure (▶ 168), put in a new resort hotel, renovated the other Disney hotels and added the Downtown Disney entertainment/shopping/dining inside-outside megamall.

Aside from bringing Tomorrowland's retro vision of the future up to contemporary speed, the changes have not altered the essence of the park. Some of the parades and shows scheduled throughout the park all day are now more directly linked to hit movies than in the past; the same goes for many of the newer rides and attractions. The awkward books of different colored tickets have been replaced with a single (high) admission fee. The FASTPASS system is a mighty effort to reduce long lines and waiting times at the more popular rides.

You enter the park at **Main Street, U.S.A.**, a Norman Rockwell-style fantasy replica of small-town America at the beginning of the 20th century. From here you can head off on foot or jump on the Disneyland Railroad trains that circle the park, climbing off at any one of the themed "lands," which between them hold about 60 rides and attractions and about the same number of stores and eating spots.

The redecorated **Tomorrowland** now offers, along with its classic Space Mountain and Star Tours attractions, new draws including the 3-D "Honey, I Shrunk the Audience" (where special effects make you feel really tiny) and the Astro Orbiter (where you pilot a spacecraft).

© Disney Enterprises, Inc.

You'll get wet on Splash Mountain

The old standards of **Fantasyland** still delight the little ones: They'll love the Mad Hatter's Tea Party, Peter Pan's Flight, It's a Small World and Sleeping Beauty Castle. The Matterhorn Bobsleds ride can be found here and it's well worth waiting for if you like your roller coasters atmospheric.

Mickey's Toontown, drawn from the 1988 "Who Framed Roger Rabbit" movie, offers rides and attractions geared toward the kindergarten set. Here, kids can meet and greet cartoon characters like Mickey Mouse, Goofy, Donald Duck and Roger Rabbit, but the most fun is simply to walk around – the whole off-kilter place is designed to put you inside a cartoon.

Adventureland's Jungle Cruise feels a bit dated these days, but Tarzan's Treehouse (based on the 1999 animated film) is a good climb-around. The Enchanted Tiki Room, with its oversized fake birds, will put you to sleep, but fear not: The popular Indiana Jones Adventure will soon wake you up and stick you right into Indy's harrowing escape from the Temple of the Forbidden Eye.

Frontierland's Big Thunder Mountain Railroad rockets through an abandoned gold mine. The kids will like the Petting Zoo, the Fantasmic! display and the Mark Twain Riverboat.

New Orleans Square features an amazing Haunted Mansion with high-tech ghost activity. As you float through an underground cave in a boat, treasure-hunting while a scruffy lot of pirates put on a show, you'll see why the Pirates of the Caribbean has emerged as a favorite attraction.

Finally, **Critter Country** offers Splash Mountain, one of the largest water-flume rides around.

How to Get the Most Out of a Visit

• **Start early**, best accomplished by spending a night or two at one of the Disney hotels.

• Purchase the **Multiday Park Hopper Tickets**. The advantages are in savings and convenience; the disadvantage is you're obliged to buy three or four days admission when you might only want one or two days.

• The **FASTPASS** system allows you to reserve a specific ride at a specific time via computer; instead of waiting, you can do something else and come back when it's time for the ride. It's a way of saving a place in line without actually being there. Look for FASTPASS machines near the major attractions at Disneyland and Disney's California Adventure.

Disney's California Adventure

If you've done Disneyland and you're still on your feet, head to Disney's California Adventure for a fantasy experience of the Golden State. Reports on Disney's California Adventure are not terrific, the bottom line being too much money for too few attractions. Although the focus here is the late teen and young adult market, time will tell how it fares and how Disney responds to its perceived success or failure. At the moment, having to pay full price twice, once for Disneyland and then again for Disney's California Adventure, feels a little like a rip-off.

You enter the 55-acre park by passing under a shrunken Golden Gate Bridge of San Francisco. And this pretty much summarizes what the park is all about – a collection of Californiana transformed into an amusement park. There are three main "lands": **Paradise Pier**, an authentic-looking but high-tech version of a California waterfront; **Hollywood Pictures Backlot**, a fantasy vision of Hollywood, focusing on Hollywood Boulevard; and the **Golden State**, which is divided into six districts representing different aspects of California: Grizzly Peak Recreation Area, Bountiful Valley Farm, Pacific Wharf, Condor Flats, The Bay Area and The Golden Valley Winery.

A dozen rides and half a dozen shows and attractions have been concocted around these icons of California. The most popular are **Soarin' Over California**, a simulated hang-glider ride over the whole shebang and the **Grizzly River Run**, a dynamic white-water thrill ride.

Downtown Disney

You can eat well in Disney's California Adventure, or head over to Downtown Disney – a flashy strip of restaurants (that serve alcohol), nightclubs, movie theaters and stores conveniently located between the two parks – and choose from 12 dining spots ranging from Y Arriba Y Arriba's Latin fare to the Rainforest Café, followed by entertainment at such stalwarts of nightlife as The House of Blues and Ralph Brennan's Jazz Kitchen.

The manufactured urbanity of Downtown Disney represents something of a change from the saccharine traditions of Disneyland; it should make the whole experience more tolerable for those who've been dragged to Anaheim by Disney-demanding children.

TAKING A BREAK

As with most theme parks, there are endless places to eat around the Disney parks. Whatever you feel like eating, you'll be able to get it here.

➕ 201 F1 ✉ 1313 Harbor Boulevard at Katella Avenue, Anaheim, off the Santa Ana Freeway
☎ (714) 781-4565 or (213) 626-8605; www.disneyland.com ⏰ Disneyland: 10–10; Disney's California Adventure: 10–9 (subject to seasonal change); Downtown Disney: daily 7 am–2 am
💲 Expensive; under 3 free. You cannot visit both parks on the same single admission

DISNEYLAND: INSIDE INFO

Top tips If you're doing both parks over two or more days, the **Grand Californian Hotel** is probably the best place to stay, although there are dozens of others close by. Designed to resemble the famed old Ahwahnee Hotel in Yosemite National Park, the hotel provides easy access to Disneyland, Disney's California Adventure and Downtown Disney.
• The parks are open **every day, year-round**. If it's possible, avoid summer, holidays and weekends, when crowds are heaviest.

Getting there If you're not driving, you can get there by **train** from Downtown L.A. via Fullerton, or take the **MTA bus** No. 460 for a 90-minute trip from Downtown. A **Greyhound bus** does the same trip in half the time, 16 times daily; buses also go to Disneyland from LAX, Long Beach, Pasadena and Hollywood.

Santa Barbara

Roughly 90 minutes' drive northwest of Los Angeles up the California coast, Santa Barbara, the bedroom community for well-off Angelenos, remains a tranquil, Spanish-tinged coastal small city. The rugged Santa Ynez Mountains rise to the east; the Pacific stretches away to the west, bedecked with its Channel Islands jewels. In between, Santa Barbara's Mediterranean-style downtown and waterfront parks and streets offer visitors a low-key yet rich assortment of attractions, ranging from white sand beaches to sophisticated galleries and museums.

Santa Barbara's mission and the splendid little natural history museum lie in the hills east of downtown, as do many of the city's most desirable residential areas. You'll find most of what you want to see and do in Santa Barbara relatively close to the waterfront.

Santa Barbara was leveled by an earthquake in 1925. During construction, the town planners decreed that all buildings would be Spanish Mediterranean in style. As a result, the city's commercial district features lovely structures with adobe-textured walls, rounded archways, glazed tilework and terra-cotta-tile rooftops. Take a self-guided **Red Tile Tour** (maps from the Visitor Information Center). Among the finer buildings are the **County Courthouse** (1929) and the **Museum of Art**, an outstanding regional museum with a surprisingly deep collection, including works by Matisse, Chagall, O'Keefe and Monet, and an exquisite assortment of

Santa Barbara's "Queen of the Missions" dates from 1786

SANTA BARBARA: INSIDE INFO

Top tips Don't miss the graceful **Santa Barbara Mission**, established in 1786 by Father Serra and built by the Chumash (➤ 14–16). Known as "The Queen of the Missions," it overlooks the city, the Pacific and the Channel Islands.
• The **Santa Barbara Museum of Natural History**, a small gem alongside Mission Creek in the hilly east side of town, has several fabulous collections, including a wonderful selection of artifacts from the Chumash and other Native Californians. It's close to the mission, so plan to do them both on the same trip.
• A **surrey cycle** is a wonderful way for families to tour Santa Barbara's 2 miles of level waterfront cycle paths. You can rent these along with cycles and inline skates at Beach Rentals, 22 State Street, tel: (805) 966-6733.
• If you can afford it, stay at the pricey Spanish hacienda-style **Four Seasons Biltmore** (1260 Channel Drive at the end of Olive Mill Road, tel: 800/332-3442 or 805/969-2261); it's one great Southern California hotel experience.

Getting there If you intend to do Santa Barbara in a single day, it's probably best to rise at the crack of dawn and get on to the Ventura Freeway (101), then head north from L.A. On the other hand, if you're planning on spending the night (there are many fine hotels, bed-and-breakfasts and inns to choose from), the drive along the coast through Malibu and Oxnard on Hwy. 1, before you pick up the freeway in Ventura, is much prettier but a bit slower. Either way, you'll arrive in Santa Barbara via 101 (Pacific Coast Highway) – a busy road, but less so since Interstate 5 opened up as the main artery from L.A. to San Francisco. The 101 slices right through downtown Santa Barbara; when you get off the freeway, you're there.

Right: A surrey cycle cruises the beachfront cycle path

Chinese ceramics. Wining, dining and strolling the stores and galleries of State Street and surrounding streets down to the waterfront is a wonderful way to spend an afternoon.

The Waterfront

Here you can roam out onto **Stearns Wharf** or stroll along Chase Palm Park and the waterfront to the **Zoological Gardens**, a nifty little zoo that can be toured in less than an hour. If you've had enough walking, take the waterfront shuttle back to State Street or take a break on **East Beach**, which stretches north from the zoo back to Stearns Wharf. The beach is clean and pretty, with volleyball courts, picnic areas with barbecue grills and the **Cabrillo Pavilion**, a bath-house and recreation center in a landmark 1925 building. Aside from the attractions listed, there are many beaches

within walking or cycling distance where you can lounge, swim, surf, sail, sunset cruise, whale watch… whatever. And the nearby hills shelter a number of lovely wineries producing some fine California vintages.

Above: Santa Barbara is lucky to have miles of white sand beaches

TAKING A BREAK

Esau's Coffee Shop (403 State Street, tel: 805/965-4416, daily 6–1) has homemade everything for breakfast or lunch.

Santa Barbara Visitor Information Center
✉ 1 Santa Barbara Street ☎ (800) 927-4688 or (805) 966-9222; www.santabarbaraca.com 🕐 Mon–Sat 9–4, Sun 10–4

Santa Barbara County Courthouse
✉ 1100 Anacapa Street ☎ (805) 962-6464 🕐 Mon–Fri 8–5, Sat–Sun and holidays 10–4:45 💲 Free

Santa Barbara Museum of Art
✉ 1130 State Street ☎ (805) 963-4364; www.smmuseart.org 🕐 Tue–Sat 11–5, Thu till 9, Sun noon–5 💲 Inexpensive; free under 6, Thu & first Sun each month

Santa Barbara Zoological Gardens
✉ 500 Niños Drive ☎ (805) 962-5339; www.santabarbarazoo.org 🕐 Daily 10–5, last admission 4; closed Christmas and Thanksgiving 💲 Moderate, free under 3

Santa Barbara Mission
✉ Laguna and Los Olivos streets ☎ (805) 682-4713 🕐 Daily 9–5 💲 Inexpensive; free under 16. Docent-guided tours $1 extra; call to arrange in advance

Santa Barbara Museum of Natural History
✉ 2559 Puesta del Sol Road ☎ (805) 682-4711; www.sbnature.org 🕐 Mon–Sat 9–5, Sun 10–5 💲 Adults moderate; seniors and students inexpensive; children 12 and under; free first Sun

Long Beach

Most tourists don't make it out to Long Beach except for devotees of maritime lore compelled to visit the magnificent *Queen Mary*, purchased by Long Beach's city managers and converted into a floating hotel/museum in 1967. She remains a world-class attraction, with lavish art-deco and Moderne interiors maintained in perfect condition. Yet there's much more than the *Queen Mary* to this hard-working port town. For starters, Long Beach is home to another must-see destination (for sea-loving souls): the stunning Long Beach Aquarium of the Pacific, a brilliantly designed facility.

Below: Long Beach's pride and joy, the *Queen Mary*

Long Beach is California's fifth largest city and for a century served as a major shipping port and an active Navy town until the Cold War ended, leading to the economically devastating closure in 1991 of the city's naval station and shipyard. In the years since, Long Beach has been hard at work replacing the sailors with tourists. The city hosts a world-class grand prix

auto race in April (➤ 193), a Cajun and zydeco music festival
in June, and a blues festival in September. But travelers
need not wait for a special event.

With 5.5 miles of beaches, the *Queen Mary*, the Long Beach
Museum of Art, the stores of Shoreline Village, the historic
architecture of old downtown and the Aquarium of the
Pacific, you'll find plenty to do here any day of the year. For
architecture aficionados there's a fine Greene & Greene
project, the **Tichenor House**, at 852 E. Ocean Boulevard.
Long Beach's **Museum of Latin American Art**, housed in a
1920s building, is the only museum in the L.A. area devoted
entirely to contemporary Hispanic art.

You could easily spend two days here, with a night aboard
the opulent **Queen Mary**. Initial suspicions that the *Queen*

is a tourist trap prove false: Elegantly detailed staterooms
constructed of tropical hardwoods, miles of bakelite hand-
rails, teak decks and memorabilia-filled exhibits everywhere –
including one devoted to sister ship the *Titanic* – make time
spent onboard the *Queen* utterly fascinating.

You'll definitely want to visit the **Aquarium of the Pacific**.
Housed in a glass structure with undulating walls and roof
designed to echo the look and movement of water, the
120,000-square-foot aquarium contains more than 12,000 sea
creatures. It examines in immaculate detail the ecology of the
Pacific Ocean.

Divided into three sections, covering Southern California/
Baja, the Tropical Pacific and the Northern Pacific, the aquarium includes some amazing exhibits, such as an underwater
tunnel that puts you inside a seal and sea lion habitat and a

**A balmy
seaside scene
at Shoreline
Village**

35,000-gallon Deep Reef exhibit populated with armadas of vividly hued tropical fish.

If indoor fish-watching isn't your thing, go outside: Watch whales, ride in a gondola, sail in a tall ship or explore a submarine. These attractions and more can be found on or near the Long Beach waterfront. San Pedro and the L.A. Harbor are right next door, and the Catalina Express boats to Catalina Island dock a few yards from the *Queen Mary*.

Overlooking the harbor and the ocean, the **Long Beach Museum of Art** resides in a 1912 Craftsman-style house and an adjacent pavilion; the focus here is primarily on contemporary work by Southern California artists. The collections are fine, but the real highlight is video: The museum owns more than 3,000 artists' videos, one of the country's largest collections, on revolving display in the video annex.

Often overlooked along the waterfront, Long Beach's old **downtown** has a rich selection of thrift shops, antiques outlets and used bookstores, many housed in vintage buildings.

TAKING A BREAK

Somewhat pricey but excellent American regional fare can be found at the **Shenandoah Café** (4722 E. Second Street, at Park Avenue, tel: 562/434-3469, Mon–Fri 5–10 pm, Sat 5–11 pm, Sun 10–2, 5–10 pm).

Museum of Latin American Art
✉ 628 Alamitos Avenue ☎ (562) 437-1689; www.molaa.com 🕐 Tue–Sat 11:30–7:30, Sun noon–6 💲 Adults moderate; students and seniors inexpensive; under 12s free

Queen Mary
✉ 1126 Queens Highway (at the end of the 710 freeway, across the Queensway Bridge from the Aquarium) ☎ (562) 435-3511 or (800) 437-2934; www.queenmary.com 🕐 Daily 10–6; extended summer hours 💲 Expensive

Aquarium of the Pacific
✉ 100 Aquarium Way ☎ (562) 951-1683; www.aquariumofpacific.org 🕐 Daily 9–6 💲 Expensive; children 3–11 moderate

Long Beach Museum of Art
✉ 2300 East Ocean Boulevard ☎ (562) 439-2119; www.lbma.org 🕐 Tue–Sun 11–5 💲 Inexpensive; under 12s free

---

LONG BEACH: INSIDE INFO

Top tip If you buy tickets to see the *Queen Mary* and the Cold War-era Soviet sub *Scorpion* docked nearby, you'll be treated to a fascinating, behind-the-scenes guided tour of both boats.

Getting there Take the Harbor Freeway (110) to the San Diego Freeway (405) to the Long Beach Freeway (710), or take 405 to 710 from the West Side. Or take the Metro Blue Line; the last four stops are in Long Beach.

Orange Coast Beaches

Orange County's coast features a number of small, independent cities strung out along the Pacific from the south end of Long Beach to the north end of San Diego County. This excursion focuses on three of them, working from north to south: Huntington Beach, the birthplace of California's surf scene; Newport Beach, home to the world's largest yacht harbor; and Laguna Beach, famed for its art scene, shopping and secluded beaches.

A visitor could trip down this coast by car (public transportation is not very reliable) in a day, or take several days to explore the area attractions, which are mostly of the sandy variety.

You'll know you're in **Huntington Beach** when you've passed Bolsa Chica State Beach and the **Bolsa Chica Ecological Preserve**, a bird sanctuary across the highway. Huntington Beach starts here and stretches south. The once-scruffy oil town has been growing upscale and inland for years, but the beach remains the focus, especially where Main Street meets the Coast Highway. Watch the surfing from the pier, check out the **Surfers Walk of Fame** and stop by the **International Surfing Museum** to get a historical perspective on the sport. It really did have its California start here, in 1907, when Henry Huntington brought surfers over from Hawaii to encourage visitors to come to the beach on his Pacific Electric Railroad.

Ten miles south, you move into one of the more expensive precincts of Southern California – **Newport Beach**, home to 10 yacht clubs and 10,000 yachts. Wrapped around a natural bay, Newport includes the Balboa Peninsula along the ocean side, pricey Lido and Balboa Islands in the bay and waterfront homes, piers, stores and boats around the bay. Among them, the **Lovell Beach House**, at W. Ocean Front and 13th Street, survives as one of architect Rudolph Schindler's most famous works. The **Orange County Museum of Art** displays contemporary Californians like Ed Ruscha, Ed Kienholz and video artist Bill Viola. At the east end of the bay you'll find one small, natural gem: the **Upper Newport Bay Ecological Reserve and Regional Park**, with 10 miles of trails winding through a sanctuary that shelters up to 30,000 birds from 160 different species throughout the year.

South of Newport you pass through Corona del Mar, then along the 3 miles of pristine coastline that forms **Crystal Cove State Park**. After Crystal Cove

---

ORANGE COAST BEACHES: INSIDE INFO

Getting there From Long Beach or from the 405 Freeway, make your way to Seal Beach, Orange County's most northerly town. Head south on Hwy. 1, the Pacific Coast Highway.

For yachtsmen, Newport Harbor can't be beat

comes **Laguna Beach** – a town with a long artsy tradition. Laguna has clung to that tradition as much as possible, given the pressures of mega-bucks real-estate realities. The PCH passes through the middle of town, just a few steps from the unpretentious Main Beach. Laguna shelters dozens of smaller, more secluded beaches. If this town beach is overcrowded, head down to the Aliso Pier, a couple of miles south. In "the Village," you'll find a colorful assortment of stores, cafés and pubs and more than 60 art galleries displaying innumerable Laguna beachscapes and landscapes, the primary inspiration for the town's artists since the late 19th century. The best of the genre can be found in the **Laguna Art Museum**.

Bolsa Chica Ecological Preserve
PCH at Warner Avenue, Seal Beach ☎ (714) 846-3460 Guided tours first Sat each month, 9–10:30 am Free; inexpensive for a guided tour

International Surfing Museum
411 Olive Avenue, Huntington Beach ☎ (714) 960-3483 Daily noon–5, summer; Wed–Sun, rest of year Inexpensive; free under 6

Orange County Museum of Art
850 San Clemente Drive, Newport Beach ☎ (949) 759-1122 Tue–Sun 11–5 Inexpensive; free Tue

Upper Newport Bay Ecological Reserve and Regional Park
Newport Bay Naturalists (for information, maps), 600 Shellmaker Drive (off Backbay Drive) ☎ (949) 640-6746; www.newportbay.org Two-hour discovery walks every Sat and Sun at 1 pm, starting from Shellmaker Island Free

Crystal Cove State Park
8471 PCH, just north of Laguna Beach ☎ (949) 494-3539 (call for information on camping and reservations) Day-use moderate

Laguna Art Museum
307 Cliff Drive, Laguna Beach ☎ (949) 494-6531 Tue–Sun 11–5 Inexpensive

Palm Springs and Joshua Tree National Park

With 85 public, private or semiprivate golf courses in the area, Palm Springs, "America's Desert Playground," offers fabulous opportunities to hit the links. If you don't play, there are plenty of other activities to keep you here for a few days. And if you like your nature a little wilder, head up into one of the Indian Canyons for a hike. Better still, make the one-hour drive to Joshua Tree National Park, 38 miles east of Palm Springs.

Palm Springs

The best bet for (well-heeled) visitors is to stay in a golf resort, such as the Marriott Desert Springs Resort, Marriott's Rancho Las Palmas or La Quinta Resort and Club – for convenience and a taste of the high life, club style. A budget option is a day at the Palm Springs Country Club, with its low green fees.

There are plenty of chances for teeing off in Palm Springs

If you don't play golf, you can hike wild canyons, ride trams into snowcapped mountain ranges, trek through a desert national park, go shopping, sunbathe, swim, play tennis, cycle or tour a compelling collection of architect-designed homes from the golden era of Modernism. The after-dark scene here is a hot one. Consult your concierge or the *Palm Springs Desert Guide* (a compendium of information on the area, free

The Best Hotels

- Marriott Desert Springs Resort
  tel: (760) 341-2211
- Marriott Rancho Las Palmas
  tel: (760) 568-2727
- La Quinta Resort and Club
  tel: (760) 346-2904
- Palm Springs Country Club
  tel: (760) 323-8625

and available all over the Palm Springs area) for this year's – or this week's – trendy nightspot.

One of the best family options is the **Palm Springs Oasis Waterpark**. With 12 waterslides, a wave pool for board and body surfing, an inner-tube ride and "beaches" with private cabanas and food service, this facility offers a complete oceanfront package, 125 miles from the ocean.

Don't miss the **Palm Springs Aerial Tramway**, rising from the desert floor to the top of 8,516-foot Mount San Jacinto, where you'll find snowshoeing and cross-country skiing trails in winter and great hiking in summer. The cars rotate during the 14-minute, 2.5-mile ascent to give spectacular panoramic views. Remember to take an extra sweater; the summit can be very cold, even in summer. Once on top, you can grab a bite in a snack bar or have a meal in the Mountain Station restaurant.

Architecture buffs will find a good selection of Modernist buildings in "The Springs." As well as the Tramway Valley Station, noted architect Albert Frey designed the Palm Springs City Hall, the Tramway gas station and his own house off Tahquitz Canyon Way. John Lautner's home for Bob Hope is another standout. For locations of these and Palm Springs' other landmarks, pick up the guide *Palm Springs: Brief History and Architectural Guide* from the visitor center.

Lovers of the wild desert have options near and far. Close at hand is the **Living Desert Wildlife and Botanical Park**, a 1,200-acre destination in nearby Palm Desert, complete with 400 species of desert animals (some, like bighorn sheep and coyotes, native; others, like cheetahs and zebras, not so native), botanical gardens, a spectacle called the Wildlife Wonders Animal Show and some fine hiking trails.

Joshua Tree National Park

The striking Joshua tree, *Yucca brevifolia,* is so-called because of its outstretched limbs, which reminded early Mormon

PALM SPRINGS AND JOSHUA TREE NATIONAL PARK: INSIDE INFO

Getting there Palm Springs lies about 120 miles east of L.A. via Interstate 10. Leave the freeway at the Palm Springs exit and take California 111 onto North Palm Canyon Drive and into town. The drive takes roughly two hours. Among the many airlines offering flights from LAX to Palm Springs Regional Airport are Alaska (tel: 800/426-0333), America West (tel: 800/235-9292) and United Express (tel: 800/241-6522).

Top tip For animal lovers, dawn or dusk is the best time for spotting any of the primarily **nocturnal creatures** that inhabit the park, including bighorn sheep, coyotes, black-tailed jackrabbits and kangaroo rats.

settlers of the biblical Joshua leading wanderers through the desert. They also called it the "praying plant." In the national park are two very different deserts: the **Colorado Desert**, to the east, dominated by the creosote bush; and the higher, cooler **Mojave Desert**, to the west, with great stands of Joshua trees. Miles of hiking and cycling trails lace through the park, allowing visitors a chance to delve deeply into the ecology of the desert.

TAKING A BREAK

Three kinds of Mexican food – Mayan, Huasteco and Aztec – make a meal at **Edgardo's Café Veracruz** an eye-opening, delicious experience (494 N. Palm Canyon Road, tel: 760/320-3558, Mon–Fri 11–3, 5:30–9:30, Sat–Sun 8 am–10 pm.

Wild desert at its best: The Living Desert Wildlife and Botanical Park

Palm Springs Desert Resorts Convention and Visitors Bureau
✉ Atrium Design Center, 69-930 Highway 111, Suite 115, Rancho Mirage
☎ (800) 41-RELAX, (760) 770-9000 or (760) 770-1992 (24-hour info line);
www.desert-resorts.com 🕐 Mon–Fri 8:30–5

Visitor Center
✉ 2781 N. Palm Canyon Drive ☎ (760) 770-8418 🕐 Daily 8–4

Palm Springs Oasis Waterpark
✉ On the Gene Autry Trail (off I-10) between Ramon Road, E. Palm Canyon
Drive ☎ (760) 325-7873; www.oasiswaterresort.com 🕐 Daily 1–6, mid-
Mar–Labor Day; 11–6 weekends only Sep–Oct 💲 Expensive over 5 feet tall;
moderate 3–5 feet tall; free under 3 feet tall

Palm Springs Aerial Tramway
✉ Tramway Road (off Highway 111) ☎ (760) 325-1391;
www.pstramway.com 🕐 Mon–Fri 10–8, Sat–Sun 8–8 💲 Expensive

Living Desert Wildlife and Botanical Park
✉ 47-900 Portola Avenue, Palm Desert ☎ (760) 346-5694;
www.livingdesert.org 🕐 Daily 9–5, Sep–Jun 15; 8–1:30, rest of year
💲 Adults/seniors moderate; children 3–12 inexpensive

Indian Canyons (Andreas, Murray and Palm Canyons)
☎ (760) 325-5673 for information 🕐 Closed in summer 💲 Moderate

Joshua Tree National Park
✉ 74485 National Park Drive, Twentynine Palms ☎ (760) 367-5500;
www.joshua.tree.national-park.com 🕐 All year daily 💲 Day-use moderate
per car; inexpensive per person; camping expensive per day

Walks and Tours

1 SANTA MONICA

Walk

This walk encompasses great views, an option for strenuous stair-climbing and a look at one of Santa Monica's pleasant residential neighborhoods. Finally, it takes you to Third Street Promenade, a stroller's haven. You'll find plenty to enjoy along the way.

1–2

Start at the south end of **Palisades Park**, where Colorado Boulevard meets the Santa Monica Pier. Head north through Palisades Park, the grassy, palm-shady strip that runs along the top of the cliffs. Stop to take a look at Santa Monica Pier and Beach below, and Santa Monica Bay and the Pacific. On a clear day you can see Catalina Island off in the distance near the peninsula of Palos Verdes. To the right of Point Dume in Malibu, the **Santa Monica Mountains** form a bumpy northern horizon.

DISTANCE 4 miles (round trip)
TIME 4 hours (round trip)
START/END POINT South end of Palisades Park at Santa Monica Pier ✚ 202 D2

2–3

As you stroll along, paralleling **Ocean Avenue**, you'll pass boulevards that run all the way from here to Downtown Los Angeles and beyond, including Santa Monica Boulevard, Wilshire Boulevard and San Vicente. The foot of Santa Monica Boulevard here is the end of the fabled **Route 66.** You'll also pass a couple of fabulous hotels – the historic

The Santa Monica Pier conjures that old-time seaside carny atmosphere – a great place to end a walk or begin a cycle ride

Miramar (101 Wilshire Boulevard) and the Streamline Moderne **Shangri-La** (1301 Ocean Avenue).

3–4

When you reach the north end of Palisades Park, head east on Adelaide. At **Fourth Street**, make a choice: If you're feeling energetic, head down the **Adelaide Steps** with the rest of the fitness buffs and then back up. If you're not feeling so fit, enjoy the views over **Santa Monica Canyon** and watch the stair-climbers do their thing.

4–5

To get to the **Third Street Promenade**, go south along Fourth Street to Wilshire, then right along Third Street and voilà! you're on this three-block stretch of cafés, movie theaters, shops, fountains, topiary dinosaurs and a good mix of locals for people-watching. It's one of L.A.'s best walks. At the south end of the Promenade, go right down Colorado Avenue, cross Ocean Avenue, and you're back at Santa Monica Pier.

Topiary dinosaurs enliven the scene on Santa Monica's Third Street Promenade

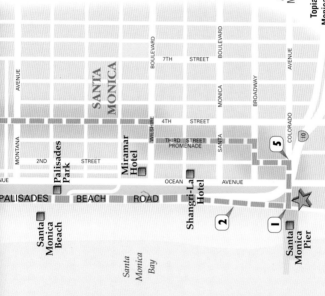

2 SOUTH BAY

Cycle ride

DISTANCE 20 miles **TIME** 2 hours
START POINT Will Rogers State Beach ✚ 202 D2
END POINT Torrance Beach ✚ 202 off E1

L.A. cycle enthusiasts range from high-tech multi-gear racers and mountain bikers to retro-style cruisers – and the 20 miles of nearly flat beachfront cycle path accommodates them all

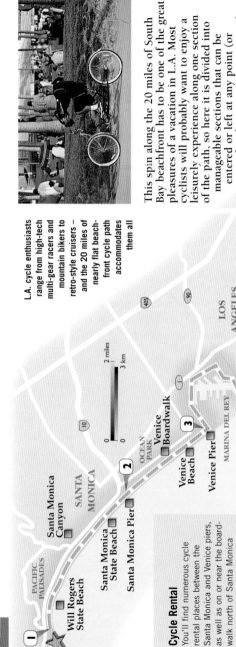

This spin along the 20 miles of South Bay beachfront has to be one of the great pleasures of a vacation in L.A. Most cyclists will probably want to enjoy a leisurely experience along one section of the path, so here it is divided into manageable sections that can be entered or left at any point (or completed in reverse). It's a good idea to start early as the path can get busy, especially on summer weekends.

Cycle Rental

You'll find numerous cycle rental places between the Santa Monica and Venice piers, as well as on or near the boardwalk north of Santa Monica Pier and near the foot of Pier Avenue in Hermosa Beach.

1–2

Start at **Will Rogers State Beach** (▶ 67) in Pacific Palisades. As you head south, the sands beckon on your right, and there you have it: the Pacific! The ocean here can range from quite rough to completely placid, depending on the weather, the wind, the time of year and the swell. South of Santa Monica Canyon, the path drops down on to the beach, which is now **Santa Monica State Beach** (you've crossed from Pacific Palisades, part of L.A., into the sovereign city of Santa Monica). Now you're closer to the ocean; look for dolphins, whales and other marine life – and watch out

for high-speed cyclists and inline skaters, especially on busy summer afternoons. On your left are beach clubs, chic homes, a couple of restaurants (including the wonderful **Back to the Beach** (445 PCH), which serves breakfasts and lunches with some Mexican influences, and bicycle rental places; beyond the highway, the cliffs rise to Santa Monica's Ocean Park. At **Santa Monica Pier** you've traveled about 3 miles.

2–3

The path now edges along the parking lots just north of Santa Monica Pier, then swoops under the pier before curving back over by the boardwalk at the edge of the beach. About a mile south of the pier you leave Santa Monica and re-enter L.A. From here to the next section at Marina del Rey is another 4 miles. There's great people-watching on the beach and boardwalk, restaurants, bars, shops and vendors

South Bay

EL SEGUNDO
EL PORTO

ROSECRANS AVENUE

(405)

MANHATTAN BEACH

(4)

Manhattan Pier

(107)

HERMOSA BEACH

(1)

Hermosa Beach Pier

KING HARBOR

Redondo Beach Pier

REDONDO BEACH

Redondo Wharf

PALOS VERDES

Torrance Beach

(5)

Safety Notes

• While the beaches of L.A. are not particularly dangerous, you might not want to ride the cycle path **at night**.

• If you dismount for a beach or food stop, **lock your cycle** or keep it in plain sight.

• Don't ride your cycle in the **"Walking Only, No Cycle Riding"** zones along the various boardwalks, where the cycling and pedestrian zones converge. You can get ticketed and there's a high fine. The zones are clearly marked.

along the boardwalk (the cycle path is distinct from the boardwalk, but parallels it for short stretches here and there). **Venice Boardwalk** and **Venice Beach** (➤ 54–56) have starred in hundreds of movies, so you may recognize spots along the way – Venice Pier, the Muscle Beach weightlifting pens and the basketball courts immortalized in the movie "White Men Can't Jump" (1992). It's a popular spot, and to avoid the worst of the crowds in the summer it's best to go on weekdays or very early in the morning – unless of course you're in it for the people. Try **Figaro's** (hearty American-style food) or the **Sidewalk Café** (food all day long, also beer, wine and cocktails) on Venice Boardwalk if you're ready for a break.

3–4

From **Venice Pier** start with a traffic-dodging detour through **Marina del Rey**. Once you get around the marina – about a 1-mile side trip through the land of fancy boats – you're back on the beach at **Playa del Rey**, a quiet little town. From here it's a straight shot down the coast to Manhattan Beach.

Along the way you pass Dockweiler Beach, El Segundo and El Porto, home to water-treatment plants, refineries and the L.A. airport flight path. But the surroundings get more

In the South Bay the cycle path slices between expensive homes on one side and public sands on the other

pleasant again as you cross **Rosecrans Avenue** to enter the increasingly pricey beachfront enclave of **Manhattan Beach**.

On the 900-foot Manhattan Pier, about 12.5 miles south of the Santa Monica Pier, is an **aquarium** (open Mon–Fri 3 pm–sunset, Sat–Sun 10am–sunset, free) with crabs, lobsters, eels and "touchable" anemones and starfish.

Pancho's (3615 Highland and Rosecrans), a popular Mexican-American diner, a few blocks off Manhattan Beach, is a good place for a break.

4–5

The last section of the path is about 6 miles from **Manhattan Pier** to Torrance Beach. Around **Hermosa Beach Pier** are surfers, surf shops and other evidence of the urban surf culture that is integral to the South Bay, and if there's a good swell, you can watch them riding the waves. At the foot of Pier Avenue in Hermosa Beach is **Hennessy's Tavern** (Pier Avenue), a bar and rooftop deck with a fine view of Hermosa Beach and much of Santa Monica Bay. To the east, Manhattan, Hermosa and Redondo are dense, low-rise, residential neighborhoods, once solidly working-class but now increasingly pricey and exclusive.

You have to navigate your way along some busy streets in King Harbor, but once you get round it you're back on the beach for another mile before passing through a parking garage and pedestrian walkway (be sure to dismount and walk your bike; ➤ 185) at **Redondo Beach Pier** – a fun, on-foot side-trip if you like old-fashioned piers. Stop for a walk on Redondo Wharf to see the Great White Shark, taken off the coast of Washington State years ago, on display in one of the curio shops. Continue on the 2-mile stretch of **Torrance Beach** – a lovely, uncrowded beach that ends at the northern edge of expensive Palos Verdes.

GETTING ADVANCE INFORMATION

Websites

- L.A. Convention and Visitors Bureau: www.lacvb.com
- www.at-la.com
- www.losangeles.com

- Los Angeles Times weekly entertainment magazine www.calendarlive.com

In the U.S.

Los Angeles Convention and Visitors Bureau 633 W. 5th Street, Los Angeles, CA 90071 ☎(213) 624-7300

CHECK WITH EMBASSIES, CONSULATES AND OTHER SOURCES FOR INFORMATION ON VISA, PASSPORT AND OTHER ENTRY REQUIREMENTS AS WELL AS NEW AIRPORT AND AIRPLANE SECURITY REQUIREMENTS.

BEFORE YOU GO

WHAT YOU NEED

- ● Required
- ○ Suggested
- ▲ Not required

	U.K.	Germany	U.S.A.	Canada	Australia	Ireland	Netherlands	Spain
Passport/National Identity Card	●	●	▲	○	●	●	●	●
Visa	▲	▲	▲	▲	▲	▲	▲	▲
Onward or Round-Trip Ticket	●	●	▲	▲	●	●	●	●
Health Inoculations (tetanus and polio)	▲	▲	▲	▲	▲	▲	▲	▲
Health Documentation (▶192, Health)	▲	▲	▲	▲	▲	▲	▲	▲
Travel Insurance	●	●	▲	○	●	●	●	●
Driver's License (national)	●	●	●	●	●	●	●	●
Car Insurance Certificate	n/a	n/a	●	●	n/a	n/a	n/a	n/a
Car Registration Document	n/a	n/a	●	●	n/a	n/a	n/a	n/a

WHEN TO GO

▢ Peak season   ▢ Off-season

JAN	FEB	MAR	APR	MAY	JUN	JUL	AUG	SEP	OCT	NOV	DEC
65°F	66°F	67°F	69°F	72°F	77°F	83°F	81°F	81°F	77°F	73°F	69°F

Very wet   Wet   Cloud   Sun   Sun/Showers

While summer remains the most popular time to visit L.A., the heat and crowds do not necessarily make it the best time to go – especially when winter temperatures can range from the mid-60s Fahrenheit up into the 80s. Winter also means less smog, although beach-lovers will find the ocean temperatures colder. Fall can be very pleasant, except when the winds off the desert – the notorious "Santa Anas" – push the temperatures into the 80s and even 90s. Spring can be beautiful, although the "June gloom" – marine fog that rolls in off the sea – can linger along the coast. Rain usually comes in late fall and winter, occasionally in torrential bouts, which cause mudslides.

In the U.K.
California Tourism
Information Office
52–54 High Holborn,
London WC1V 6RB
☎(44) 20 7242 3131

In Canada
Embassy of the U.S.A.
490 Sussex Drive,
Ottawa, Ontario
K1N 1G8
☎(613) 238-5335

In Australia
Consulate General of
the U.S.A.
19–29 Martin Place,
Sydney, NSW 2000
☎(612) 9373 9200

GETTING THERE

By Air All international flights to L.A. arrive at Los Angeles International Airport (LAX).
From the U.K. and Ireland: The following offer daily non-stop direct flights to L.A. from
London: Air New Zealand, British Airways, United Airlines, Virgin Atlantic, American, United
Airlines. The following offer one-stop direct flights to L.A. from Gatwick: Continental,
Delta, Northwest. Direct flights from regional airports to the U.S. (but not direct to L.A.):
American Airlines and British Airways from Manchester and Glasgow, Northwest from
Glasgow. Delta from Manchester. Delta and Aer Lingus both fly direct from Ireland to L.A.
From Australia and New Zealand: There are direct flights on United Airlines and Qantas out
of Sydney, although fares are better on flights originating in Auckland, New Zealand, with
stops in Hawaii or the South Pacific.
Within the U.S.: All major U.S. carriers serve LAX and John Wayne; other regional airports
(Ontario, Long Beach, Santa Barbara, Burbank) offer excellent service and (often) less
expensive round-trip fares. Non-stop, direct or stopover flights are readily available from
practically every large city in the U.S. and Canada. Check travel agents, flight brokers,
travel sections in newspapers and the Internet for the best deals and special offers.

By Rail and Bus Amtrak operates various train lines into L.A. from the north and east. The
Southwest Chief originates in Chicago; the *Sunset Limited* starts in Florida. The *Coast
Starlight* runs along the Pacific Coast from Seattle to San Diego via L.A. For information
on Amtrak routing and scheduling tel: (800) USA872-RAIL7245; www.amtrak.com.
Bus is not the greatest way to see the country. The main operator is **Greyhound** (tel: 800/
231-2222; www.gryehoundgreyhound.com), but be prepared for bus stations in the dingier
parts of towns, often frustratingly slow travel and more expensive than you expect.

TIME

 Los Angeles is on Pacific Standard Time (PST), eight hours behind Greenwich
Meantime (GMT -8). Daylight Savings Time, from April through November, moves
the clocks up one hour to GMT -7.

CURRENCY AND FOREIGN EXCHANGE

Currency The basic unit of currency in the United States is the dollar ($1). One dollar is
100 cents. **Bills** come in denominations of $1, $5, $10, $20, $50 and $100. All bills
are green and are the same size, so look carefully at the dollar amount on them. **Coins** are
1 cent (penny), 5 cents (nickel), 10 cents (dime), 25 cents (quarter) and 50 cents (half-
dollar). There are also one-dollar coins, but these are comparatively rare. An **unlimited
amount** of U.S. dollars can be imported or exported.
U.S. dollar **travelers' checks** are the best way to carry money, and they are accepted as
cash in most places (not taxis), as are **credit cards** (Amex, VISA, MasterCard, Diners Card).

Exchange There are foreign exchange bureaus in the major terminals at LAX, but it might
be easier to obtain American dollars or travelers' checks at your own bank in your home
country. If you intend to obtain American dollars from ATMs, your bank will provide you
with details of where your cards will be accepted in Los Angeles.

GMT/U.K. 12 noon	← **Los Angeles** 4 am	← **New York** 7 am	← **Chicago** 6 am	→ **Spain** 1 pm	→ **Australia** 10 pm

WHEN YOU ARE THERE

CLOTHING SIZES

U.K.	U.S.A.	
36	36	
38	38	
40	40	**Suits**
42	42	
44	44	
46	46	
7	8	
7.5	8.5	
8.5	9.5	**Shoes**
9.5	10.5	
10.5	11.5	
11	12	
14.5	14.5	
15	15	
15.5	15.5	**Shirts**
16	16	
16.5	16.5	
17	17	
8	6	
10	8	
12	10	**Dresses**
14	12	
16	14	
18	16	
4.5	6	
5	6.5	
5.5	7	**Shoes**
6	7.5	
6.5	8	
7	8.5	

NATIONAL HOLIDAYS

Jan 1	New Year's Day
Third Mon Jan	Martin Luther King Jr. Day
Third Mon Feb	Presidents' Day
Mar/Apr	Easter (half day Good Friday, whole day Easter Monday)
Last Mon May	Memorial Day
Jul 4	Independence Day
First Mon Sep	Labor Day
Second Mon Oct	Columbus Day
Nov 11	Veterans' Day
Fourth Thu Nov	Thanksgiving
Dec 25	Christmas Day

Some stores are open for business on national holidays.

OPENING HOURS

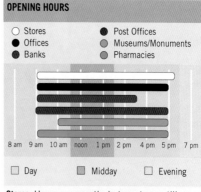

○ Stores	● Post Offices
● Offices	● Museums/Monuments
● Banks	● Pharmacies

8 am 9 am 10 am noon 1 pm 2 pm 4 pm 5 pm 7 pm

☐ Day   ☐ Midday   ☐ Evening

Stores Hours vary greatly, but most open till 9 pm on one day. Some open Sun noon–5.
Banks Some banks open till 4 pm, or Fri 6 pm. Most are closed Sat; all are closed Sun.
Post Offices Open Mon–Fri 9–5, till 1 pm Sat. Smaller offices keep shorter hours.
Museums Hours vary. Most open 9:30 or 10 am to 5 or 6 pm. Some keep longer hours Thu, Fri or Sat. Many are closed Mon.
Places of Worship See the *Yellow Pages*.

POLICE 911

FIRE 911

AMBULANCE 911

PERSONAL SAFETY

Crime levels in Los Angeles have fallen sharply over recent years, but it is still wise to take sensible precautions:

- Avoid the notorious South-Central district and East L.A.
- Don't walk alone in quiet streets or Venice Beach after dark.
- Carry only the cash you need; leave other cash and valuables in the hotel safe.
- Report theft or mugging to the police to provide a reference in case of an insurance claim.

Police assistance:
☎ **911** from any phone

TELEPHONES

There are pay-phones on many street corners and most are coin oper-ated. From public phones dial 0 for the operator and give the name of the country, city

and number you are calling. You will need at least $5.50 in quarters for an overseas call. Some phones take prepaid phone cards, available at drug-stores and newsstands, and some take credit cards. Dial 1 plus the area code for numbers within the U.S. and Canada. Dial 411 to find U.S. and Canadian numbers.

International Dialing Codes
Dial 011 followed by

U.K.:	44
Ireland:	353
Australia:	61
Germany:	49
Netherlands:	31
Spain:	34

POST OFFICES

L.A.'s main branch post office: 7101 S. Central Avenue. For location of nearest branch, tel: (800) ASK-USPS. The LAX branch is located at 9029 Airport Boulevard, Inglewood. Some branches are open on Saturday mornings.

ELECTRICITY

The power supply is 110/120 volts AC (60 cycles).

Sockets take two-prong, flat-pin plugs. An adaptor is needed for appliances with two-round-pin and three-pin plugs. European appliances also need a voltage transformer.

TIPS/GRATUITIES

Tipping is expected for all services. As a general guide:

Restaurants (service not included)	15–20%
Bar service	15%
Tour guides	discretion
Hairdressers	15%
Taxis	15%
Chambermaids	$1 per day
Porters	$1 per bag

CONSULATES

U.K.
(310) 477-3322

Ireland
(415) 392-4214
(San Francisco)

Canada
(213) 346-2700

Australia
(310) 229-4800

New Zealand
(310) 207-1605

HEALTH

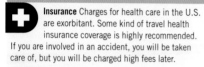

Insurance Charges for health care in the U.S. are exorbitant. Some kind of travel health insurance coverage is highly recommended. If you are involved in an accident, you will be taken care of, but you will be charged high fees later.

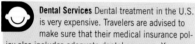

Dental Services Dental treatment in the U.S. is very expensive. Travelers are advised to make sure that their medical insurance policy also includes adequate dental coverage. You may have to pay up front at the time of service, so save all bills for later compensation from your provider.

Weather Los Angeles is nearly always warm and sunny. Sunscreen is highly recommended, especially if you're going to the beach. Evenings in spring, fall and winter can be chilly, so it's a good idea to take an extra sweater if you go out at night.

Drugs Like most large American cities, L.A. seems to have huge drugstores on every other block. Most of them are chains, like Rite-Aid, and many stay open 24 hours a day, dispensing prescription and non-prescription drugs as well as everything from shampoo to dog food. Consult the phone book's *Yellow Pages* for a drugstore nearest your hotel.

Safe Water L.A.'s tap water is clean and safe to drink. Bottled water or seltzer is available in supermarkets, drugstores, convenience stores and most restaurants and bars.

CONCESSIONS

Students Holders of an International Student Identity Card are entitled to discounts on many attractions. Contact tourist information for details.

Senior Citizens Senior citizens (seniors) will find discounts on many services and attractions. Qualifying age varies from 55 to 65. You need to request a discount up front and may be asked to show proof of age. Contact AARP on (800) 424-3410, www.aarp.org for more information.

TRAVELING WITH A DISABILITY

Most L.A. facilities have been retrofitted to provide access for people with disabilities. This includes accessible toilets, and buses equipped with lifts and space inside for wheelchair users. Amtrak trains provide sleeping and seating areas for passengers with disabilities. Many car-rental companies offer cars with special hand controls. Call the L.A. County Commission on Disabilities for more specific local information, tel: (213) 974-1053.

CHILDREN

L.A. is generally very child-friendly, with the exception of chic and/or trendy restaurants with attitude. Look for listings in the *Los Angeles Times* and other local sources for children's activities.

RESTROOMS

There are good public restroom facilities at all public beaches along the L.A. coast. Otherwise, try in hotel lobby areas for the best options.

CUSTOMS

The import of wildlife souvenirs from rare or endangered species may be illegal or require a special permit. Before buying, check your home country's regulations.

As the "entertainment capital of the world," Los Angeles has no shortage of fairs, festivals and parades to delight its visitors, whatever the season. The **L. A. Convention and Visitors Bureau**'s multilingual events hotline (tel: 213/689-8822; www.lacvb.com) will provide additional information and the "Calendar" section in the *Los Angeles Times* every Sunday has comprehensive listings for all events in the city each week (latimes.com).

JANUARY
• 1st – **Tournament of Roses Parade**: Hugely popular parade in Pasadena featuring marching bands and extravagant floats adorned with thousands of blooms. Every four or five years the Rose Parade is followed by the final of the inter-collegiate football championship watched by 100,000 in the striking Rose Bowl Stadium.

FEBRUARY
• Dates vary – **Chinese New Year Festival**: A colorful carnival and parade feature dragon dancers and fireworks in L.A.'s Chinatown.

MARCH
• 1st Sunday – **Los Angeles Marathon**: The city is host to 20,000 runners in this popular annual event, with street entertainers, bands and cheering crowds lining the route.
• Late March/Early April – **Academy Awards (Oscars)**: L.A.'s most famous celebration of the movie industry and its achievements now takes place in a purpose-built theater in the new Hollywood and Highland shopping and entertainment complex – the Kodak Theatre. Oscar night has the city buzzing for weeks, with everybody who's anybody attending or throwing a glitzy party.

APRIL
• Mid-April – **Toyota Long Beach Grand Prix**: The streets of downtown Long Beach are the setting for this world-class auto race. Visitors come to cheer on the teams and also enjoy a pro/celebrity race featuring many famous movie and TV faces.

MAY
• 5th – **Cinco de Mayo**: This festival marking the Mexican victory over the powerful French army at the Battle of Puebla in 1862 celebrates Hispanic heritage and culture with music, dancing and a wealth of culinary delights. A huge Cinco de Mayo fiesta is also held on the last Sunday in April along Broadway, Hill and Spring Streets in Downtown.
• Late May – **Old Pasadena Summerfest**: A lively festival with plenty of music, arts, crafts, foods and sports events.

JUNE
• Mid-June – **Sunset Series Sailboat Races**: Colorful sailboats race from the marina to the California Yacht Club in pretty Marina del Rey.
• Mid- to Late June – **Lesbian and Gay Pride Celebration**: West Hollywood Park is the venue for this colorful weekend festival featuring a glittering parade on Sunday morning that winds its way to the park along Santa Monica Boulevard.
• Third weekend – **Mariachi USA Festival**: Celebrate mariachi music with more than 200 world-class performers. Ballet folklorico and fireworks are also featured.
• June to August, Sundays – **Woodland Hills Concerts in the Park**: Each Sunday through the summer every kind of music from classical to jazz to rock (and most things in between) is performed outdoors in a series of concerts at Warner Ranch Park.

JULY
• 4th – **Independence Day**: Impressive fireworks displays (most spectacular at Marina del Rey), parades and local festivities help mark this favorite national holiday.
• July to Mid-September – **Hollywood Bowl Concert Season**: The excellent acoustics and gorgeous outdoor setting of this world-famous concert theater charm visitors from near and far. Bring a picnic and enjoy the music on a balmy L.A. evening.
• Second Weekend – **Lotus Festival**: The attractive Echo Park Lake is the setting for this celebration of

Asian-Pacific culture featuring music, dance, food, flowers and dragon boat races.
• Late July/Early August – **Central Avenue Jazz Festival**: Central Avenue was the heart of L.A.'s vibrant jazz scene of the 1920s through the 1950s and this is celebrated with a weekend of performances in and around the Dunbar Hotel.

AUGUST
• 4th – **Festival of the Chariots Parade**: Venice Beach is the setting for this parade of giant chariots, which also features traditional Indian dance and ethnic food.
• Early August – **Watts Summer Festival**: An annual event since 1966, this established African-American festival of arts and culture features a carnival, a parade and a great deal of live music.
• Early August – **Nisei Week Japanese Festival**: Japanese arts and culture in L.A.'s Little Tokyo.
• Early August – **International Surf Festival**: The fabulous Hermosa, Redondo and Manhattan beaches host championship surfing competitions over a week.
• Mid-August – **Venice Beach Showcase Celebrations**: This Boardwalk festival has something "Venetian" for everyone with plenty of children's activities, music, power-lifting demonstrations and skating and skateboarding competitions.
• Last Three Weekends – **African Marketplace and Cultural Fair**: A celebration of the cultural and economic development of African-American communities in the U.S., the Marketplace features arts and crafts, concerts, exhibitions, traditional food, a film festival and a soccer tournament.
• Late August – **Klon Blues Festival**: This annual Long Beach festival showcases top blues musicians from around the world.
• Late August – **Sunset Junction Street Fair**: This weekend-long party celebrates the diverse local community in L.A.'s Silver Lake district. Live music takes place on three stages, plus several carnival rides and more than 200 craft, artisan and food stands.

SEPTEMBER
• Mid-September – **Los Angeles County Fair**: More than a million people visit the world's largest county fair, held each year in Pomona, west of Los Angeles.Livestock, old-style sideshows and horse races are among the many attractions.
• Late September – **Lobster Festival**: Redondo Beach is the attractive location of this feast of crustaceans including Maine lobsters, local seafood, ethnic cuisine, arts, crafts and children's rides.

OCTOBER
• Mid-October – **AFI-LA International Film Festival**: Features from around the world are shown at this major Film Festival.
• Last Sunday – **International Festival of Mask**: Ethnic costumes and masks are worn to great effect in this popular parade through Hancock Park.

NOVEMBER
• 2nd – **Dia de los Muertos (Day of the Dead)**: This Mexican religious festival honoring the dead is celebrated with music, art exhibitions and other festivities in L.A.'s El Pueblo district.
• Sunday before Thanksgiving – **Doodah Parade**: This parody of Pasadena's Rose Parade takes place in the same town and features local people lampooning just about anything of a topical nature.

DECEMBER
• Sunday after Thanksgiving – **Hollywood Christmas Parade**: Hundreds of celebrities and flamboyant floats are the draw for 1 million plus visitors to this famous parade along Hollywood and Sunset Boulevards, held annually since 1931.
• First week – **Downtown Tree Lighting Ceremony**: Once lit, a 70-foot fir tree in the Citicorp Plaza is the picturesque setting for carol singing and other seasonal events.
• Mid-December – **Las Posadas**: Candlelit processions accompany a nine-day reenactment of Mary and Joseph's journey to Bethlehem, which takes place at Olvera Street, Downtown Los Angeles. Traditional Mexican Christmas music as well as children's parties complete the celebrations.

Atlas

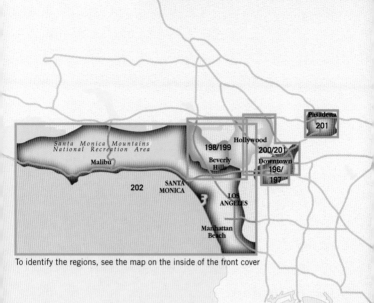

To identify the regions, see the map on the inside of the front cover

Metropolitan Maps

🛣 295	Interstate highway	▓	Built up area
🛣	Federal highway	▓	Park
🛣 295	Other highway	◼	Featured place of interest
✈	Airport	▪	Place of interest

City Plans

	Highway	▓	Park
	Main road	▓	Important building
	Other road	◼	Featured place of interest

Downtown Los Angeles

196

WILSHIRE BOULEVARD

WESTLAKE

OCEAN VIEW AVENUE

MacArthur Park

KOREATOWN

LOS ANGELES

Staples Center

Los Angeles Convention Center

Mount St Mary's College

Los Angeles Trade-Technical College

Shrine Auditorium

University of Southern California

Natural History Museum

Rose Garden

Aerospace Museum

Exposition Park

California Science Center

African American Museum

Memorial Coliseum

Sports Arena

Trinity Park

EXPOSITION BOULEVARD

200   201

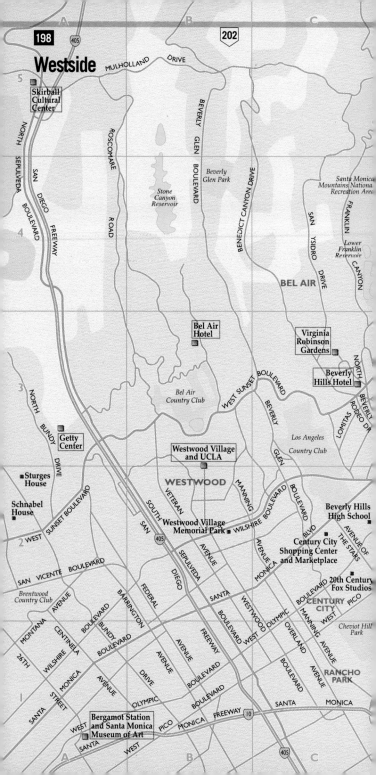

198

202

Westside

MULHOLLAND DRIVE

BEVERLY GLEN BOULEVARD

NORTH SEPULVEDA BOULEVARD

SAN DIEGO FREEWAY

ROSCOMARE ROAD

Skirball
Cultural
Center

Stone
Canyon
Reservoir

Beverly
Glen Park

BENEDICT CANYON DRIVE

SAN YSIDRO DRIVE

FRANKLIN CANYON

Santa Monica
Mountains National
Recreation Area

Lower
Franklin
Reservoir

BEL AIR

Bel Air
Hotel

Virginia
Robinson
Gardens

NORTH BEVERLY

Beverly
Hills Hotel

WEST SUNSET BOULEVARD

Bel Air
Country Club

BEVERLY GLEN

LOMITAS

BEVERLY

RODEO DR

Los Angeles
Country Club

NORTH BUNDY DRIVE

Getty Center

Westwood Village
and UCLA

WESTWOOD

MANNING

WESTWOOD BOULEVARD

BOULEVARD

Beverly Hills
High School

AVENUE OF THE STARS

Sturges
House

VETERAN

Schnabel
House

WEST SUNSET BOULEVARD

Westwood Village
Memorial Park

WILSHIRE

SOUTH

SAN

405

AVENUE

MONICA

BLVD

Century City
Shopping Center
and Marketplace

2 WEST

SEPULVEDA

DIEGO

AVENUE

WESTWOOD

20th Century
Fox Studios

SAN VICENTE BOULEVARD

Brentwood
Country Club

FEDERAL

SANTA

BOULEVARD WEST

OLYMPIC

OVERLAND

MANNING AVENUE

PICO

**CENTURY
CITY**

Cheviot Hill
Park

MONTANA AVENUE

CENTINELA

BUNDY BOULEVARD

BARRINGTON

AVENUE

FREEWAY

BOULEVARD WEST

**RANCHO
PARK**

WILSHIRE

26TH

SANTA MONICA AVENUE

AVENUE

DRIVE

BOULEVARD

SANTA MONICA AVENUE

1

SANTA STREET

OLYMPIC

BOULEVARD

MONICA

FREEWAY

SANTA

10

Bergamot Station
and Santa Monica
Museum of Art

WEST

SANTA

WEST

PICO

MONICA

405

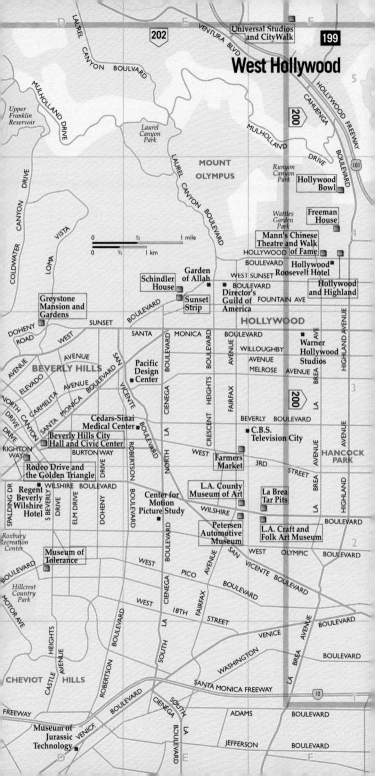

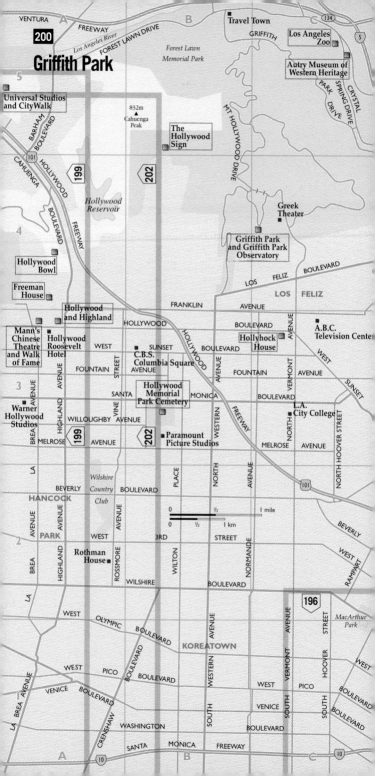

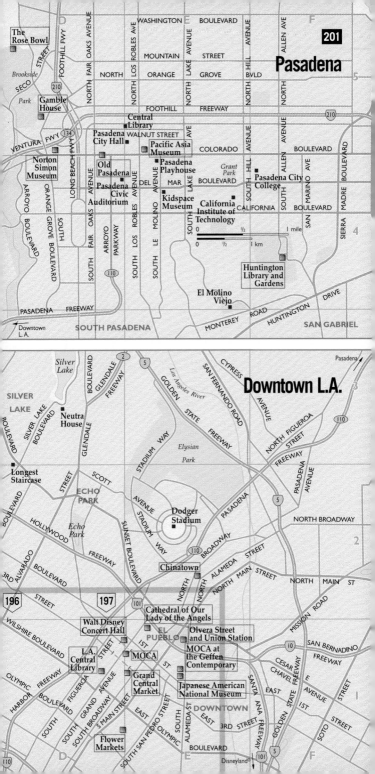

Pasadena

The Rose Bowl

Brookside
Park

Gamble
House

WASHINGTON

E

BOULEVARD

ALLEN AVE

F

MOUNTAIN

STREET

NORTH

ORANGE

GROVE

BLVD

5

NORTH FAIR OAKS AVENUE

NORTH LOS ROBLES AVE

NORTH LAKE AVENUE

NORTH HILL AVENUE

NORTH ALLEN AVE

FOOTHILL FWY

SECO STREET

FOOTHILL FREEWAY

Central
Library

VENTURA FWY

Norton
Simon
Museum

WALNUT STREET

Pasadena
City Hall

Pasadena
City College

Pacific Asia
Museum

COLORADO

BOULEVARD

Old
Pasadena

Pasadena
Playhouse

Grant
Park

Pasadena Civic
Auditorium

DEL MAR

BOULEVARD

Kidspace
Museum

California
Institute of
Technology

CALIFORNIA

BOULEVARD

ARROYO

ORANGE GROVE BOULEVARD

SOUTH

FAIR OAKS

ARROYO PARKWAY

SOUTH LOS ROBLES

SOUTH EL MOLINO

SOUTH LAKE AVENUE

SOUTH HILL

SOUTH ALLEN

SAN MARINO

SIERRA MADRE BOULEVARD

BOULEVARD

½   1 mile

0   ½   1 km

Huntington
Library and
Gardens

El Molino
Viejo

PASADENA   FREEWAY

Downtown
L.A.

SOUTH PASADENA

MONTEREY   ROAD

HUNTINGTON   DRIVE

SAN GABRIEL

4

Downtown L.A.

Pasadena

3

Silver
Lake

SILVER
LAKE

Neutra
House

Longest
Staircase

SILVER LAKE BOULEVARD

BOULEVARD

GLENDALE

2

5

GLENDALE   FREEWAY

Los Angeles River

STADIUM WAY

GOLDEN   STATE   FREEWAY

SAN FERNANDO ROAD

CYPRESS

AVENUE

NORTH FIGUEROA STREET

PASADENA   AVENUE

110

ECHO
PARK

Echo
Park

SCOTT STREET

HOLLYWOOD   FREEWAY

SUNSET BOULEVARD

AVENUE

STADIUM WAY

Elysian
Park

Dodger
Stadium

110

PASADENA

BROADWAY

5

NORTH BROADWAY

2

3RD

ALVARADO BOULEVARD

BOULEVARD

196

WILSHIRE BOULEVARD

197

Walt Disney
Concert Hall

L.A.
Central
Library

OLYMPIC

HARBOR   FREEWAY

BOULEVARD

STREET

101

Chinatown

EL
PUEBLO

MOCA

Grand
Central
Market

Flower
Markets

SOUTH FIGUEROA STREET

SOUTH GRAND AVENUE

SOUTH BROADWAY

S MAIN STREET

SOUTH SAN PEDRO STREET

1ST ST

NORTH ALAMEDA STREET

NORTH MAIN STREET

NORTH   MAIN   ST

Cathedral of Our
Lady of the Angels

Olvera Street
and Union Station

MOCA at
the Geffen
Contemporary

Japanese American
National Museum

DOWNTOWN

3RD   STREET

EAST   BOULEVARD

SOUTH OLYMPIC

EAST

EAST ALAMEDA ST

MISSION ROAD

SAN BERNARDINO

10

FREEWAY

CESAR CHAVEZ AVENUE

GOLDEN STATE FREEWAY

SANTA ANA FREEWAY

EAST   1ST   STREET

SOTO   STREET

10

1

110

D

Disneyland

E

101

5

F

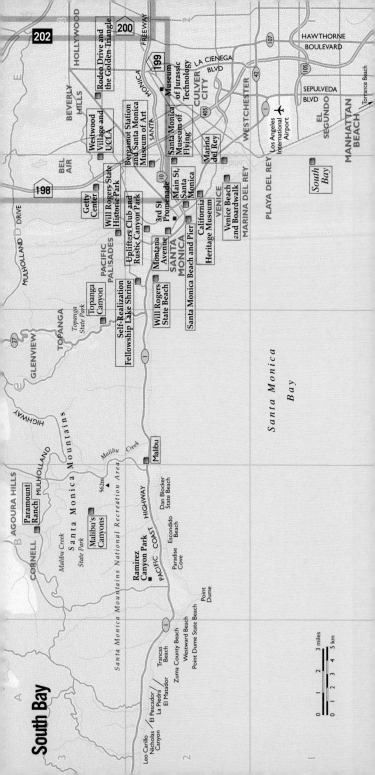

South Bay

200

199

198

202

07

105

42

405

27

17

HOLLYWOOD

BEVERLY HILLS

BEL AIR

PACIFIC PALISADES

TOPANGA

GLENVIEW

AGOURA HILLS

CORNELL

MULHOLLAND DRIVE

MULHOLLAND

MULHOLLAND

Santa Monica Mountains

PACIFIC COAST HIGHWAY

Santa Monica Mountains National Recreation Area

Topanga State Park

Malibu Creek State Park

Malibu Creek

562m

HAWTHORNE BOULEVARD

LA CIENEGA BLVD

CULVER CITY

SANTA MONICA FREEWAY

WESTCHESTER

SEPULVEDA BLVD

EL SEGUNDO

MANHATTAN BEACH

PLAYA DEL REY

MARINA DEL REY

VENICE

SANTA MONICA

Torrance Beach

Los Angeles International Airport

Rodeo Drive and the Golden Triangle

Westwood Village and UCLA

Museum of Jurassic Technology

Bergamot Station and Santa Monica Museum of Art

Santa Monica Flying

Marina del Rey

Getty Center

Will Rogers State Historic Park

Uplifters Club and Rustic Canyon Park

Main St, Santa Monica

3rd St Promenade

Montana Avenue

California Heritage Museum

Venice Beach and Boardwalk

Self-Realization Fellowship Lake Shrine

Will Rogers State Beach

Santa Monica Beach and Pier

Topanga Canyon

Malibu's Canyons

Ramirez Canyon Park

Malibu

Dan Blocker State Beach

Escondido Beach

Paradise Cove

Point Dume

Paramount Ranch

South Bay

Santa Monica Bay

Leo Carrillo Beach

Nicholas Canyon

El Pescador

La Piedra

El Matador

Trancas Beach

Zuma County Beach

Westward Beach

Point Dume State Beach

miles

km

0 1 2 3

0 1 2 3 4 5

STREETPLAN INDEX

Ave Avenue
Blvd Boulevard
Dr Drive
E East
Fwy Freeway
Hwy Highway
N North
Pde Parade
Pl Place
Rd Road
S Suth
St Street
W West

Index

Picture credits

Abbreviations for terms below: (t) top; (b) bottom; (l) left; (r) right; (c) center
The Automobile Association wishes to thank the following photographers, libraries and
associations for their assistance with the preparation of this book.
Front and back cover: (t) AA Photo Library/Clive Sawyer; (ct) AA Photo Library/Phil
Wood; (cb) AA Photo Library/Max Jourdan; (b) AA Photo Library/Clive Sawyer; Spine AA
Photo Library/Max Jourdan.
BRIDGEMAN ART LIBRARY, LONDON 82/3 Irises, 1889 by Vincent van Gogh (1853-
90), J. Paul Getty Museum, Malibu, CA, USA, 84 An Old Man in Military Costume (for-
merly called Portrait of Rembrandt's Father), c.1630 (panel) by Rembrandt Harmensz,
van Rijn (1606-69), J. Paul Getty Museum, Malibu, CA, USA, 150 Waiting, c.1882 (pas-
tel) by Edgar Degas (1834-1917), Norton Simon Collection, Pasadena, Ca, USA; BRUCE
COLEMAN COLLECTION 26l (Pacific Stock), 27r; CORBIS UK LTD 13 (Bettmann), 14
(David Muench), 16t (Don Wiechec), 16b (Nik Wheeler); © DISNEY ENTERPRISES,
INC. 167t, 167b, 168; THE GAMBLE HOUSE 153b, 153r (photos by Timothy Street-
Porter); GETTY IMAGES 12t, 12b, 21t, 21b; RONALD GRANT ARCHIVE 19t, 29b; THE
HUNTINGTON LIBRARY 141t, 154; CATHERINE KARNOW 11l, 11r; THE KOBAL
COLLECTION 8b, 17, 18/19, 68; LOS ANGELES CONVENTION & VISITORS BUREAU
25b/gr, 26/7b/gr, 28, 129 (photos by Tom & Michelle Grimm); LOS ANGELES COUNTY
MUSEUM OF ART 109b Portrait of Mrs Edward L. Davis and her Son, Livingston Davis,
1890, by John Singer Sargent, Los Angeles County Museum of Art, Frances and Armand
Hammer Purchase Fund, 110/1 Mulholland Drive; The Road to the Studio, 1980, by
David Hockney, Los Angeles County Museum of Art, Purchased with funds provided by
the F. Patrick Burns Bequest; MUSEUM OF CONTEMPORARY ART, LOS ANGELES
144/5 Map, 1962, by Jasper Johns, encaustic and collage on canvas, 60 x 93 inches. (Gift
of Marcia Simon Weisman) photo by Paula Goldman, (©Jasper John/VAGA, New
York/DACS, London 2002); PETERSEN AUTOMOTIVE MUSEUM 124; SANTA BAR-
BARA MUSEUM OF NATURAL HISTORY 15b; SANTA MONICA MUSEUM OF FLYING
65; THE SKIRBALL CULTURAL CENTER 79t; NIK WHEELER 25, 27l, 96, 178; © UNI-
VERSAL STUDIOS 120b, 121t, 121b, 122t, 122b, 123; COURTESY VENTURA COUNTY
MUSEUM OF HISTORY & ART 15t; WORLD PICTURES 107t.

The remaining photographs are held in the Association's own photo library (AA PHOTO
LIBRARY) and were taken by CLIVE SAWYER with the exception of the following:
Max Jourdan 3(i), 3(v), 8tl, 8tr, 8cr, 20/21b/gr, 20, 22/3b/gr, 22, 24/5b/gr, 24t, 29t, 30t,
30b, 32b, 52b, 53bl, 53br, 55t, 59l, 59r, 76, 78t, 78bl, 78br, 80/1, 81t, 81c, 88c, 88b, 90tl,
90tr, 91, 92, 94, 103, 106b, 107b, 116t, 116b, 117, 118t, 119, 128t, 140b, 142/3, 143t,
143r, 146, 148, 157, 158, 182, 183, 187; Rob Holmes 3(iii), 129b, 165, 170, 180; Ken
Paterson 26r; Phil Wood 24b, 64, 85t, 95t, 95b, 120t, 147.

Clive Sawyer would like to thank the following for their help in the taking of photographs in and around Los Angeles: Connie Nash-Millette of Carmel-by-the-Sea, Sandra
Milstein from Bel Air and Gregg Donovan, Ambassador to Beverly Hills.

SPIRAL GUIDES

Questionnaire

Dear Traveler

Your comments, opinions and recommendations are very important to us. So please help us to improve our travel guides by taking a few minutes to complete this simple questionnaire.

Send to: Spiral Guides, MailStop 66, 1000 AAA Drive, Heathrow, FL 32746–5063

Your recommendations...

We always encourage readers' recommendations for restaurants, nightlife or shopping – if your recommendation is added to the next edition of the guide, we will send you a FREE AAA Spiral Guide of your choice. Please state below the establishment name, location and your reasons for recommending it.

_____

_____

_____

_____

_____

Please send me AAA Spiral_____

(see list of titles inside the back cover)

About this guide...

Which title did you buy?

_____ AAA Spiral

Where did you buy it? _____

When? mm/ y y

Why did you choose a AAA Spiral Guide? _____

_____

_____

_____

Did this guide meet your expectations?

Exceeded ☐   Met all ☐   Met most ☐   Fell below ☐

Please give your reasons_____

_____

_____

_____

continued on next page...

Were there any aspects of this guide that you particularly liked?

_____
_____
_____
_____
_____

Is there anything we could have done better?

_____
_____
_____
_____
_____

About you...

Name (Mr/Mrs/Ms) _____

Address _____

_____

_____ **Zip** _____

Daytime tel nos. _____

Which age group are you in?

Under 25 ☐ 25–34 ☐ 35–44 ☐ 45–54 ☐ 55–64 ☐ 65+ ☐

How many trips do you make a year?

Less than one ☐ One ☐ Two ☐ Three or more ☐

Are you a AAA member? Yes ☐ No ☐

Name of AAA club _____

About your trip...

When did you book? m m / y y   **When did you travel?** m m / y y

How long did you stay? _____

Was it for business or leisure? _____

Did you buy any other travel guides for your trip? ☐ Yes ☐ No

If yes, which ones? _____

_____

Thank you for taking the time to complete this questionnaire.